Enjoy This Book!

Manage your library account and explore
all we offer by visiting us online at
www.nashualibrary.org.

Please return this on time, so
others can enjoy it, too.

If you are pleased with all that the
library offers, tell others

@ Nashua Public Library
2 Court Street, Nashua, NH 03060
603-589-4600, www.nashualibrary.org

GAYLORD

FACEBOOK® & TWITTER® FOR SENIORS FOR DUMMIES®

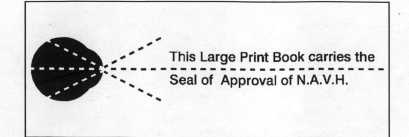

This Large Print Book carries the
Seal of Approval of N.A.V.H.

FACEBOOK® & TWITTER® FOR SENIORS FOR DUMMIES®

MARSHA COLLIER

THORNDIKE PRESS

A part of Gale, Cengage Learning

GALE
CENGAGE Learning™

Detroit • New York • San Francisco • New Haven, Conn • Waterville, Maine • London

Thorndike Press, a part of Gale, Cengage Learning.

Thorndike Press® Large Print Health, Home & Learning.

The text of this Large Print edition is unabridged.

Other aspects of the book may vary from the original edition.

Set in 16 pt. Plantin.

LIBRARY OF CONGRESS CATALOGING-IN-PUBLICATION DATA

Collier, Marsha.
   Facebook and Twitter for seniors for dummies / by Marsha Collier. -- Large print ed.
     p. cm.
   ISBN-13: 978-1-4104-3407-4 (hardcover : large print)
   ISBN-10: 1-4104-3407-9 (hardcover : large print)
   1. Facebook (Electronic resource) 2. Twitter. 3. Internet and older people. 4. Large type books. I. Title.
  HM743.F33C65 2011
  006.7'540846--dc22

2011000625

Published in 2011 by arrangement with John Wiley & Sons, Inc.

Printed in Mexico
4 5 6 7 15 14 13 12 11

Dedication

To all the future online citizens who have purchased this book to get a taste of how much fun joining the online party can be. I look forward to seeing you on Twitter and Facebook, hearing your stories, and learning from you.

I dedicate this book also to my daughter, Susan Dickman, who's always been there to help me get "cool." Heather Meeker, who's there with support and love — thank you. And to my dear friends on Twitter and Facebook who have embraced me as part of their community, I want to thank all of you for your help and support; you make the online world a fun place to visit for millions of people. Keep on doing what you're doing.

Author's Acknowledgments

This book couldn't have been written without input from the thousands of wonderful people that I've met online from all over the world. You inspire me to work harder and do my best to help as many people as possible.

I've made so many friends along my eBay, Facebook, and Twitter travels: If not for them, this book wouldn't be here. Thanks to the rest of my Twitter buddies — who always seem to have a lightning-fast response when I send them a tweet.

I particularly want to thank my freaking brilliant editors at Wiley Publishing, Inc. who helped make this book as much fun as it is: my über-smart project editor Leah Cameron, my super editor Barry Childs-Helton, and my tech editor Mark Justice Hinton; Steven Hayes, my acquisitions editor, who is always there for support and ideas; and Andy Cummings, my publisher, who — lucky for me — still takes my calls!

Thank you all!

About the Author

Marsha Collier spends a good deal of time online. She loves buying and selling on eBay, as well as meeting online denizens from around the world. As a columnist, author of the best-selling For Dummies books on eBay, and a radio host, she shares her knowledge of the online world with millions. Before her eBay career took off, Marsha owned and operated her own marketing and advertising firm, a company that won numerous awards and earned her "Small Business of the Year" accolades from several organizations. She got started online during the Internet's early years, and quickly mastered the art making friends online.

Marsha is one of the foremost eBay experts and educators in the world — and the top-selling eBay author. In 1999, Marsha created the first edition of *eBay For Dummies,* the bestselling book for eBay beginners. Then she followed up the success of the first book with *Starting an eBay Business For Dummies,* targeting individuals interested in making e-commerce their full-time profession. That book became an instant nationwide hit, making several notable bestseller lists.

Currently, Marsha has 20 books in print on her favorite subject — eBay. Her *eBay For Dummies* was published in special versions for the United Kingdom, Canada, Germany, China,

France, Spain, and Australia. Marsha's books have sold over 1,000,000 copies (including the special editions in foreign countries as well as translations in Spanish, French, Italian, Chinese, and German). These books are updated regularly to keep up with site and market changes.

Along with her writing, Marsha is an experienced e-commerce educator. She was the lead instructor at eBay University (teaching seminars all over the United States), as well as a regular presenter at the eBay Live national convention since its inception. Marsha also hosted "Make Your Fortune Online," a PBS special on online business that premiered in 2005. The show was the basis for her PBS premium five-DVD set, "Your Online Business Plan." In 2006, she was invited to address the Innovations Conference in Singapore to present the ideas of e-commerce to a new market.

In 2008, she was dubbed one of twenty influential iCitizens in Kelly Mooney's *The Open Brand: When Push Comes to Pull in a Web-Made World,* and was invited to speak at a leading e-commerce conference attended by Coca-Cola, Hewlett Packard, Procter & Gamble, Victoria's Secret, and other e-commerce leaders.

She hosts Computer & Technology Radio on KTRB 860 AM in San Francisco, as well as on the Web at www.computer andtechnologyradio.com. She also makes regular appearances on television, radio, and in print to discuss customer needs and online commerce.

Marsha currently resides in Los Angeles, CA. She can be reached via her Web site, www.marshacollier.com.

Publisher's Acknowledgments

We're proud of this book; please send us your comments through our online registration form located at `http://dummies.custhelp.com`. For other comments, please contact our Customer Care Department within the U.S. at 877-762-2974, outside the U.S. at 317-572-3993, or fax 317-572-4002.

Some of the people who helped bring this book to market include the following:

Acquisition and Editorial
Senior Editorial Manager: Leah P. Cameron
Senior Copy Editor: Barry Childs-Helton
Acquisitions Editor: Steven Hayes
Technical Editor: Mark Justice Hinton
Editorial Assistant: Amanda Graham, Leslie Saxman
Sr. Editorial Assistant: Cherie Case
Cartoons: Rich Tennant (`www.the5thwave.com`)

Composition Services for Original Edition
Project Coordinator: Patrick Redmond
Layout and Graphics: Carl Byers, Christin Swinford
Proofreaders: Melissa Cossell, Evelyn C. Wellborn
Indexer: Sharon Shock

Publishing and Editorial for Technology Dummies

Richard Swadley, Vice President and Executive Group Publisher

Andy Cummings, Vice President and Publisher

Mary Bednarek, Executive Acquisitions Director

Mary C. Corder, Editorial Director

Publishing for Consumer Dummies

Diane Graves Steele, Vice President and Publisher

Composition Services for Original Edition

Debbie Stailey, Director of Composition Services

Get More and Do More at Dummies.com®
Start with **FREE** Cheat Sheets

Cheat Sheets include

- Checklists
- Charts
- Common Instructions
- And Other Good Stuff!

To access the Cheat Sheet created specifically for this book, go to www.dummies.com/cheatsheet/facebooktwitterforseniors

Get Smart at Dummies.com

Dummies.com makes your life easier with 1,000s
of answers on everything from removing wallpaper
to using the latest version of Windows.

Check out our
- Videos
- Illustrated Articles
- Step-by-Step Instructions

Plus, each month you can win valuable prizes by entering
our Dummies.com sweepstakes.*

Want a weekly dose of Dummies? Sign up for Newsletters on
- Digital Photography
- Microsoft Windows & Office
- Personal Finance & Investing
- Health & Wellness
- Computing, iPods & Cell Phones
- eBay
- Internet
- Food, Home & Garden

Find out "HOW" at Dummies.com

*Sweepstakes not currently available in all countries; visit Dummies.com for official rules.

Contents at a Glance

Table of Contents

Cartoons at a Glance

by Rich Tennant

The 5th Wave — By Rich Tennant

"It worked, honey! I'm connected to the network!"

page 35

The 5th Wave — By Rich Tennant

"I know it's a short profile, but I thought 'King of the Jungle' sort of said it all."

page 113

The 5th Wave — By Rich Tennant

"I'd respond to this person's comment on Twitter, but I'm a former Marine, Bernard, and a Marine never retweets."

page 227

The 5th Wave — By Rich Tennant

"These are the parts of our life that aren't on YouTube."

page 293

Introduction

I've been working and playing online since the mid-'80s. I started out using CompuServe from my old Kaypro II with a 300-baud modem. I'd log on to my computer in the evenings when I had some quiet time after work, after my daughter was asleep.

The online world I found through CompuServe had no fancy pages, videos, or even photos. Just phosphor-green text on a tiny screen. The early onliners didn't know any better technology, so we communicated with people by sending words across the country and across the world. We chatted with each other and joined groups to discuss our hobbies and our families.

Drawing an analogy here, there have been related social communities online for as long as there have been connected computers. Even though the kids today may think they invented the current online world, today's social media are just the 21st-century continuation of a community we've known for quite a while.

Many people who were online then (in the early '80s) are still online now. People *of a certain age* may also (after a long career) want to jump back into the family feeling of an online community. So, even though this book title says *For Seniors,* you should know I don't like that term. This book is for those with experience.

Although a persistent rumor claims that only the youngsters go online, actually online participation is growing faster in people over 50. There are more online users over 40 than under 25. Perhaps these people were so busy living their lives and bringing up their children that they didn't have extra time for themselves then — but they do now. And just as in the '60s or '70s, they don't want to be left out of anything. They want to be smack dab in the middle of the online revolution.

Unfortunately, a lot of what they encounter when they go online is unfamiliar stuff. So (naturally enough) some of the experienced, graying generation experience a feeling of trepidation when it comes to the Internet — most of all, they're a bit unsure about getting on Twitter and Facebook.

I have to say: *Why?* Participating in social media is freeing — and can bring so much into your life! You can't *not* be there!

I encourage you: Join your extended family, your children, and your friends online. By participating in social media, you'll find many of your old friends. I reconnected with my first boyfriend on Twitter, and we share family photos on Facebook. In a world where people don't chat on the phone much anymore, the online arena is the perfect place to connect.

And you will also make *new* friends. I am blessed enough to have met many of my online friends in person. The online world has given me a whole new group of people that I can call on for advice — or, better yet, go out to brunch with — in the real world.

Twitter is pretty straightforward — once you get the hang of it, you'll be tweeting like a pro in no time. But a Web site that's as complex as Facebook has many nooks and crannies that can confuse new users (and even experienced ones). Think of this book as a roadmap that can help you find your way around in the social media, getting just as much or as little as you want from the trip. Unlike an actual road map, however, you won't have to fold it back to its original shape (whew). Just close the book and come back any time you need a question answered.

About This Book

Remember those open-book tests that teachers sprang on you in high school? Well, sometimes you may feel like Facebook pop-quizzes you while you're online. Think of *Facebook & Twitter For Seniors For Dummies,* as your open-book-test cheat sheet with the answers. You don't have to memorize anything; just keep this book handy and follow along whenever you need to.

With this in mind, I've divided this book into pertinent sections to help you find your answers fast. I'll show you how to

➡ Set up your computer for the ultimate online experience.

➡ Learn to use online searches and tools to widen your online reach.

➡ Set up a new account on Gmail to handle all your new communication.

27

➤ Get online and register to start meeting old (and new) friends.

➤ Post to your friend's Facebook walls and send special messages.

➤ Find people you haven't heard from in years and catch up with their lives.

➤ See what's going on with your children and grandchildren online — and join the party.

➤ Share photos and videos online.

➤ Become a part of a unique community of people!

 Do not reach for your glasses. To protect the privacy of the online community, the screen images (commonly called *screen shots*) that I've used in this book blur e-mail addresses on purpose. That's to protect the innocent (or not so . . . what the heck, cue the *Dragnet* theme).

Conventions Used in This Book

Anyone born before 1960 grew up in an analog age. Televisions were big, bulky affairs; the first remote controls ca-chunked each time they changed the channel (and they only had four buttons). Families woke up and went to sleep seeing a test pattern. Cameras (the good ones) were solid, heavy devices — and movie cameras whirred along with a comfortable mechanical hum. Typewriters clacked in a danceable rhythm.

Then life turned digital without anyone's permission — even without folks noticing until it happened. The com-

28

fortable mechanical sounds of everyday appliances seemed to go away. Whirring, buzzing, and beeping replaced the familiar sounds. Everything got more complex: the button count on my remote control went from four to a gazillion! It seems as if everything we use has gotten smaller. Some of those little digital cameras look so small and cheesy that I'm shocked they can take a good picture — but they do. (They take great ones!) Even the type on a page, it seems, has gotten smaller — which is why my publisher has graciously set this book in a type that will permit you to read something, glance at your computer, and look back again without having to pick your glasses off the top of your head.

Here are a few conventions to look out for as you read this book:

➤ **Online addresses:** The online location (or address) of a Web site is called a Uniform Resource Locator (URL). These online addresses — as well as e-mail addresses — appear in a `monofont` typeface, as follows:

`www.facebook.com`

➤ **What to type:** When instructions for a task require that you type something on your keyboard, that something appears in **bold** typeface.

➤ **On-screen buttons with long labels:** When an on-screen button is labeled with a phrase instead of a single word, I put it in title case, like this: Click the Do This Silly Digital Thing Now button. That ought to head off confusion at the pass.

Foolish Assumptions

I'm thinking that you've picked up this book because you heard that the immediate world has jumped online and maybe you feel a little left out. Perhaps you already like to send text messages and think this Twitter thing might be for you? If either of these assumptions is true, this is the right book for you.

Here are some other foolish assumptions I've made about you (I'm famous for my foolish assumptions . . . you too?):

➥ You have access to a computer and the Internet (or plan to get it soon!) so you can get online and start to socialize.

➥ You have an interest in communicating with people, and you want to find out more about what you can do online — without asking your children.

➥ You want tips to help you get online without looking like a newcomer, or *newbie* (the kids call them *noobs*). I can relate. We have a lot in common.

➥ You're concerned about maintaining your privacy and staying away from shysters.

How This Book Is Organized

This book has four parts. The chapters stand on their own, meaning you can read Chapter 5 after you read Chapter 10 or skip Chapter 3 altogether. It's all up to you. If you've already dipped your toe into the online pool, you can fly ahead to get good tips on advanced tasks. Don't wait for permission from me or think that you have to read the entire book from start to finish. Feel free to go directly to the sections you're interested in. Following is a general break-down of the book's content.

Part I: Computer and Internet Basics

Consider Part I a refresher course if you're experienced in using computers. I tell you about computer basics that give you the foundation for a good online experience. I explain the shortcuts and features in Web browsing, and show you the advantage of having an online e-mail account. You also discover some of the top social networking sites to get you talking the talk quickly.

Part II: Putting Your Face onto Facebook

If you're ready to dive into Facebook with both feet (or headfirst if you're really impetuous), check out Part II, which gives you the lowdown on everything you need to get up and running as an online denizen.

You find out how to register, share photos and videos, join groups, post messages to your friends (both privately and publically), and so much more. The world of Facebook is ever-expanding, and this part gives you all the tools you need to lead the pack. Once you learn the basics, the rest just falls into place.

Part III: And Now, It's Twitter Time

From registering to becoming a Twitter-maven, it's all here. You've got enough information to get you tweeting in no time. I show you how to meet people (which is just a little more difficult on Twitter than Facebook) and benefit from Twitter traditions — such as Follow Friday.

Part IV: The Rest of the Social Networking Story

In this part, I show you some other sites you might like to visit to share music and read (and post) online reviews of businesses, products, and services. I've included a tutorial on how to blog — and show how you can have your own blog on the Internet without it costing you a penny.

It's all so much fun. I can't wait for you to get started.

Where to Go from Here

Like everything else in the world, Twitter and Facebook have an ever-changing nature. And for Facebook — because the Web site is more complex — this is even truer. (That's annoying, isn't it?) These social networking sites are always trying to improve the user experience, but sometimes such changes can be confusing. My job is to arm you with an understanding of basic functions, so you won't be thrown by any minor course corrections on the site's part. If you hit rough waters, just look up the troublesome item in the book's index.

Most of all, don't get frustrated! Keep reviewing topics before you feel fully comfortable to take the plunge on Twitter and Facebook. Perhaps even start off with baby steps — with either site there's no need to start off with a bang. No one will notice that you're just a beginner.

A persistent piece of Internet lore quotes Albert Einstein as saying, "I never commit to memory anything that can easily be looked up in a book." But nobody seems to know exactly when he said that. No problem. You and I know that books are handy to have around when you're learning new things. I'm all about that. So is this book.

Feedback, Please

I'd love to hear from you: your successes and your comments. I'm on Twitter every day as @MarshaCollier (http://twitter.com/marshacollier). Feel free to join me on Facebook: I have my personal page, a book fan page, and a community page set up by Facebook with my biography. I love making new friends and will be glad to help you whenever I can.

Contact me at talk2marsha@coolebaytools.com or on my site, www.marshacollier.com. I can't always answer each and every question you send. But do know that I promise to read each e-mail and answer when I can.

Visit my blog at http://mcollier.blogspot.com, and if you'd like to learn about eBay, check out my Web site at www.coolebaytools.com. I also wrote *eBay For Seniors For Dummies,* so if you're looking to make a little spare cash, that book will definitely simplify selling (and buying) on eBay for you.

Every Saturday from noon to 2:00 p.m. Pacific Time, I co-host the *Computer and Technology Show* on radio with Marc Cohen. You can also call in and speak to us live during the show at 877-474-3302 if we can ever help you with your computer problems. The show is also archived online at www.computerandtechnologyradio.com and on iTunes.

Welcome to the future. It's actually kind of a fun place.

Part I

Computer and Internet Basics

The 5th Wave   By Rich Tennant

"It worked, honey! I'm connected to the network!"

Chapter 1

Getting a Computer Ready for the Internet

Don't worry, I'm not going to tell you that you need really fancy equipment to get started online, but you must *have* a computer. These days, there are more choices than you can imagine for joining the online social scene. If you're in the market for a computer, you've got a few choices, which I tell you about in this chapter.

Shopping for a computer can be a dizzying experience. As a matter of fact, it's downright confusing. I suggest you go to a store and kick a few tires (or try out a few keyboards) before you make a decision. Also, recognize that your decisions about computer equipment depend on how and where you plan to use your computer. Follow my advice in this chapter to evaluate your computer use and find the right source for your equipment.

Along with your hardware of choice and an Internet connection (see Chapter 2), you need just one more item — a software program — to interact with online social sites (such as Facebook and Twitter). When you get a computer, you get an Internet browser for free. A browser is the software program that lets your computer talk to the Internet. It's like having your own private cyberchauffeur. In this chapter, I also tell you a little about the common browsers that are readily available.

Pick Hardware to Match Your Computer Use

1. I confess, I have a desktop, a laptop, *and* a netbook computer — and I use each one at different locations and for different reasons. You certainly don't need to have all three varieties to work with Facebook and Twitter; simply decide on which type is right for you before you buy. Think through the scenarios in this section and see which one matches your plans. Then go find the computer hardware that fits.

2. If you are one who likes to sit at a desk or table, or wants a regular place to use your computer, you'll be happy with a desktop variety. Also, if you like to have all the power of today's computing at your disposal, you'll have to get a desktop. *Desktop* computers are larger than their portable cousins, and can hold more bells and whistles.

    These days you can buy a package that combines a monitor, keyboard, and a computer module. But with all the great deals on the Internet, you may want to make these purchases separately. See the section "Shop for Your Computer of Choice" for more about where to purchase.

3. If you're looking for a computer that will allow you to sit seductively at Starbucks — looking cool — you'll have to get a laptop. Okay, how about if you just want to use Twitter or Facebook from *anywhere* in your home other than your desk (say, the kitchen counter)? The major difference between a desktop and a *laptop* (as shown in **Figure 1-1**) is that everything you need is combined in one compact, lightweight package. Also, you'll be able to use your laptop (called *notebook* by some) to go online anywhere a wireless (WiFi) connection is available. WiFi readiness is built into all laptops these days.

Figure 1-1

Also consider the following if you're leaning toward getting a laptop:

- You'll find that keyboards can get progressively smaller, depending on the size of notebook you buy. So if you have big fingers, be sure to test out the notebook offerings in a store prior to buying one.

- You'll find smaller monitors on today's laptops, so they can be portable. It somewhat defeats the portability purpose when you have to lug around a 26-inch, 6-pound behemoth. Keep in mind that Web browsers allow you to easily increase the size of the text you see (more about that in the task "Browse for a Browser" later in this chapter).

 I've taken my laptop out by the pool when I'm on vacation, and at home, I sometimes *tweet* (send a message on Twitter) from my garden. Portability is a wonderful thing.

4. If you're looking for extra portability and convenience, think netbook. *Netbooks* are smaller than desktops or laptops (they generally have 10-inch screens), you can stick them in a purse or shopping bag, and you can buy one for as little at $300. They are a great deal. My netbook, shown in **Figure 1-2** (nail polish is for scale), is an Asus Seashell, and it weighs a little over two pounds.

Figure 1-2

Due to size limitations, there are a few tasks that a netbook can't perform, as illustrated in **Table 1-1**.

Table 1-1	What a Laptop and a Netbook Can Do	
Task	*Netbook*	*Laptop*
E-mail, chat, instant messaging	x	x
Social networking, blogging, Twitter, and Facebook	x	x
Surfing the Web	x	x
Streaming audio or video	x	x
Using word processors, spreadsheets, and small business programs	x	x

Capturing live action with a built-in Web cam	x	x
Playing games	Online Games	PC Games
Editing videos and photos	Lower resolution photos only	x
Converting music from CDs to Mp3 files		x
Seamlessly watching HD movies		x
Running complex software		x

 My laptop gets the most use, but my netbook always travels with me. But don't think that netbooks are just for traveling; they can easily fulfill your every need for using online services.

5. If you really want to Tweet or Facebook from your pocket, you can do so from any of the current smartphones. A *smartphone* is truly a mobile personal computer that fits in your hand, and you can also use it to make phone calls. Smartphones often contain mini versions of almost every piece of software you have on your laptop. When your WiFi connection is out, or if you have the need to connect from a restaurant, your smartphone can do the trick.

Popular smartphones include the iPhone, Blackberry, Android, and the Palm Pre. **Figure 1-3** shows my phone ready for action.

Figure 1-3

Know What Hardware Options to Look For

1. Before you purchase one of the different types of
equipment I outline in the previous section, think
about some of the options you need to look for on any
computing device that you plan to use for interacting with
your pals on Facebook and Twitter. Look for a computer
with a large hard drive. The more time you spend using
— and storing stuff on — your computer, the more Blob-
like your hard drive's contents become. (Remember that
1950s horror movie, *The Blob,* where an alien life form
just grows and grows?)

43

A hard drive with at least 60 gigabytes (GB) of storage space should keep your computer happy, but you can get hard drives as big as 500 GB. You're probably going to be storing photos and videos (yes, you will — I promise), so I suggest that you buy one with the biggest hard drive you can afford.

2. One USB port is *never* enough. These days, it seems like every peripheral device you need connects to your computer through a Universal Serial Bus (USB) connection. You may end up with an external hard drive for backup, a mouse, a printer, and a digital camera that you need to connect (so you can download pictures). **Figure 1-4** shows a common peripheral device: a USB flash drive. Make sure that the desktop, laptop, or netbook computer you get has at *least* two USB ports (you can plug and unplug from these at will).

Figure 1-4

3. Make sure the computer's central processing unit (CPU) is fast. A *CPU* (also known as a *chip*) is your computer's brain. It should be the fastest you can afford. You can always opt for the top-of-the-line, but even a slower 900MHz (megahertz) processor *could* suffice. The

popular Atom processor from Intel is in most netbook computers, and that clocks at 1.6 GHz (gigahertz). If you want lightning-fast speed (imagine a Daytona 500 race car with jet assist), you have to move up to one that boosts to at least 3.6 GHz.

4. Get a CD/DVD drive; a disc burner is standard equipment. You use the drive to load new software programs into your computer from compact discs. You can also use the CDs or DVDs for your backups. These days, all models play and record DVD movies on your computer, and most new software comes in the CD or DVD format.

5. You must have a keyboard. No keyboard, no typing. The basic keyboard is fine. They do make funky ergonomic models that are split in the middle. But if the good old standard keyboard feels comfortable to you, stick with it.

6. Multiple media-card reader. Your digital camera will no doubt have a memory card in it where it holds all the pictures you take. It's a lot easier to pop out the card and slip it into your computer than mess around with connecting cables so you can download your photos. Different cameras take different sizes of media cards, and camera manufacturers haven't really conformed to a standard yet. So it's a plus when the computer accepts multiple cards — because you'll probably get a new camera before you get a new computer.

7. You need a pointing device that moves the pointer around the computer screen; it's usually a *mouse*. Laptops and netbooks come with touchpads or trackballs designed to do the moving and give you a quick way to select options by clicking or tapping. I personally find that a mouse is a better choice.

To save possible pain in your hands, I recommend you use an ergonomic mouse like the Contour Mouse from Contour Design (`http://ergo.contourdesign.com`). I've used one for over a decade. See **Figure 1-5**. The Contour Mouse fits your hand and is available in seven different sizes, for right and left hands. This mouse reduces or eliminates the grip force required to navigate and click traditional mice. This sculpted mouse is designed to support your hand comfortably without the need to clutch the mouse to control it.

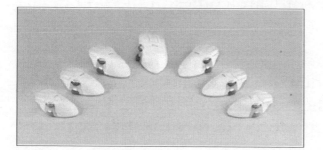

Figure 1-5

8. When buying a monitor to go with a desktop computer, size counts! An LCD (Liquid Crystal Display) monitor that has at least a 17-inch screen can make a huge difference in your comfort level after several hours of rabid tweeting or reading your friends' Facebook posts. Anything smaller, and you could have a hard time actually seeing the words and images. The good news: Monitors have become so inexpensive that you can find a 20-inch or larger variety for about $200.

Shop for Your Computer of Choice

1. These days you can find computers at many retailers, including Office Depot, Staples, Apple Store, Sony Style,

and my favorite, Costco. Try out each computer and ask questions. Every brick-and-mortar retailer these days is more than willing to show you the options they offer.

2. You can also get online and find sellers who have even better deals on new, used, or refurbished computer equipment. Some Web sites that include computers for sale are Amazon (www.amazon.com), Buy.com (www .buy.com), BestBuy.com (www.bestbuy.com), and even at Costco.com (www.costco.com).

3. If you don't feel comfortable buying a used machine (but want to save money), you may want to consider a factory-refurbished model. These are new machines that were returned to the manufacturer for one reason or another. The factory fixes them so they're nice and spiffy, and then sweetens the deal with a terrific warranty. Some companies even offer optional, extended, on-site repairs. What you're getting is a new computer at a deep discount because the machine can't be resold legally as new. Here are some things to know about refurbished computers:

- **They're rebuilt and come with warranties.** For the most part, refurbished computers are defined as returns, units with blemishes (scratches, dents, and so on), or evaluation units. The factories rebuild them to their original working condition, using new parts (or sometimes used parts that meet or exceed performance specs for new parts). They come with 60- to 90-day warranties that cover repairs and returns. Warranty information is available on the manufacturers' Web sites, so be sure to read it before you purchase a refurbished computer.

- **You can get name brands.** Major computer manufacturers such as Dell, IBM, Sony,

Hewlett-Packard, and Apple provide refurbished computers. Check whether their Web site has an outlet store (**Figure 1-6** shows one example). I visit `shopping.hp.com/outlet`, `www.sony style.com/outlet`, and `www.dell.com/outlet`, and check the sites for closeouts and refurbished goods all the time — and I've never been burned!

 Because the inventory of refurbished computers changes daily (as do the prices), there's no way of telling exactly how much money you can save by buying refurbished instead of new. I suggest that you find a new computer system you like (and can afford) in a store or a catalog, and then compare it with refurbished systems of the same brand and model.

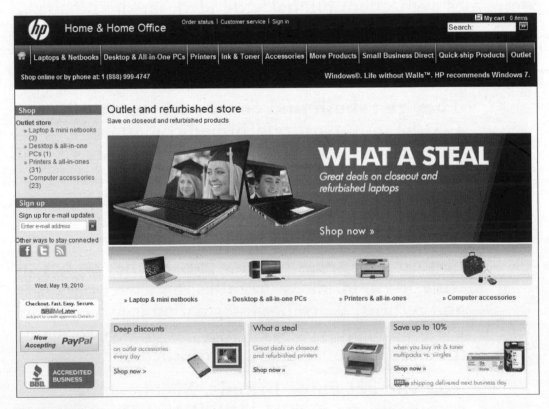

Figure 1-6

If you're thinking about buying from the Web or a catalog, don't forget to include the cost of shipping in the total price. Even with shipping costs, however, a refurbished computer may save you between 30% and 60%, depending on the deal you find.

Browse for a Browser

1. The two most popular *browsers* (the software programs that help you read what's on the Internet) are Firefox (available both for MAC and the PC) and Microsoft Internet Explorer. (They are to browsers what Coca-Cola and Pepsi are to the cola wars.) Both programs are powerful and user-friendly. Type the address (also known as the *URL,* for *Uniform Resource Locator*) of the Web site you want to visit, and boom, you're there. For example, to get to Twitter's home page, type **www.twitter.com** in the browser's address box and press Enter. (It's sort of a low-tech version of "Beam me up, Scotty!" — and almost as fast.)

According to recent statistics, the most popular browsers are Internet Explorer, Firefox, Chrome, and Safari. **Figures 1-7** and **1-8** show you the first two browsers and how they show pages in the same way. (Sit, browser! Now shake! *Good* browser!) The one you choose is a matter of preference — I use them both!

A Web page in Firefox

Figure 1-7

The same page in Internet Explorer   Icons on the toolbar

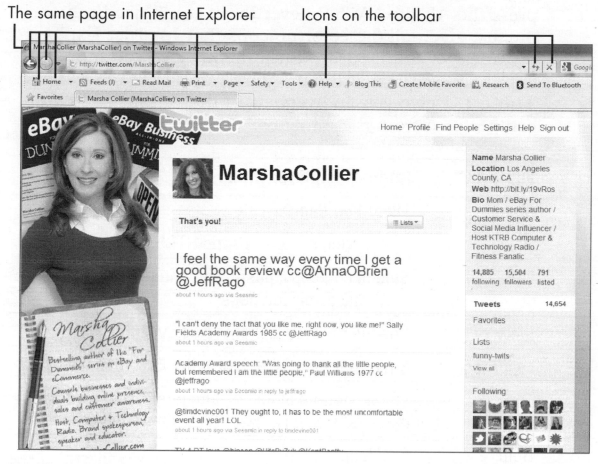

Figure 1-8

2. You can get Microsoft Internet Explorer and Firefox for free. To find out more information (or to make sure you're using the most up-to-date version of the software), go to:

- `www.microsoft.com` for Microsoft Internet Explorer

- `www.mozilla.com/firefox` for Firefox

3. If you've ever wondered what all those buttons and drop-down lists at the top of your browser do, now's the time to check it out. At the top of almost all Microsoft-enabled programs are standard drop-down menus that invoke various functions. (If they don't appear on your version,

press the Alt key.) Who'd ever think you'd need to use menus, given all the colorful icons that Internet Explorer provides? Well, the drop-down menus give you more in-depth access to what the program can do. **Table 1-2** and **Table 1-3** give you an overview of the various tasks you can perform from these menus.

Table 1-2	Internet Explorer Menus
Menu	*What You Can Do*
File	Open, print, save, and send HTML Web pages
Edit	Select, cut, copy, paste, and find text on the currently displayed page
View	Change the way Explorer displays Internet pages
Favorites	Save your favorite pages in the Favorites file
Tools	Enable pop-up blockers, add filters, and clear your machine's history of the Web sites you've visited
Help	Find help

Table 1-3	Firefox Menus
Menu	*What You Can Do*
File	Open, print, save, and send HTML Web pages
Edit	Select, cut, copy, paste, and find text on the currently displayed page
View	Change the way Firefox displays Internet pages
History	See and navigate back and forth among the sites visited in your current session
Bookmarks	Bookmark a page or access your saved bookmarks (same as "favorites" in Internet Explorer)

Tools	Enable features, install add-on programs, clear Private Data, and set browser options
Help	Find help

4. As a *graphical interface*, Internet Explorer also presents you with colorful icons that allow you to invoke programs or tasks with a click of the mouse. You find these icons on the toolbars at the top of your browser window (refer to Figure 1-8).

5. If you want to add speed to your browsing and cut down your desk time, get comfy with using keyboard and mouse shortcuts. I'm all about using keystrokes instead of always pointing and clicking! I also love the controls available on my mouse. **Table 1-4** and **Table 1-5** give you a list of all the shortcuts I could find. You'll see that Internet Explorer and Firefox share some shortcuts.

Table 1-4	**Internet Explorer Shortcuts**
Press This	*Explorer Will*
F1	Open a help window
F3	Open the Search box so you can perform a search for a specific word on the current page
F4	Open your URL list so you can click back to a site that you just visited
F5	Refresh the current page
F11	Display full screen, reducing the number of icons and amount of other stuff displayed
Esc	Stop loading the current page
Home	Go back to the top of the Web page

53

End	Jump to the bottom of the current page
Backspace	Go back to the last Web page you viewed
Ctrl and + (plus sign); Ctrl and – (minus sign)	Enlarge or reduce the text on the screen
Ctrl and D	Add the current page to your Favorites list. (Don't forget to organize this list once in a while!)

Table 1-5	**Firefox Shortcuts**
Press This	***Firefox Will***
Backspace	Go to the previous page you've viewed
Ctrl and O	Open a window to open files from your computer
F5	Refresh current page
Ctrl and U	View Page source (to study HTML)
F11	Display full-screen, reducing the amount of icons and stuff displayed
Esc	Stop loading the current page
Ctrl and P	Print the page
Ctrl and S	Save the current page to a file on your computer
Backspace	Go back to the last Web page you viewed
Ctrl and + (plus sign) or Ctrl and – (minus sign)	Enlarge or reduce the text on the screen
Ctrl and F	Find a word on the current Web page

Chapter 2

Hooking Up to the Internet

You're settled on your computer, and you're ready to get started with social connections on the Web. Before you start checking out sites such as Facebook and Twitter, you need *access* to the Internet. (Details, details. . . .) The way to access the Internet is through an *Internet service provider,* or ISP, such as Earthlink, AT&T, or RoadRunner. If you don't already belong to one of these, don't worry; joining is easy, as I describe in this chapter.

ISPs offer two basic types of connections: dial-up (slower,

but less expensive) and broadband (faster and pricier). In this chapter, I fill you in on some details to help you decide what's right for you. Also, I tell you about the wired or wireless networking methods that complete the setup you need for easy access to Facebook and Twitter.

Over the years, I have written what seems like volumes of tips to keep people safe online. But I know this book won't have to give you all the whys and wherefores — you've been around the block (as have I) — so I give you just a few easy-to-follow rules for staying safe during your online social interactions.

Select an Internet Service Provider

1. If you plan to join a telephone dial-up ISP (because dial-up requires no additional equipment or connections in most — usually older — computers), just load the freebie software that comes with a computer and follow the registration steps that appear on your computer screen. (Also see the next section in this chapter.) A new computer may come with a free trial of America Online (AOL) or some other ISP. Before you put up your credit card, use your free trial to scout the Web for the best deals on getting hooked up to the Internet.

 When you go to a computer store or buy a computer, you're hit with all kinds of free trial offers that beg you to "Sign up now, first month free!" You can find free introductory deals everywhere! If you're new to the Internet and not sure which ISP to go with, your best bet may be to start with NetZero HiSpeed. NetZero has been around for years, and offers accelerated speeds on their dial-up connections.

2. If you have a need for speed, you may want to look into getting a broadband connection. The quality of the different types of broadband (DSL and cable) can vary greatly from area to area and even from street to street. Before you decide what kind of broadband connection you want, use your local library or friend's computer and go to the following Web site, shown in **Figure 2-1**:

www.broadbandreports.com

Type your ZIP code, press Enter, and read the reports for other users in your area. You can e-mail, post questions, and get all the information you need to decide what kind of high-speed connection will work best for you.

Type your ZIP code here.

Figure 2-1

3. If you decide that your time is worth a bit more than an increase in ISP cost, broadband (high-speed) connections can save you bunches of time when you're flying through Facebook photos. Here's the skinny on the different types:

- *DSL:* Short for *Digital Subscriber Line.* For as little as $19.95 a month, you can get rid of your pokey, analog dial-up connection and always be connected to the Internet. A DSL line can move data as fast as 6 MB per second — that's six *million* bits per second, or 140 times as fast as a 56K modem. At that speed, a DSL connection can greatly enhance your interaction with Facebook and Twitter, as well as any other Internet experience. For more information about what DSL is and how to get it, visit www .dslreports.com.

- *Cable:* An Internet cable connection is a reliable method for Internet access if you have digital cable TV. Your Internet connection runs through your television cable to a modem, and is regulated by your cable TV provider. With the advent of digital cable, this reliable and speedy Internet connection is an excellent alternative. (See my speed report from my wireless network in **Figure 2-2**.) Most cable accounts include several e-mail addresses for everyone in your family.

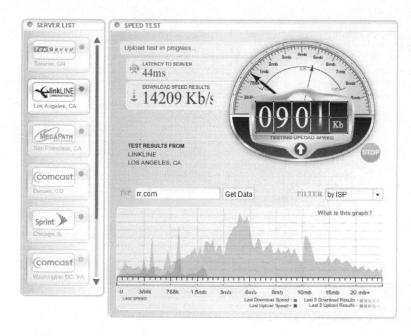

Figure 2-2

4. You have one more type of Internet connection to consider: public WiFi. *WiFi* stands for Wireless Fidelity, which describes a particular (and common) wireless technology for local networking without wires (that is, via a radio frequency). Believe it or not, there are lots of public places where you can find wireless Internet access that's free or has a very low fee. That's right — depending on the computer system you choose (see Chapter 1) and how much time you intend to spend online, you may not need an ISP of your own. All you need is a portable computer — netbook or laptop — that has a wireless connection (and all the new ones do these days).

To find free WiFi when you want to go portable, find your nearest coffee house and ask whether they have a free WiFi connection. If so, get connected and visit www.wi-fihot spotlist.com. At this site, as shown in **Figure 2-3**, type where you plan to be and you'll find any local WiFi hotspots.

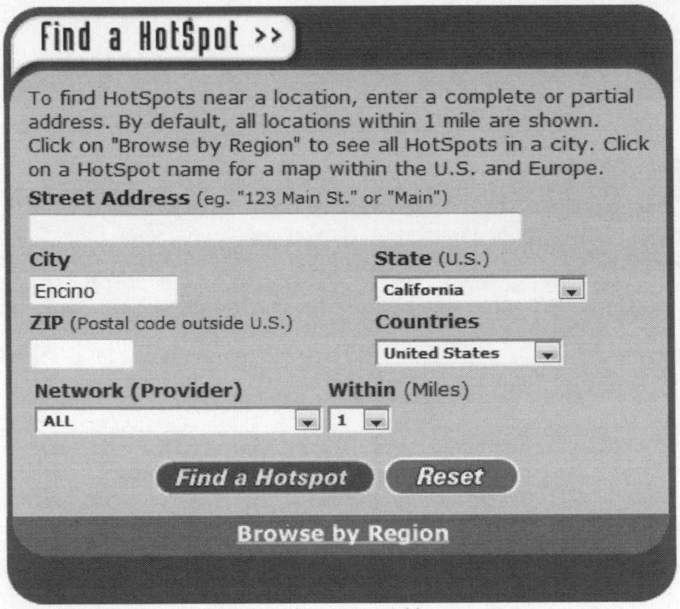

Find a HotSpot >>

To find HotSpots near a location, enter a complete or partial address. By default, all locations within 1 mile are shown. Click on "Browse by Region" to see all HotSpots in a city. Click on a HotSpot name for a map within the U.S. and Europe.

Street Address (eg. "123 Main St." or "Main")

City

Encino

State (U.S.)

California

ZIP (Postal code outside U.S.)

Countries

United States

Network (Provider)

ALL

Within (Miles)

1

Find a Hotspot   **Reset**

Browse by Region

Figure 2-3

Set Up a Dial-Up Connection

1. If you want to set up a dial-up connection, follow these simple steps. Run the free dial-up software that comes on your computer. It will prompt you through a registration process, so be sure to fill in all the blanks.

2. When prompted, get a phone cable and plug it into your computer's modem card and into a phone jack on the wall nearby.

3. Following the software instructions, you should merely need to wait until you hear some strange sounds coming from your computer (connecting noise) and your computer will connect with the service.

> Even if you start out with a standard dial-up connection, I honestly don't expect you to stay with it for too

long. Once you get the hang of running from profile to profile on Facebook or tweeting to your heart's content on Twitter, you're going to want some serious speed. Don't worry; the next section in this chapter tells you how to hook up to broadband and get the speed you need.

Choose a Broadband Network Option

1. When you set up your Internet connection with anything other than a direct dial-up connection to your computer, you're actually setting up the beginnings of a home network. By networking your home, you can save time — not to mention gain convenience — because you add the flexibility of taking your laptop into different rooms or locations. You can also tweet from out by your pool (or in your backyard) during summer!

 A *network* is a way to connect computers so they can communicate with each other as if they were one giant computer with different terminals. The best part of this idea is that a network lets several computers share a high-speed (broadband) Internet connection — and you can share printers and gaming devices as well. When you set up a computer network, your home can become a WiFi hotspot!

2. You have a choice of three types of home networks: Ethernet, powerline, and wireless. See **Table 2-1** for a quick rundown of some pros and cons of each.

61

Table 2-1	Network Pros and Cons	
Network type	**Pros**	**Cons**
Ethernet	Fast, cheap, and easy to set up	Everything must be wired together, cables run everywhere
Powerline	Fast, because your home is prewired with electrical outlets	Electrical interference may degrade signal
Wireless network	Fast, no ugly cables to deal with	More expensive, possible interference from electrical devices

While you make a decision about the type of network you want to use, consider the following points:

- The wireless network is currently the hot ticket and is becoming a standard. If you have a laptop and a high-speed connection, you deserve to have WiFi in your home. Any day now, you'll want to stream video from your notebook to your television. WiFi can do that and more!

- With broadband over powerline networking, you get high-speed Internet directly into your home electrical system. Just plug in your powerline boxes (more on that later) and you're up and running!

3. Regardless of the type of network you choose, all networks need the following two devices:

- **Router:** A router allows you to share a single Internet connection among multiple devices. A router does exactly what its name says: It routes signals and data to and from the different devices on your network. If you have one computer, the router can act as a firewall or even as a network device, allowing you to have a wireless printer (I have one — it's great) and a connection for a gaming device.

 You can connect as many computers, printers, or game systems (Wii, Xbox, or PS3 — yours or the kids') as you like, and reach the Internet from anywhere in your home. You can even hook up your laptop from the bedroom if you don't feel like getting out of bed.

- **Modem:** You need a broadband modem for a high-speed Internet connection, and you get one from your cable or phone company. To install, plug the modem into an outlet with cable (just like your TV) or into a phone jack with the phone line for DSL. The modem connects to your router with a short length of Ethernet cable.

 If you have broadband, and have more than one computer, you don't need to have a main computer turned on to access the connection from anywhere in the house.

Connect a Powerline Network

1. An ingenious invention, a powerline network uses your existing home power lines to carry your network and your high-speed Internet connection. You access the network by plugging a powerline adapter from your computer into an electrical outlet in the wall. Powerline networks have been around for a while and are in their second round of technological advances.

2. When deciding what kind of network to set up, consider these benefits of a nifty little powerline system:

- **It's inexpensive.** The requisite powerline magic box costs around $40, but you'll need one for each computer.

- **It's fast, as fast or faster than other network connections.** You could stream DVD movies from one room to another.

- **The networking connection is made through your existing electrical wiring.** It doesn't consume extra electricity.

- **Installation is easy.** Just plug a cable into your computer, and connect the cable to the powerline adapter. Plug the powerline adapter into the wall outlet.

3. To set up a powerline network, you need the following items in addition to a router and modem (which you need for any network):

- **Electrical outlets:** I'll bet you have more than one in each room.

- **An Ethernet connection on each computer:** All new computers come with an Ethernet outlet.

- **Powerline Ethernet bridge for each computer:** You plug an Ethernet cable from your computer into the powerline Ethernet bridge, a small box about the size of a pack of cigarettes that plugs into any two- or three-prong electrical outlet. See **Figure 2-4.**

Figure 2-4
Photo courtesy of Netgear

4. Hooking up a powerline network is so easy that it's a bit disappointing — you'll wonder why it isn't more complicated. If you have a high-speed Internet connection, you received a modem when you signed up. Because it's not common to connect the modem directly to your computer (a router does the network routing for you), you may already have a router.

The integration works like this:

1. *The high-speed connection comes in through your DSL or cable line.*

2. *The cable (or DSL) line plugs into your modem.*

3. *An Ethernet cable goes from your modem into a router.*

4. *One "out" Ethernet cable connection from the router goes to a local computer.*

5. *Another "out" Ethernet cable goes to the powerline adapter.*

6. *The powerline box plugs into a convenient wall outlet.*

5. When you want to connect the computers in other rooms to the network, just plug in a magic powerline

box. **Figure 2-5** shows you the basic setup for (say) a home office. Other rooms need only a powerline adapter that you hook up to a computer, game device, and so on, running an Ethernet cable from the adapter to the device's network card.

Connect a Wireless Network

1. Wireless networking (also known as WiFi) is the hot technology for all kinds of networks. It's an impressive system, with no cables or connectors to bog you down. You're probably more familiar with wireless technology than you may think at first. If you've ever used a wireless telephone at home, you've used a technology similar to a wireless network. Most home wireless phones transmit on the radio frequency band of 2.4GHz (gigahertz) and offer an option to choose from several channels automatically to give you the best connection.

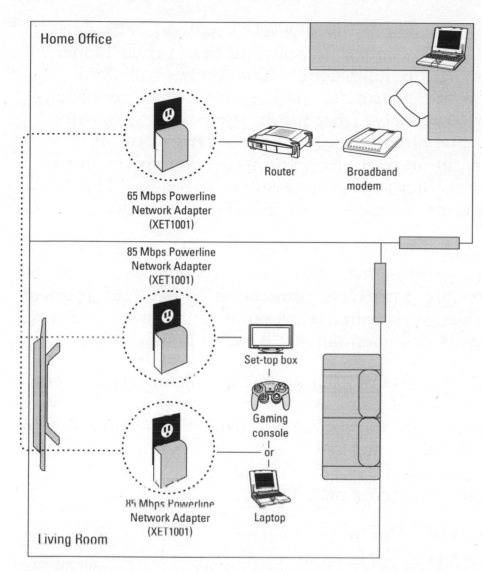

Home Office

65 Mbps Powerline
Network Adapter
(XET1001)

Router

Broadband
modem

85 Mbps Powerline
Network Adapter
(XET1001)

Set-top box

Gaming
console

or

85 Mbps Powerline
Network Adapter
(XET1001)

Laptop

Living Room

Figure 2-5

Figure courtesy of Netgear

 Here's an FYI on all those signals running around and about your house. AM radio broadcasts from 53KHz (kilohertz) to 1.7MHz (megahertz), and FM radio, television, cell phones, GPS, and the space station broadcast in megahertz. One gigahertz (GHz) is a thousand kilohertz, so it won't be interfering with other radio frequency signals.

2. The two prevalent forms of wireless networks also work on the 2.4GHz band; you'll need to preset the channel when you set up the system. There are basically four types of wireless formats, and the newer types are usually *backward-compatible* (that means the newer types work well with the older types). Be sure to check out the various computers, routers, and so on that you want to connect together in your network; in particular, find out which wireless format(s) they use. Those formats are

➤ **802.11a:** This wireless format works really well; fast with good connectivity. It's used when you have to serve up a wireless connection to a large group of people, such as in a convention center or a dormitory. This isn't something you'll use at home.

➤ **802.11b:** My old laptop has a built-in 802.11b connector, so I can connect to the ever popular WiFi hotspots in Starbucks and airports. The b version is slower than the newer versions (mentioned later in this list) and can transfer data at only 11 Mbps (11 megabits of data per second).

➤ **802.11g:** This is the next incarnation of WiFi that uses the 2.4GHz band; its nickname is "the g band." It speeds data to a possible 54 Mbps, and is backward-compatible with 802.11b service. Many older WiFi networks and gaming devices work on the g band.

➤ **802.11n:** This mode — the newest — builds on the previous standards by adding multiple-input multiple-output (MIMO) technology. MIMO uses multiple antennas (usually built into the router) to carry more information than previously possible with a single antenna. It uses the 5GHz band (an improvement on the old 2.4GHz band). It also increases speed through connection to 100 Mbps.

 For maximum speed, your entire network needs to be an 802.11n, 5GHz network. In my house, my 802.11n network doesn't work at full speed because I have existing laptops on 802.11b/g. I'll continue with a mixed 802.11b/g/n network until I replace all my laptops with 802.11n. And until I do that, my system won't run at the top advertised speeds.

3. Before you start worrying about sending your data over the airwaves, you'll be glad to know that wireless networks are protected by their own brand of security.

- **WEP (Wired Equivalent Privacy):** This original technology led the way in home WiFi security. WEP encrypts your wireless transmissions and prevents others from getting into your network. Sadly, it got so that a high school kid could crack this system, so now home WiFi users have WPA (and even WPA-2) instead. For more about those, read on.

- **WPA (WiFi Protected Access)** utilizes a *pre-shared key* (PSK) mode, where every user on the network is given the same passphrase. In the PSK mode, security depends on the strength and secrecy of the passphrase. So to link your laptop or desktop to a wireless network with WPA encryption, you need to find out the predetermined passphrase. Just enter it during setup on every computer that uses the network, and you should be good to go.

 Most WiFi hotspots you come across may not have any encryption, and some may be free for all to use. Just be aware that some miscreants drive through neighborhoods with a WiFi scanner looking for open wireless networks. These war-driving scammers then attempt to connect to an unprotected network to hack into personal information. Be sure to set your security settings to protect your network.

4. With a wireless network, you have to hook your computer (a laptop works best) to a wireless router to perform some beginning setup tasks such as choosing your channel and setting up your WPA passphrase. When you complete the setup and turn on your wireless router, you have created a WiFi hotspot in your home or office. Typically, your new hotspot will provide coverage for at *least* 100 feet in all directions, although walls and floors cut down on the range. Even so, you should get good coverage throughout a typical home. For a large home, you can buy signal boosters to increase the range of your hotspot.

5. The following steps, although simplified, outline the process for how you configure your wireless network. **Figure 2-6** shows a wireless network diagram from Netgear.

   1. *Connect an Ethernet cable from your laptop to your router.*

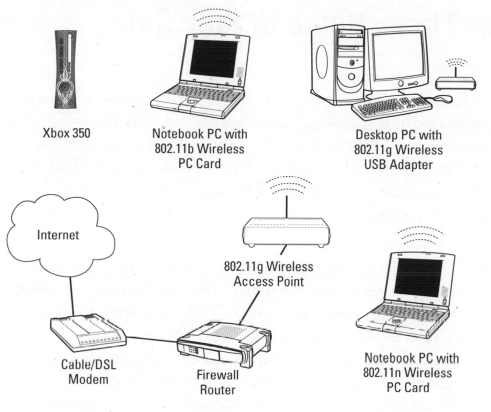

Xbox 350

Notebook PC with
802.11b Wireless
PC Card

Desktop PC with
802.11g Wireless
USB Adapter

Internet

802.11g Wireless
Access Point

Cable/DSL
Modem

Firewall
Router

Notebook PC with
802.11n Wireless
PC Card

Figure 2-6

Figure courtesy of Netgear.

2. *The setup program may run automatically (or the documentation that came with your router will tell you how to invoke it). Set your security protocol and passphrase.*

3. *Follow router instructions as to whether you need to reboot the router.*

4. *Run a cable from your DSL or cable jack to your modem.*

5. *Connect an Ethernet cable from your modem to your router.*

6. *Type in the passphrase to all computers on the network, one at a time.*

Remember These Rules to Stay Safe Online

1. Don't click links you receive in e-mail messages. Even if you get an e-mail message from someone you know, don't click any links. There's no way to know for sure that their account hasn't been hacked and you're being directed to a site that can do you serious damage. Here are specific examples of e-mail messages with links that you might receive:

   • **Phishing e-mails:** These e-mails purport to be from your bank, your investment broker, or even your insurance company. They ask you to click a link and when you do, you arrive on a page where you have to log in. *Do not log in* (if you've gone this far). Bad-deed doers can replicate a Web page to look very official, and what they really want is your log-in information — in particular your passwords, account information, or Social Security Number.

   • **E-mails that you think are from friends:** You may get a link in an e-mail message that you think is from a friend. Don't click it unless you are sure! Sometimes these links take you to a Web site where you can get a Trojan (a sneaky program that gives a hacker remote access to your computer), a virus (when unknowingly downloaded, replicates itself to wreck havoc on your programs or data), a worm (a variant of a virus that replicates itself transparently until it takes over all your computer's memory and possibly your hard drive), or heaven knows what. Stay safe.

- **E-mails from your bank or someone that you do business with:** Instead of clicking a link in the e-mail, go to the bank or business Web site by typing the Web address in your browser address bar as you usually do. If the bank or business has some sort of special message for you, it will show up when you sign in to your account. Most times, you will not receive an e-mail link unless you sign up with the business for automatic payments or notices.

2. Stay safe with friends. You'll find that you will have more "friends" on Twitter because Twitter is a bit more impersonal. The fun of Twitter is being able to hear from many people from different places. Also, your Twitter bio is only a sentence long and it doesn't (or at least shouldn't) give much away about you.

 Facebook's info page does show a lot of information. You might not want everyone on your friend list to be able to see everything — perhaps only your closest friends. Use Facebook's security controls (see Chapter 6) to set controls for who can see what when they visit your Facebook pages.

3. Don't give away too much information. Don't give away any bit of information that makes you feel uncomfortable. Be careful who you trust online with your home address and other contact information. *And never give away your Social Security Number!* I don't want to scare you, but someone with just a few bits of information about you can get a lot more data than you can imagine. The Internet has plenty of sites (for example, Google maps) that will even show people a photo of your house. Always be cautious.

Chapter 3

All About E-Mail

I know, I know, you've got sending and receiving e-mail down. But did you know there's a bit more to it? You can not only use e-mail to send messages, but you can also subscribe to news lists and feeds on the Internet. And in fact, Facebook and Twitter use your e-mail account to send you notifications of activity on your (and your friends') pages, private messages, and more. You'll be surprised when your e-mail becomes your pipeline to the news your friends post on the sites. Let's get into the full picture now!

Know that your e-mail address consists of two parts. The part before the @ sign is the local part (so the server knows who to send the e-mail to). After the @ sign is the *domain address* — which tells the domain name system which mail transfer agent accepts mail for that domain.

Every Web site has a URL (its address online), and every e-mail address has a domain component. When requests for Web pages or e-mails are launched into the ethers of the Web, the routing system needs to know where they should be sent. So if you're using the e-mail address your Internet service provider (ISP) assigned you, the e-mail is sent to your user ID (your name) @ your ISP domain — literally your address on the Web.

Then the mail transfer agent (MTA, a type of software) uses your online name and address to transfer electronic mail messages from one computer to another.

Also know that your e-mail address (the local part) can use any name you want, as long as someone else at the domain isn't using it. It's usually best to have at least one address with your real name for public and official use. You might want to add a second (or third, fourth, or fifth) address with different *noms de plume* for family members, friends, and specific projects. For example, I have the following names on different services:

mcollier1	eBay4Dummies
Marsha.Collier	eBayGal
Talk2Marsha	Cre8ive

There may be six different names, and all are accessible online, but they all download daily into Outlook, my e-mail program on my PC.

In this chapter, I tell you about where you can get e-mail

service and take you through the basics of signing up and using Gmail, the free e-mail service from Google. Having a Gmail account is not only cool, but it's very convenient. You might prefer to give out this anonymous e-mail address to online sites for privacy reasons. It's just an extra (*and free*) convenience. Check out this chapter for more of the benefits.

Check Out Places to Get Your E-Mail Service

1. You can start your search for an e-mail account with your Internet service provider (ISP). When you signed up for your Internet service, you were probably allotted up to five e-mail accounts for different members of your family. Your ISP also assigned you a user name when you signed up. My ISP gave me my user name, but I wasn't aware that it would be the name in my e-mail address, too. (Seriously, *mcollier1* doesn't have much of a ring to it.)

 Your ISP will have a Web interface where you can check your e-mail online, but it's far more efficient to use a software program on your computer for *all* your e-mail.

2. Understand that the e-mail account from your ISP has pluses and minuses, as follows:

> • **Minus:** You may change Internet service providers in the future. Hence, if you're using the ISP e-mail address as your own, you'll have to change it. This will force you to contact everyone who has that e-mail address to change it in their records. I've been with my ISP for over seven years; the thought of having to send

a change of address to *every single one* of my contacts is, well, loathsome.

- **Plus:** Your ISP is going to be a lot more helpful when you have a problem or a question than the Web-based free services I mention in the next step. Service providers are invested in keeping you as a paying customer. They have a customer-support staff that you can contact with problems.

3. You can also consider using a Web-based e-mail service. More and more people have found Internet-based e-mail accounts the convenient way to go. They can access these accounts online from any computer, anytime day or night. And these services are offered at no charge.

 Notice that (in the preceding step) I didn't say Web-based e-mail accounts were *free*. Although the providers don't ask for money, they do expose you to ads while you go through your e-mail. Most services have settings that allow you to download your e-mails to your home e-mail program and to your smartphone.

4. The benefits of having a Web-based e-mail address is that you can change your home ISP anytime you wish, and you won't have to notify hundreds (perhaps thousands) of connections to give your new e-mail address. In the next section, I give you an overview of the leaders in the online e-mail arena who are jockeying for your business.

Meet the Big Three Web-Based E-Mail Providers

1. Yahoo! Mail from industry veteran Yahoo! (founded in 1994, which is ancient by Internet standards) has been ratcheting up its offerings. The home page for your e-mail

is a mélange of news tips, weather reports, trendy topics from the Internet, an editable calendar, ads (of course), and (finally) your e-mail boxes, as shown in **Figure 3-1**. It's a very popular service with the following features:

- **Unlimited e-mail storage.** This means you can keep your e-mails on Yahoo! forever. (I'm not sure why you'd want to keep all your mail around, but diff'rent strokes. . . .)

- **Huge file attachments.** If you want to attach videos or other large files to your e-mails, it's easy on Yahoo! Many servers limit the size of the files you can send through e-mail. Yahoo! limits attachment size to a 25MB (megabyte) maximum.

- **Thumbnails of images.** You may want to attach pictures to e-mails you send to your friends and family. Here you can rotate the image (ever have any photos come out sideways?) and get thumbnail-size reductions of your pictures.

- **Yahoo! Messenger.** If you're familiar with the old AIM (AOL Instant Messenger) feature, you'll be right at home with the similar online-chat service that Yahoo! offers. You can talk to contacts in chat format who have accounts in the Yahoo! service — either from the Yahoo! Web site or from a smartphone.

Check, compose, and search e-mail.

Find top stories.

Read your e-mail messages.

Share your status.

Find help.

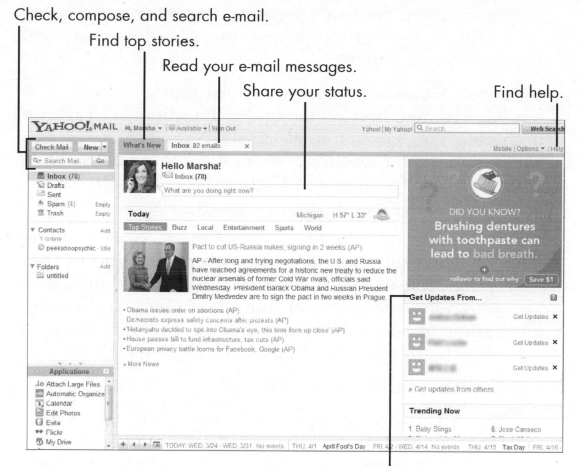

Get updates from friends and family.

Figure 3-1

- **Robust Help area.** Notice the Help link in the upper-right corner of the screen. Click it to be transported to a simple-to-understand tutorial and help area.

 To access Yahoo! Mail, go to `http://mail.yahoo.com`.

 The major drawback of Yahoo! Mail is that if you want to download your e-mail to your personal computer, you have to upgrade to the Plus service. Plus service costs $19.99 a year, but also does away with ads on your page.

2. Microsoft Hotmail is another popular online e-mail service. Hotmail lives online under the Microsoft Live umbrella. You can sign in at http://home.live.com, where you have a landing page for any other Live services you might use (as shown in **Figure 3-2**). You can also access Hotmail directly at www.hotmail.com.

 First off, you need to know that the service is only run by Microsoft; they don't fuss over what kind of computer you use. You can use either a Mac or a Windows PC and still avail yourself of Hotmail. You may know of people who have msn.com e-mail domains, which are also served up by the Hotmail servers.

Here are the special features of the no-cost Hotmail service:

- **5 GB storage space to start.** That's gigabytes — 1,024 megabytes *times five!* Not unlimited, but certainly more than you'll probably need to use.

- **Instant Messenger service for all Hotmail accounts.** All online mail services offer IM to their subscribers.

- **Integration with Outlook and Outlook Express** for e-mail and calendar, using the Outlook Hotmail Connector tool.

- **25 GB of online storage space for photos or documents in the SkyDrive function.** You can set the pictures and documents you store here to be private or to be shared. It's a very handy (and free) way to back up documents and pictures.

- **Import from other online e-mail services.** With an easy tool, you can import other online e-mail services into your Hotmail home page.

 If you want to upgrade — so you don't see ads, can send large (20MB) files, and get 10GB of storage — you can sign up for Hotmail Plus for $19.95 a year.

Windows Live™   Home   Profile   People   Mail   Photos   More ▾   MSN ▾   Search People or web   bing 🔍   Marsha ▾
sign out

Wednesday, March 24ᵗʰ

Northridge, CA 72°
Private messages | Invitations
People you might know
Your calendar

Mail   Options ▾   Help

✉ Windows Live Hotmail Member Services   2 hours ago   ⬚ Marsha
Getting started with Windows Live Hotmail   Loving this app
Go to inbox (1) | Send a message
                                                              Add people | Edit profile
                                                              Share photos | Add web activities
What's new with your network   Do more ▾

: Arketi Group | Post a note   Mar. 3   MSN

has a new Messenger picture   Mar. 3   MSNBC top news

| Post a note   Threats linked to health votes prompt
                                                          security
                                                          U.S. Mint unveils new national parks
                                                          quarters
                                                          Supreme Court halts Texas execution

More updates | ✉ Feed | Options   MSN Entertainment: News
                                                          Robert Culp, who starred in 'I Spy,' dead at 79
                                                          Megan Mullally leaves Broadway's 'Lips Together'
                                                          Megan Mullally leaves Broadway's 'Lips Together'

                                                          FOXSports.com News

Figure 3-2

3. Google Mail (Gmail) — the newcomer begun in 2004 as an invitation only test — has surpassed Yahoo! Mail (the longest-running free e-mail service) in popularity. Your Google home page has a bar at the top where you can easily access any of Google's other free services. What

makes Gmail popular is the array of features:

- **7GB of storage and growing.** Google's founders say no one will ever run out of storage space. (*Ever?* Hmmm . . . we'll see.)

- **Google Chat, which is the Google instant message service.** Unlike the other free online mail services, you can also log into the more popular AIM on your Google mail page. You also have the option of using your Webcam to have a live video chat with one of your contacts.

- **SMS (Short Message Service), or text messages, which you can send to any phone through Gmail e-mails.** All you need to know is the phone number and you can enable SMS messaging in your settings.

- **A great spam filter.** *Spam* is the name for advertising e-mail that is sent to you unsolicited by unscrupulous vendors to try to sell you goods or even to defraud you. Gmail smartly places spam in your Spam folder for you to review and delete at will. It's scathingly good at its job, check **Figure 3-3** to see all the e-mail that's been (thankfully) yanked from my Inbox.

- **Google Calendar,** an online calendar that is automatically yours when you have a Gmail account. You can opt to share your calendar with someone, or keep it private. And you see a Calendar window on your mail page. If you have a smartphone, you can view — and interactively update — your calendar from your phone.

Click to delete all spam.

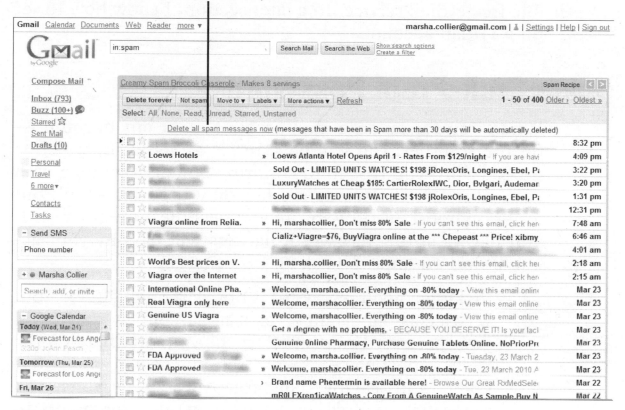

Figure 3-3

- **Connectivity features, such as instant synchronizing (sync) with smartphones and connecting with the e-mail program on your computer.** Gmail sends your e-mail to your desktop and keeps a copy on the Gmail server until you choose to delete it. The sync function on smartphones works interactively with your phone. (When you delete an e-mail from your phone, the e-mail disappears from your screen and goes into your trash on your Gmail Web page; you can always retrieve it if you've deleted it in error.)

All that said, Gmail is currently the most popular and flexible free e-mail service. In a later section, I show how to set up a Gmail account.

Pick a Pick-Proof Password

When you set up an e-mail account — or any account — on the Internet, you will have to set a *password,* which is the keyword you type in to confirm your sign-in along with your user ID. Passwords are not only used in e-mail, but also on almost every Web site you become a member of. If you have a strong password, hackers will pass by your account and attempt to hack an easier target.

 Picking a good password is not as thought-free — but *is* twice as important — as it may seem. Whoever has your password can (in effect) *be you* anywhere on the Web — posting comments, sending spam e-mail messages, and leaving dangerous messages (which can range from pranks to scams or worse) for others to see. Basically, such an impostor can ruin your online reputation — and possibly cause you serious financial grief.

With any online password, you should follow these common-sense rules to protect your privacy:

➤ Don't pick anything too obvious, such as your birthday, your first name, your address, or (never, never!) your Social Security number. (**Hint:** If it's too easy to remember, it's probably too easy to crack.)

➤ Make things tough on the bad guys — combine numbers and letters and create nonsensical words. Use upper *and* lower cases.

➤ Don't give out your password to *anyone* — it's like giving away the keys to the front door of your house.

➤ If you even suspect someone has your password, immediately change it.

➤ Change your password every few months just to be on the safe side. Maybe rotate a group of passwords over the various accounts you use?

Sign Up for a Gmail Account

1. I like Gmail above the other online e-mail service providers because it has great features and is easy to use. So start here to set up a Gmail account. Open your Web browser and type this URL in the address line:

```
http://mail.google.com
```

You'll see a page that looks like **Figure 3-4**. Read the information on the page and then click the New Features link at the lower right. Should there be any updates you need to know about, the latest news will be on this page.

2. Again, in the lower-right part of your screen, see the box that reads: *New to Gmail? It's Free and Easy. Create an Account?* Yep, that's the one, click the Create an Account button and get ready for the magic to happen. By getting your own Gmail account, you get access to Google's world of magic Web tools, such as Google calendar (an interactive online calendar you can share with your family), free Blogger blogs (more on that in Chapter 15), and Google Docs (a suite of free online programs very similar to Microsoft Office).

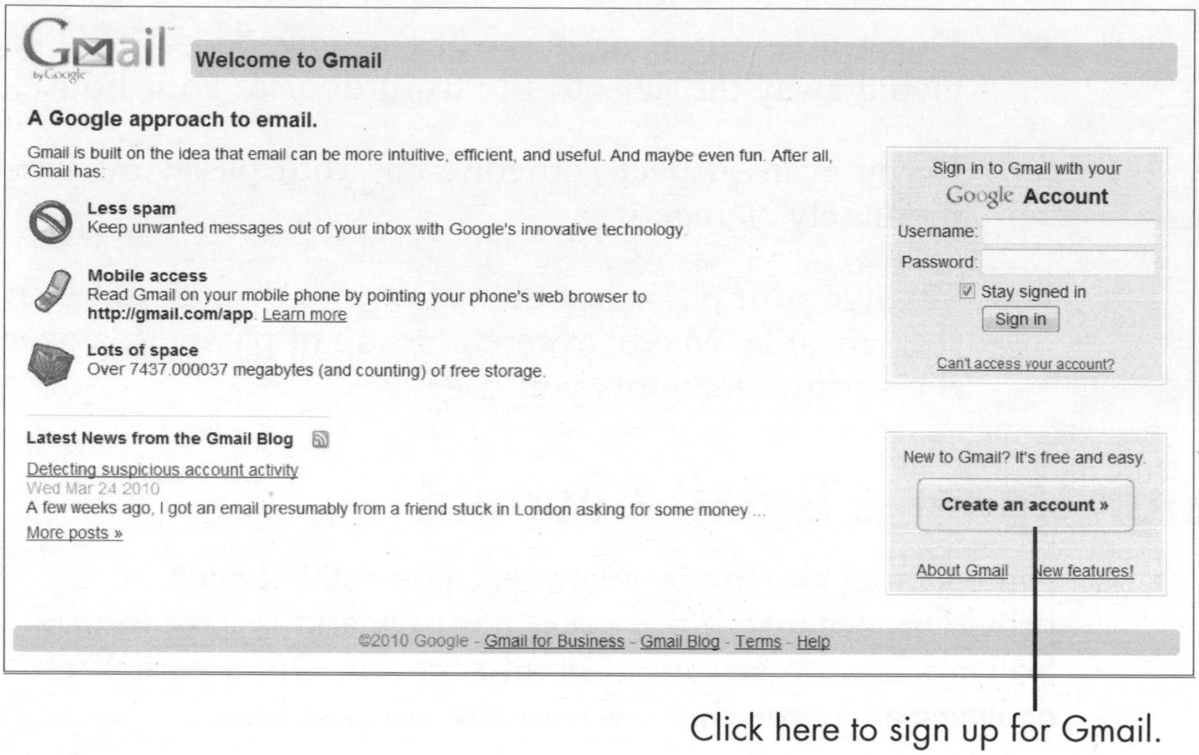

![Gmail Welcome to Gmail screen showing "A Google approach to email" with features Less spam, Mobile access, Lots of space, Latest News from the Gmail Blog, a Sign in box, and a "Create an account »" button.]

Click here to sign up for Gmail.

Figure 3-4

3. The resulting Get Started with Gmail page (see **Figure 3-5**) is where you type in your information:

- **Your name.** First and Last.

- **Desired Login Name.** Fill in what you want to become your local address and name at the Gmail domain. In Figure 3-5, I selected OnlineCustServ as my sample name. My e-mail address will be OnlineCustServ@gmail.com. (I chose this because I have another book — it's about online customer service — published by Wiley.)

 After you type in your desired name, click the Check Availability button. If that name is available, Google

86

will tell you so. If it isn't, Google will make suggestions that you probably won't like. Put on your thinking cap and come up with a good login name. This name will be with you for a long time; there's no changing it later.

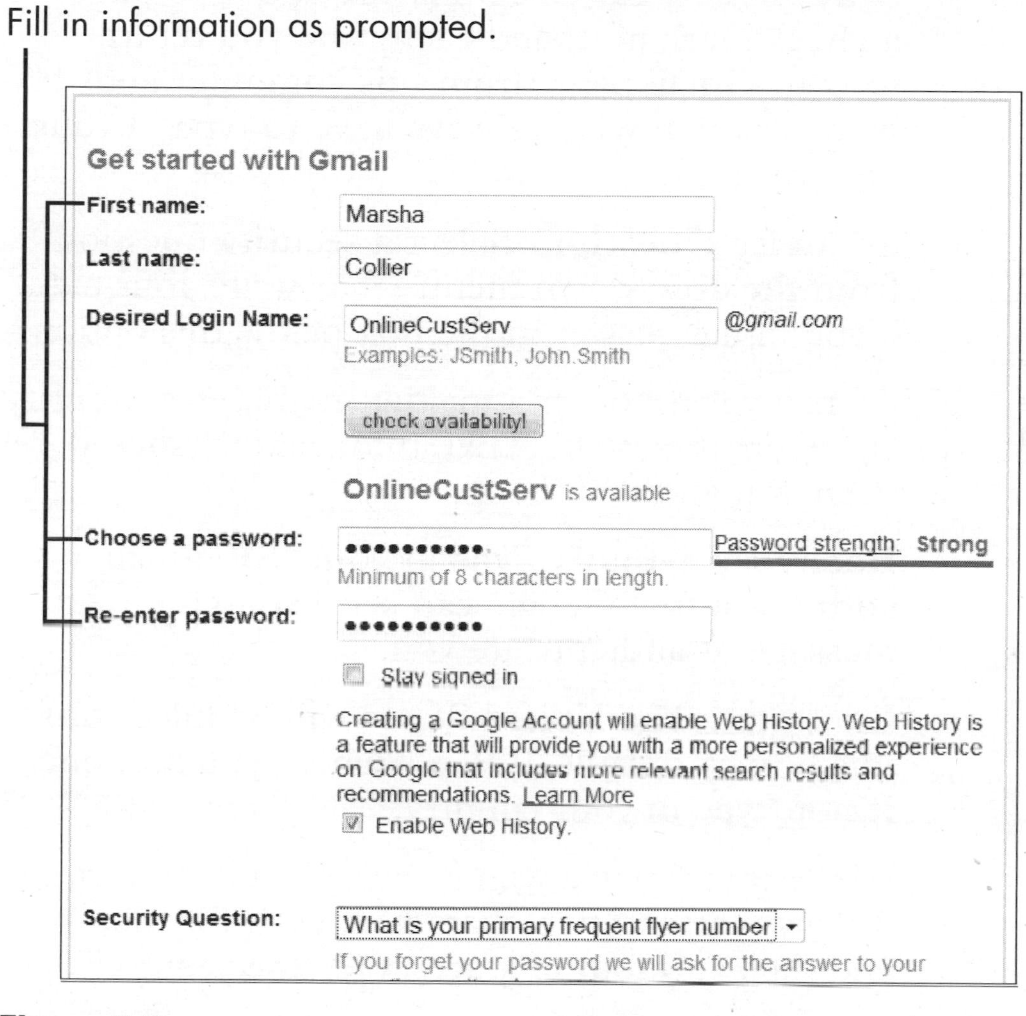

Fill in information as prompted.

Get started with Gmail

First name: Marsha

Last name: Collier

Desired Login Name: OnlineCustServ   @gmail.com
Examples: JSmith, John.Smith

check availability!

OnlineCustServ is available

Choose a password: ••••••••••.   Password strength: **Strong**
Minimum of 8 characters in length.

Re-enter password: ••••••••••

☐ Stay signed in

Creating a Google Account will enable Web History. Web History is a feature that will provide you with a more personalized experience on Google that includes more relevant search results and recommendations. Learn More

☑ Enable Web History.

Security Question: What is your primary frequent flyer number ▼
If you forget your password we will ask for the answer to your

Figure 3-5

- **Choose a Password.** Refer to the preceding section and type your password in the box; make sure it's at least eight characters long. You'll notice (as you're typing) that Google tells you whether your selected password is Weak or Strong. Go Strong! Also, type in your password again — carefully! — to confirm it where prompted.

- **Stay Signed In.** Click this check box to put a check mark in it, and each time you return to your Gmail page (from this computer and browser), you won't always have to type in your password.

- **Security Question.** Select a security question from the drop-down menu — or write your own. Type in the answer in the box below this option.

 Never use your mother's maiden name as a security question on the Web. That information should be between you and your bank.

- **Recovery e-mail.** Type in your ISP e-mail address so that Google can send you an e-mail message to authenticate you.

- **Location.** The United States will be filled into this box by default. If that's where you are, fine. If not, type in your country.

- **Birthday.** Google wants your birth date in mm/ dd/yyyy format: two characters each for month and day, and four characters for the year.

 It's okay to fib about your age, but be sure you remember the date you give Google. Should you ever forget your password, or if your account gets messed up in some way, you're going to have to supply this information. If you can't remember it, you're out of luck.

- **Word verification.** You'll see a bunch of semi-legible letters in a box. (They're called Captcha codes, and you can find out more in Chapter 5.) Try to read them — and if you can make them out, type them in as prompted. If you're wrong, the page will refresh and you'll get a new set of letters. (I had to do this three times until I got it right.)

- **Terms of Service.** Here Google outlines their Terms of Service (TOS). Any Web site you sign up with has them. Read the TOS and print them if you'd like, but if you don't agree to them, you can't have a Gmail account.

Click the I Accept. Create My Account button under the Terms of Service, and you're done.

4. Check your e-mail. Google immediately sends you an e-mail verification that your account has been established. The e-mail also contains an important verification code that you may need should you ever encounter problems or forget your password.

 Print out your Google verification e-mail so you have a record of that 30-digit verification number. While you're at it, save a copy to your documents folder; you can never be too secure.

5. The next page congratulates you for opening a Google account. On the right side of the page is a Show Me My Account button. Click it!

6. Google then offers to integrate Google Buzz into your Gmail account. *Buzz* is Google's foray into the social-networking market. Since you're already busy learning Twitter and Facebook, you might want to deal with Buzz

at a later date. Click the small link next to the big blue bar; it says *Just Go to My Inbox, I'll Try Buzz Later*. Sounds good to me.

7. The next page? It's your Gmail home page!

Add Your Contacts

1. When you first arrive at your Gmail page, take a deep breath and look around before you start to click anything. **Figure 3-6** shows you some of the important points to take in. Get familiar with the page; there's a lot to look at. You'll notice that the fine folks at Google have sent you some introductory e-mails. So why not start there?

2. One of the e-mails you have received has instructions on how to import your contacts. Move your cursor over the e-mail list. Your cursor turns into a small hand with a pointing finger. Click your mouse once and the e-mail opens!

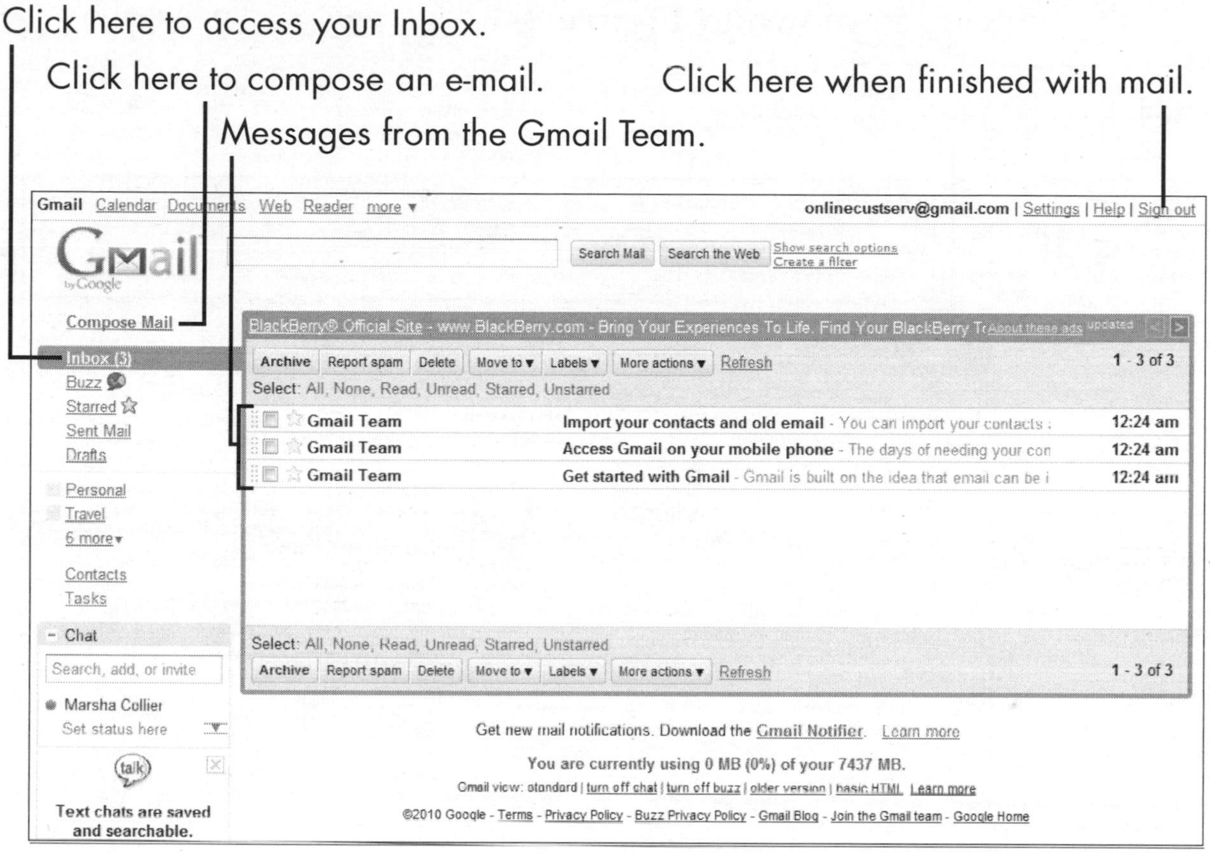

Click here to access your Inbox.

Click here to compose an e-mail.   Click here when finished with mail.

Messages from the Gmail Team.

Figure 3-6

3. You can import your contacts and existing mail from Yahoo!, Hotmail, AOL, and your ISP accounts. If you indicate that it's okay to do so, Gmail will continue to import your mail from the other servers for the next 30 days. For now, I suggest that you just close the e-mail by clicking the Back to Inbox link on the top left of the e-mail. You may just want to input your contacts manually.

4. When you're back at the Inbox, scroll down the page and look at the column on the left side. Just below your folder list and above Chat is a small Contacts link. Click it and prepare to add a contact. Your Add Contact page will

appear, as shown in **Figure 3-7**.

Click here to add a new contact.

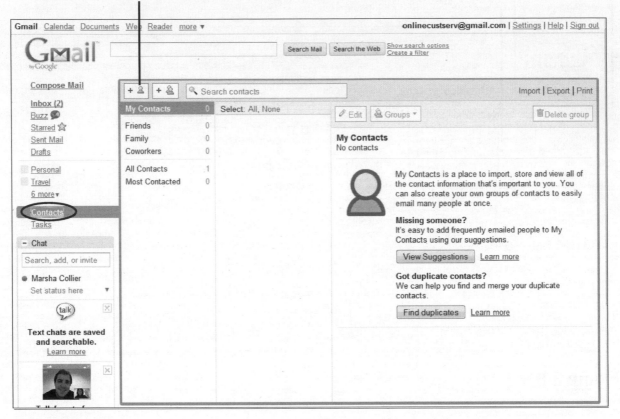

Figure 3-7

5. Click the icon with the plus (+) mark near the upper left, and another page opens; that's where you fill in your contact's information. You can add the name, company name, title, phone, address, Web site (if the person has one), birthday, and any notes you want to make. When that's done, click Save, and you'll have your new contact.

6. Click the Edit button at any time to make changes or to add information to the contact. Return to your Inbox by clicking the Inbox link at the left side of your page.

Compose and Send an E-mail

1. If you're following along, then you're probably about to send your first Gmail e-mail. Click the link that says Compose Mail (at the upper left of the screen), as shown in **Figure 3-8**.

Fill in a recipient, subject, and message.

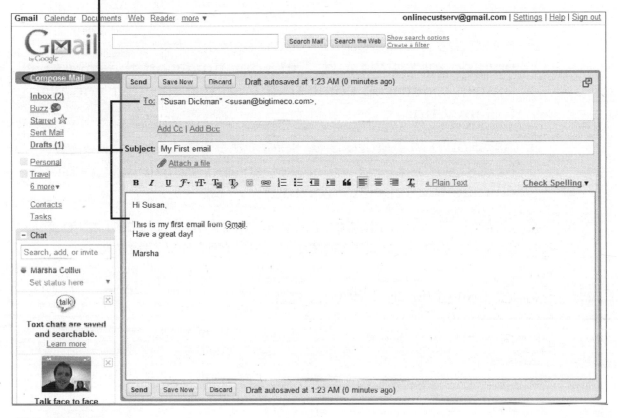

Figure 3-8

2. The e-mail form opens. In the To box, type in the name of one of your contacts or type in someone's e-mail address.

3. Type the subject of the e-mail in the Subject line.

4. Type your e-mail message into the text box below the Subject line. If you want to add interest to your text, you can change the typeface, its size, make it Bold, Italic, Underlined, or change colors by using the format bar at the top of the text box. Want to get fancy? Try these tricks on for size:

1. *Highlight the text by clicking your mouse button (and holding it down) at the beginning of the text you want to edit.*

2. *Keep the mouse button down as you drag the mouse pointer across the text.* Lift your finger off the mouse button when you come to the end of the text you want to fancy up.

3. *As shown in **Figure 3-9**, select the attribute you want to apply from the format bar.* In this example, I plan to change the typeface (or font).

4. *Select the font (or color if you're using the color selector) by clicking it, and magically your text will change.*

Click a tool to change the look of your text.

Figure 3-9

5. When you finish writing and formatting your e-mail, click the Send button in the lower-left corner of the e-mail form.

Chapter 4

Speaking the Social Networking Language

Get ready to . . .

You probably suspect that the online social network includes a whole lot more than Twitter and Facebook. And you're right! I suspect that once you get involved on the Web, you're going to want to spread your wings and take off to some other fun venues.

96

There are quite a few more sites (other than Facebook and Twitter) where you might want to participate with your friends. In this chapter, I give you a very quick overview of the most fun sites I've found in the *interwebs,* or *world-wide webbytubes* — both terms are slang for the Internet. Just to keep you up on what the cool kids say and where they hang.

So, in no special order. . . .

Gather on Facebook

Since a large section of this book is about Facebook, I won't go into a lot of detail, but know that the site (as of this writing) gets 124.1 million visitors per month according to Quantcast. That's a lot of people. You never know who is going to show up on the pages.

Facebook is a place where you can find your family (I just connected with distant relatives across the country), new people with common hobbies and ideas, as well as old school chums. Best of all? You can view old friends' photos and see how they aged over the years. Since anyone over the age of 13 with a valid e-mail address can join, most kids are members. Which gives us parents a nice benefit: We can benevolently "stalk" our kids' and grandkids' pages to see some of what they're doing and watch out for them a bit. (I love looking at my daughter's page.)

Facebook is a community where you can share online contact on a daily basis. You can check in at any time and see what's happening in your friends' and family's world. The benefit of Facebook over Twitter is that you can see all your friends' posts on one page — your home page.

Figure 4-1 shows my profile page. I've been a Facebook member for quite a while so there's always lots happening on my page.

Figure 4-1

Figure 4-2 shows you the Fan Page that the *For Dummies* people set up for me. You can find Fan Pages for some of my favorite public figures, products, and businesses. Joining a Fan Page makes you part of an online community; the posts that the pageholder makes will appear on your home page, just like the posts from your friends. Feel free to find my pages on Facebook and post, I always love meeting my readers.

Figure 4-2

Communicate through Twitter

Have you sent a text message on your phone? If not, it's time to get with it; people send more text messages than they make phone calls these days. As far back as September 2008, Nielsen reported that a typical U.S. mobile subscriber placed or received 204 phone calls each month. In comparison, the average mobile customer sent or received 357 text messages per month (a 450% increase over the number of text messages during the same period in 2006).

Twitter is basically an SMS (for Short Message Service) on the Internet. I'll tell you more about it in Part III of this book, but I know you'll have lots of fun checking in every day to see what the rest of the world has to say.

Figure 4-3 shows my Twitter profile page, along with some of my *tweets* — the online term for Twitter posts or short messages. Though these can't go over 140 characters, you may be surprised at how much information fits into that format. It makes you a more concise writer.

Figure 4-3

After you set up a Twitter account, you can start to "follow" other Twitter members (a process I explain in Chapter 12) and have other members follow you, as well. Once you begin to tweet, you will be able to have real-time conversations with people from the online community that you build this way.

Find a Spot on MySpace

MySpace was the first online social-media community to gain wide usage. It was the most popular social networking site in 2006 but was overtaken by Facebook two years later. It's rumored that MySpace has approximately 57 million (at one time 300 million) unique active users in the United States who are heavily engaged on the site.

MySpace is pretty much dominated by high-schoolers, to the point that if grown-ups join, they might find themselves wandering aimlessly throughout the site wondering what to do. Recently the CEO of MySpace (a division of Newscorp), Owen Van Natta, told the media that the site planned to focus on entertainment content. Indeed, you find many bands and other artists using MySpace to promote their brands and sell downloads.

I have a page on MySpace (**Figure 4-4**) that I visit every once in a while, but very few of my friends are active on the site.

So if time is somewhat of the essence (who really has spare time anyway?), MySpace might not be on your list of sites to visit. It's really not my cup of tea anymore.

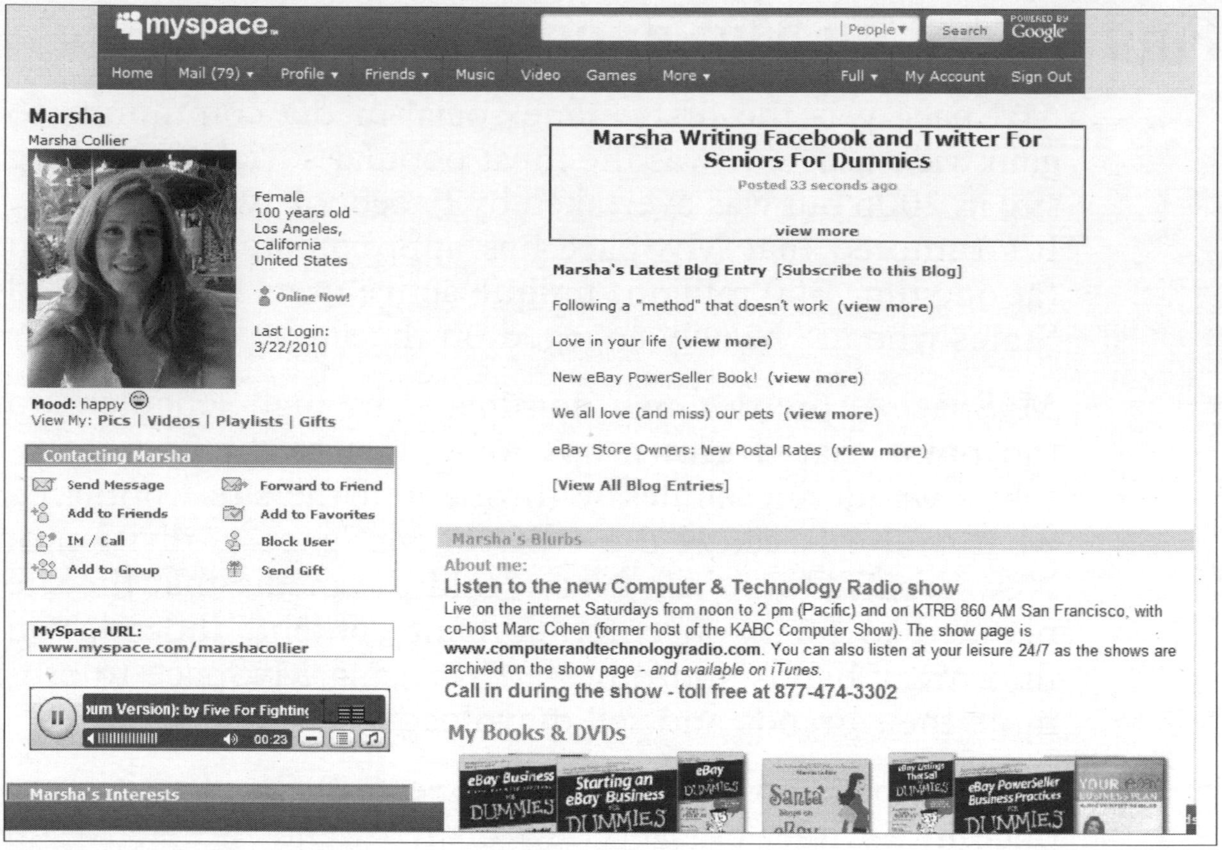

Figure 4-4

Get Connected on LinkedIn

If you have (or had) a business career, I know you're going to love LinkedIn. It's a business-oriented social network with over 60 million users. If you have a job, you should be on the site. If you're currently "at liberty," semi-retired, or interested in consulting, you should also be on the site. Just think — you can probably connect with most of the colleagues and heavy hitters you've worked with over the years. Your friends may be connected to some smart new

102

folks who just might be looking for your kind of experienced help.

After you register with LinkedIn, you can upload your resume, fill in information about yourself and your talents, and look for former acquaintances whom you've lost track of. You can search (try to remember everyone you've ever worked with) and connect with people you know and trust in business. These become your *connections*. You can invite anyone (whether a site user or not) to become a connection.

 Connections are not automatic. When you locate someone you know on LinkedIn, you have to ask them to connect with you. And don't attempt to connect with someone you don't know. Instead, find someone you already know, connect with him or her, and let that person connect you with new parties. That's the purpose of making connections.

My LinkedIn profile is shown in **Figure 4-5**. I enjoy being connected to the people I've worked with and get notices when they change jobs, update their profiles, or join one of the many groups on the site.

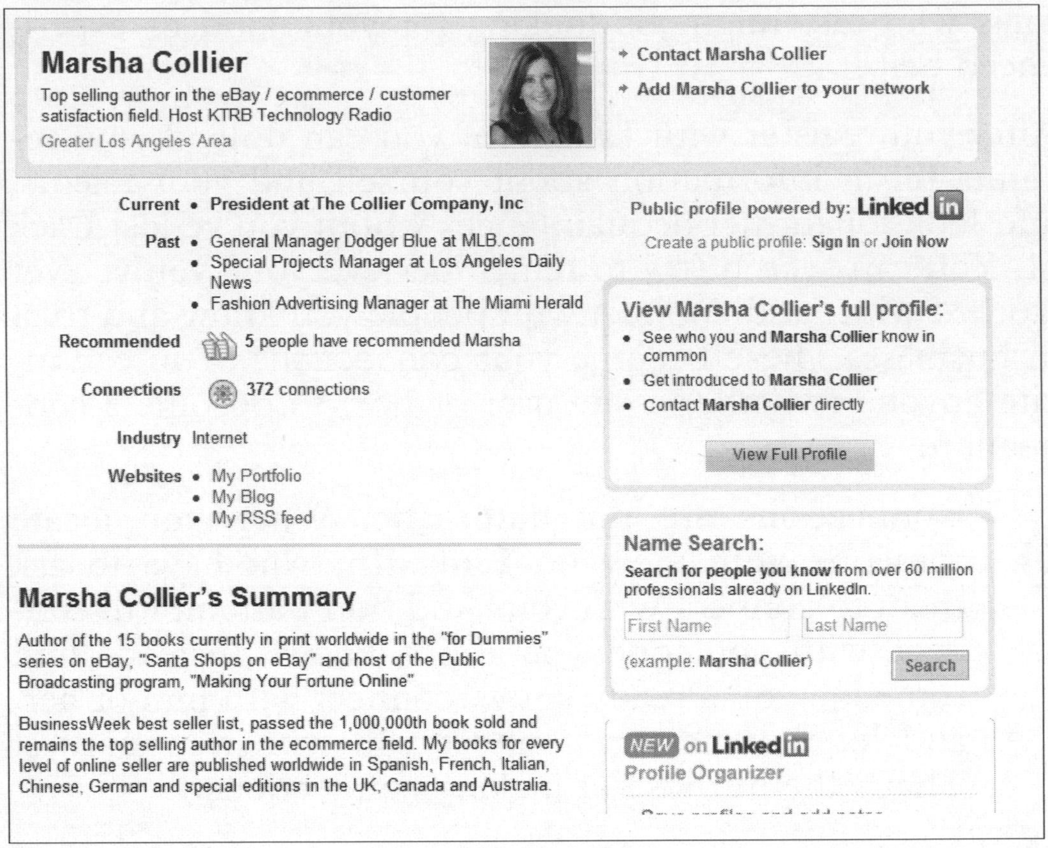

Marsha Collier

Top selling author in the eBay / ecommerce / customer satisfaction field. Host KTRB Technology Radio

Greater Los Angeles Area

→ Contact Marsha Collier
→ Add Marsha Collier to your network

Current • President at The Collier Company, Inc

Past • General Manager Dodger Blue at MLB.com
• Special Projects Manager at Los Angeles Daily News
• Fashion Advertising Manager at The Miami Herald

Recommended 5 people have recommended Marsha

Connections 372 connections

Industry Internet

Websites • My Portfolio
• My Blog
• My RSS feed

Public profile powered by: **Linked in**

Create a public profile: **Sign In** or **Join Now**

View Marsha Collier's full profile:
• See who you and **Marsha Collier** know in common
• Get introduced to **Marsha Collier**
• Contact **Marsha Collier** directly

[View Full Profile]

Name Search:
Search for people you know from over 60 million professionals already on LinkedIn.

[First Name] [Last Name]

(example: **Marsha Collier**) [Search]

NEW on **Linked in**
Profile Organizer

Marsha Collier's Summary

Author of the 15 books currently in print worldwide in the "for Dummies" series on eBay, "Santa Shops on eBay" and host of the Public Broadcasting program, "Making Your Fortune Online"

BusinessWeek best seller list, passed the 1,000,000th book sold and remains the top selling author in the ecommerce field. My books for every level of online seller are published worldwide in Spanish, French, Italian, Chinese, German and special editions in the UK, Canada and Australia.

Figure 4-5

See It All on YouTube

You're going to love YouTube — a video-sharing Web site where users can upload and share videos. You can browse almost any subject and find a video you'll enjoy. Want to watch a Harrier take off from an aircraft carrier? Check. Want to see Susan Boyle's performance from *Britain's Got Talent*? Check.

Want to see your grandchild take his first steps? That's up to your son or daughter. Most content on YouTube is uploaded by individuals, but the major media corporations including CBS, BBC, and other organizations offer some

104

of their videos on the site. YouTube is the fourth most visited Web site on the Internet, right behind Google, Yahoo! and Facebook.

 I really hope you set up an account on YouTube. You don't have to register to watch videos, but if you'd like to comment and rate videos, you need to have an account. *Entertainment Weekly* magazine put YouTube on its "Best of the Decade" list, saying, "Providing a safe home for piano-playing cats, celeb goof-ups, and over-zealous lip-synchers since 2005." It's really a lot of fun!

When you register on the site, you get your own Channel. **Figure 4-6** shows my channel and some of my favorite videos. I just know you'll spend hours on the site watching vintage commercials, TV shows, and more.

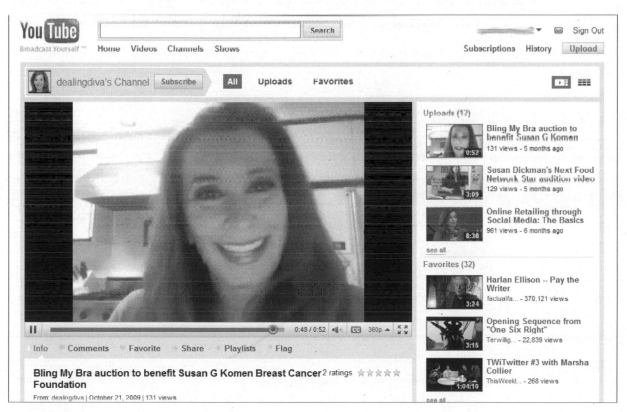

Figure 4-6

Have Your Say on BlogSpot

Have you ever considered writing a blog? The term *blog* is a shortened version of *Web-log,* originally a place where people would write and post short stories on the Web. Your blog could be that (short stories) — or a personal journal, random musings, or writings devoted to a specific subject (perhaps a hobby of yours)? It's free to set up and run a blog on Blogspot.com.

As you join more social networking sites, you can link to any blogs as you post them. And you may be surprised at the number of readers you draw. You could develop your own community where regular readers comment on your blog posts (if you wish).

I have a blog on Blogspot (see **Figure 4-7**). Check it out — maybe you'll get an idea of what you'd like to write on yours.

MARSHA COLLIER'S MUSINGS

HI! I'M THE AUTHOR OF THE "FOR DUMMIES" SERIES OF BOOKS ABOUT EBAY AND HOST OF COMPUTER AND TECHNOLOGY RADIO. I BLOG ON EBAY, USEFUL PRODUCTS AND ANYTHING FUN. ALSO PLEASE VISIT MY EBAY BOOK WEBSITE COOL EBAY TOOLS

ABOUT MARSHA

MARSHA COLLIER
LOS ANGELES,
CALIFORNIA, UNITED
STATES

I love connecting with all my readers on the web. Aside from writing books, I host a Computer & Technology Radio show with Marc Cohen Saturdays on the web and on KTRB San Francisco. When I take a break from work, I visit my garden, do some weight lifting with my trainer and enjoy my friends. Visit my online profile www.MarshaCollier.com to

TUESDAY, MARCH 02, 2010

My Life Online: Join me for a Sauvignon Blanc wine tasting

This couldn't be more creative! My buddy Rick Bakas, Director of Social Media for St. Supery winery came up with a brilliant idea to bring wine lovers together on Twitter. The virtual wine tasting is scheduled for 5 to 7 pm PST and everyone is invited.

It will be attended by wineries from all over the world who will share interesting info about their wine growing region as it relates to Sauvignon Blanc.

Join in and taste some wine and share your opinions on Twitter. Try to tweet in under 120 characters so others can "retweet" your tweets. It will be easier to follow the hectic tweetstream in a room I set up on Tweetchat.

Here are all the details from Rick. I'll see you on Twitter

Figure 4-7

Share Photos on Flickr

Flickr is a photo- and video-sharing site that's been on the Web since 2004. In 2005, the site was acquired by Yahoo! — and now you can join Flickr for free and upload photos to share with your friends and family. If you already have a Yahoo! e-mail address, that will become your user name on Flickr. Once you set up your account on Flickr, you can change your screen name to a nickname or your own name.

When you post photos on Flickr, you can *tag* them so your friends and family can find the photos by doing a search for your name or keyword. Tagging is a way to use keywords or names to identify important points about your uploaded

107

images — for example, who's in a photo, where it was taken, and so on. **Figure 4-8** shows some photos taken on my trip to France. You can use your screen name to find your photo stream (assuming your screen name is your given name) or photos where other people have tagged you by name in their images.

 If you join as a Pro member (for $24.95 a year), you won't have to look at ads, and you can upload an unlimited number of images.

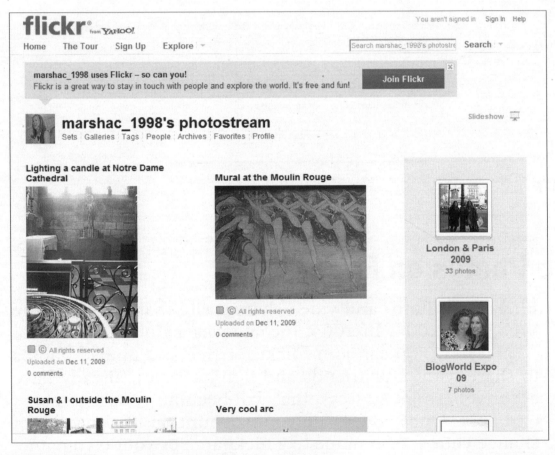

Figure 4-8

Stream Music on Pandora

Visiting Pandora.com is like having a radio in your computer. When you arrive at the home page, just type in a favorite song or artist, and Pandora will build a radio station for you; it will broadcast songs that you will like. (I promise.)

This magic result is based on the Music Genome Project, the most comprehensive analysis of music ever undertaken. Pandora's team of 50 musician-analysts listens to music, one song at a time, to study and collect hundreds of details on every song. According to the Pandora site, it takes the analysts "20-30 minutes per song to capture all of the little details that give each recording its magical sound — melody, harmony, instrumentation, rhythm, vocals, lyrics, and more — close to 400 attributes!"

Amazing, no? Once you register, you can create up to 100 stations to fit your many moods. If the music Pandora selects isn't just what you want, let the team know with a click of your mouse and they'll refine the choices selected for your station.

Figure 4-9 shows that I started a Lady Gaga channel, and it's coming up with just the sort of music I want to listen to right now.

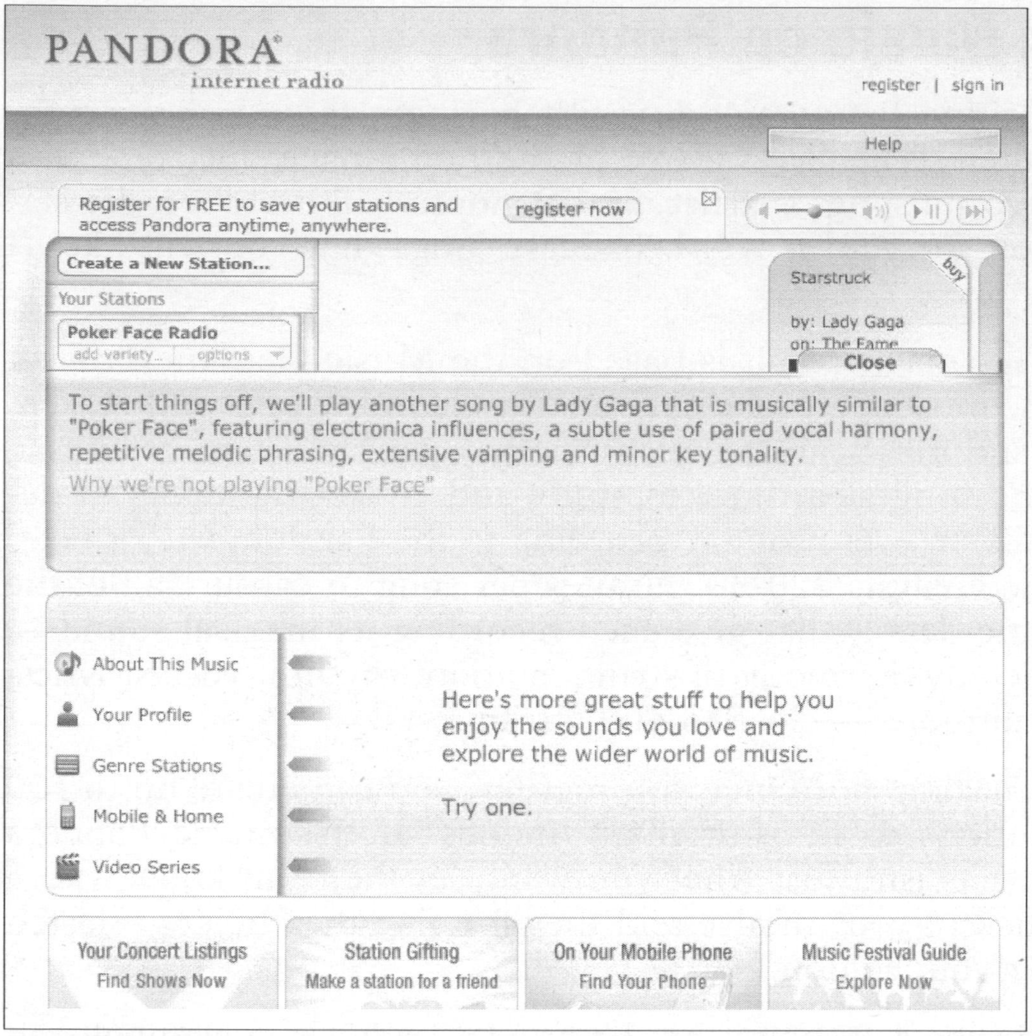

Figure 4-9

Watch TV and Movies on Hulu

Having a quiet night? Point your Web browser over to www.hulu.com, where you can find TV shows and movies online — from old favorites to the latest. It's a great place to catch up on shows that you may have missed from your favorite series. You'll find commercial-supported streaming video of TV shows and movies from NBC, Fox, ABC, and many other networks and studios.

When you arrive on the Hulu site, you see promotions for the latest shows added to the site, as shown in **Figure 4-10**. You can browse, by title, the thousands of TV shows and movies on the site by using the buttons at the top of the page.

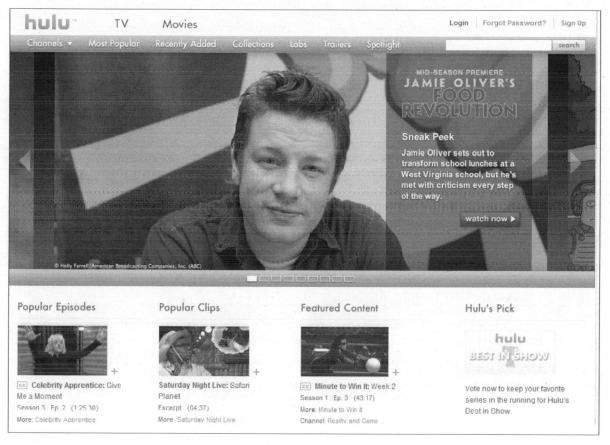

Figure 4-10

Trust me, you're going to love this site. So excuse me for a moment, I'm going to watch one of the 72 episodes of the old *Mary Tyler Moore* show.

Part II
Putting Your Face onto Facebook

The 5th Wave   By Rich Tennant

"I know it's a short profile, but I thought 'King of the Jungle' sort of said it all."

Chapter 5

Preparing Your Facebook Profile

You've heard about it. Your kids and maybe (if you have them) grandkids all have Facebook pages, and now it's your turn. I think that Facebook is the best first place to start connecting online because of the friendly atmosphere. I bet you'll be surprised when you see how many of your friends, past co-workers, and perhaps even past romantic interests await your contact.

To get yourself into the action, you need to sign up and put together your Facebook *profile,* which is where everyone

115

looks to learn more about you. You don't have to fill in your profile information all at once, so don't worry that it's going to be a time consuming task. After you sign up, your Profile page awaits your visits for leisurely updates.

Getting started on Facebook may seem daunting. But when you're ready to take the plunge, I can help you to discover what needs to be done. This chapter lays out all the Facebook setup instructions in sets of easy steps that enable you to master the basics before jumping in with both feet.

By the time you're done reading these pages, you'll have all the knowledge and tools necessary to navigate the site like a pro. All you need to add are friends and family! I tell you more about making a Facebook connection with friends and family in Chapter 7.

Let's get moving.

Sign Up for a Facebook Account

1. Open your Internet browser and type in the URL (Universal Resource Locator, the Web address) for Facebook, **www.facebook.com**. When you arrive on the Facebook home page, you find the Sign Up area, as shown in **Figure 5-1**, which asks you to fill in several important facts:

    - **Your first and last name.** D'oh, that's the very easiest part.

    - **Your e-mail address.** You may have more than one e-mail address, but decide which one will become the hub for your Facebook doings, and enter that address where prompted.

    - **Your password.** A very important feature, your

password is private, and *encrypted* (a technical way of hiding what you type from anyone other than the inner workings of the site itself — think Jack Bauer from the TV show 24). Never give your password to anyone. You might want to make note of it for your own reference; write it down and put it in a safe place (**not** taped to your computer monitor). You'll have to know your password to sign in to your Facebook account.

- **Your gender.** Okay, this is probably the easy part. Nothing much to decide on here.

- **Your birth date, including the year.** Click the down arrow next to the drop-down menus and select your month, date, and year of birth. Facebook requests your actual date of birth to encourage authenticity and provide only age-appropriate access to content.

 If you're a bit shy of exposing your *real* age, don't feel alone. My age is a secret that I guard tighter than the feds guard the gold at Fort Knox. There is a way around the Facebook requirement. If you use the drop-down menu to select your birth month and date, you can just indicate a year waaaaay back in history. In **Figure 5-1**, I selected a pretty outrageous year — 1900. (Heh, that'll keep 'em guessing.)

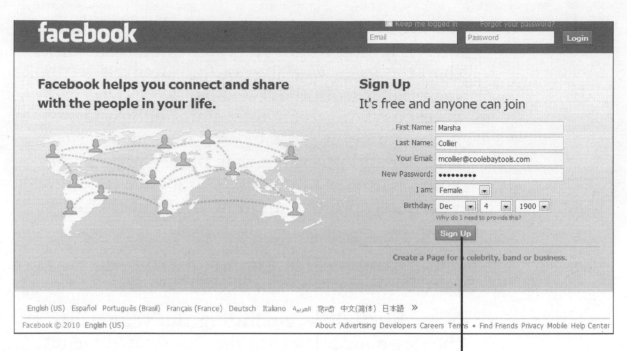

Fill in your facts and click here.

Figure 5-1

2. After you enter the information in Step 1, click the Sign Up button. Facebook runs a type of security check by asking you to type a pair of sometimes-difficult-to-read words into a text box to authenticate that you are, in fact, a human being (and not a computer program). This authentication is called a *Captcha* and is shown in **Figure 5-2**.

 You see Captchas used all over the Internet in various forms. These pesky little tests are used to prevent automated programs from signing up on the site. When those programs (often called *bots* for *robots*) sign up for sites, they can degrade the quality of service for the legitimate users on the site.

3. If you have a problem reading the Captcha words, you can try two things:

118

➡ Click the Try Different Words link, and Captcha will present you with a new set of tough-to-read words that might be easier to read (though the bots still can't read 'em). Some sites with Captcha codes have a small circular version of the recycling symbol you can click to refresh for new text.

➡ Click the Audio Captcha link (and be sure your computer's speakers are on) and a disembodied voice will read the words to you over your speakers.

If you can read this...type it here.

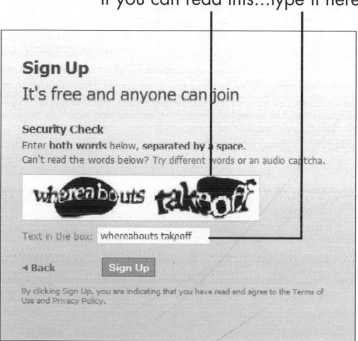

Sign Up
It's free and anyone can join

Security Check
Enter **both words** below, separated by a space.
Can't read the words below? Try different words or an audio captcha.

whereabouts takeoff

Text in the box: whereabouts takeoff

◄ Back   Sign Up

By clicking Sign Up, you are indicating that you have read and agree to the Terms of Use and Privacy Policy.

Figure 5-2

4. Type the Captcha words you see (or hear) in the text box and click the Sign Up button. Facebook then lands you on a page designed to lead you through a step-by-step process of adding friends, finding even more friends, and

filling in profile information (including your picture).

 I cover Facebook's prescribed friend-finding process in the upcoming sections, but I want you to know that you also have the option to skip some of the steps and come back to them later.

Find Friends Initially

1. After you conquer the Captcha code, Facebook takes you to an Add Friends page — not unlike the one shown in **Figure 5-3** — that will suggest friends to you. I'm not sure where this list comes from, but if you see anyone you know, you can click the Add Friend button next to his or her name.

2. If you don't see anyone you know, scroll to the bottom of the page and click Skip, which tells Facebook that you will add your friends later.

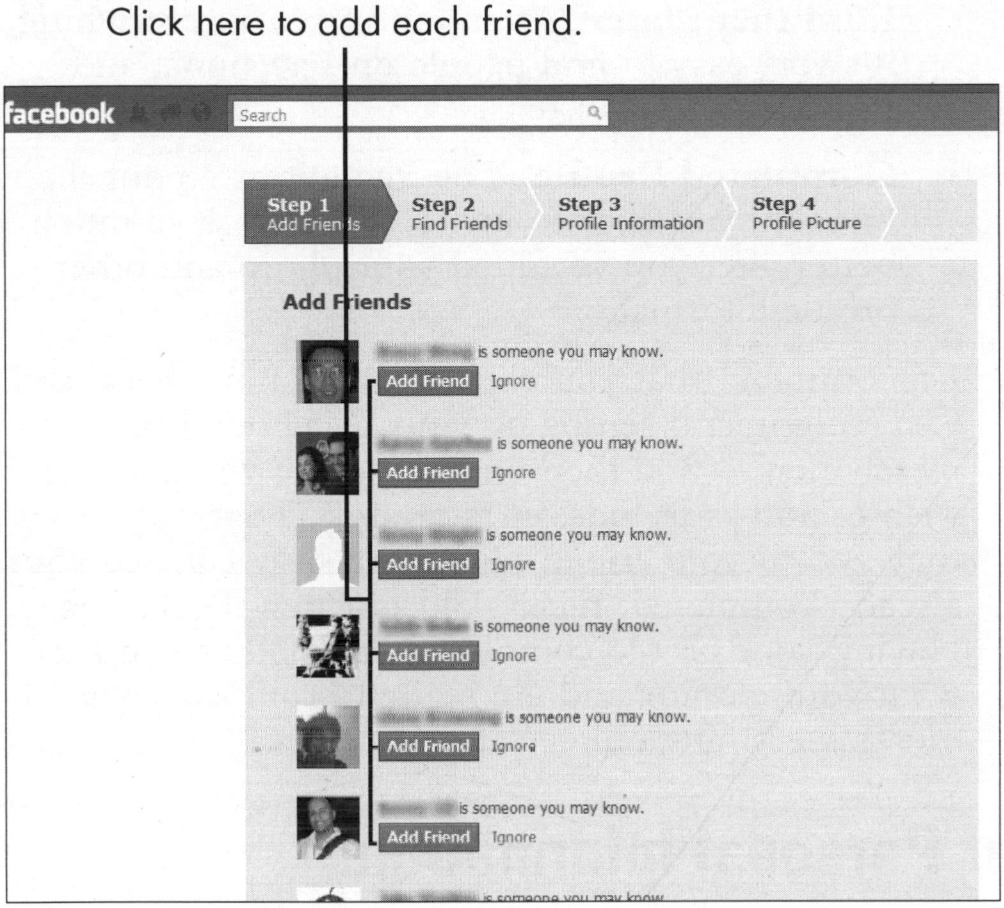

Click here to add each friend.

Figure 5-3

3. Okay, you may have skipped adding friends, but Facebook won't give up. On the next page (the Find Friends page), Facebook prompts you to type in your e-mail address and your password. If you do this, it links your e-mail account and contacts to Facebook, and allows you to send Facebook friend invitations en masse. You could do so, but I suggest you skip this step for a few reasons:

- **Privacy.** I'm a big believer in privacy. I don't want to expose my contacts to the Facebook linking.

121

- **Find them later.** After you've set up everything, it's very easy to find people on Facebook, and I'm a fan of baby steps.

- **Completed Profile.** The invitations go out the moment you click to invite. It will look so much better after you've added your photo and other profile information.

 I recommend that you click Skip for now, because I also recommend setting up your Facebook page completely first — and then finding people you know and wish to add as friends on Facebook. That way, when they accept your friend invitation, they can see your already completed, nicely-laid-out new Profile page. Having your profile completed shows that you know what you're doing and are ready to roll! Image is (almost) everything online.

Add Your Personal Information

1. This is where Facebook content gets *really* personal. Facebook asks you to enter your basic profile information, beginning with

- **The high school you attended** and your year of graduation. When you begin to type your school name, Facebook suggests schools that match, as shown in **Figure 5-4.**

- **Your college** (if any) and graduation year.

- **The company** you work (or worked) for.

 If you want to keep your age private, you wouldn't choose your year of birth from a drop-down menu when prompted. (I didn't, and Facebook let me pro-

122

ceed.) Of course, if you specify your graduation year(s), that's a pretty big hint about your age. But you knew that.

Choose your school from this list.

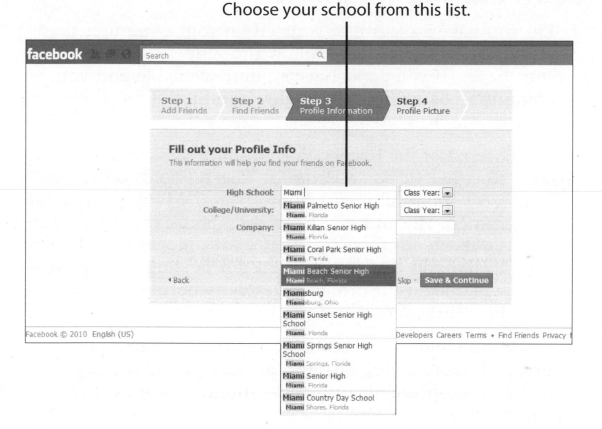

Figure 5-4

2. After you enter the requested personal information, up pops a window with suggested friends similar to the one you saw earlier in the sign-up process. You may want to add some or all of these suggested friends based on your school and employment life. You can choose to befriend any or all by clicking their names. Doing so will *immediately* send a friend request to them. (Be sure you want to connect *before* you click — there's no turning back.)

If you want, you can skip this step and go on to the next task. You can always search for friends later.

Upload Your Profile Photo

1. Do you have a picture of yourself on your computer that you'd like to share? If so, follow the simple steps that start here. (If you don't have a photo available and your computer has a camera, skip down to Step 8 for those instructions.)

 Step 4 of the Facebook sign-up process says it's time to either *Upload a Photo* or *Take a Photo* to personalize your profile and home pages. Many people are camera-shy and don't put up a photo for their Facebook friends to see. If that's your inclination, I want to tell you that I think that not posting your picture will make your profile page pretty boring. So why not be a little daring and put up your picture?

2. Click the Upload a Photo link, and the Upload Your Profile Picture dialog box appears and prompts you to select an image file on your computer, as shown in **Figure 5-5**.

3. Click the Browse button to start your picture selection. The File Upload window opens and a directory of your computer's contents will appear. Go to the folder where you store your photos. **Figure 5-6** shows the folder where I store my pictures.

Click here to look for a profile picture.

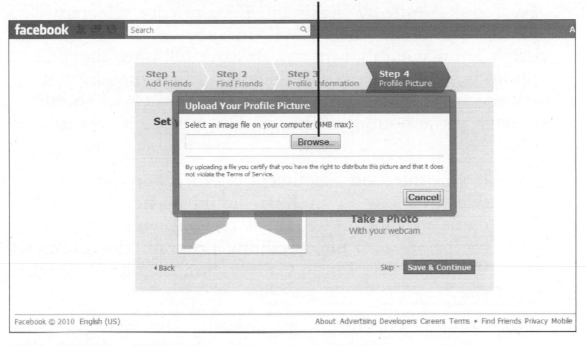

Figure 5-5

Figure 5-6

4. Select an image that you'd like to display on your Facebook profile by clicking it. Be sure your selected photo is no bigger than 4 MB (megabytes) in size. (If you don't know what that means, or can't tell how big your photo is, don't worry; Facebook will reject the photo if it's too large.) The name of the photo you chose should appear at the bottom of the window in the File Name text box.

 If you question whether a photo is too large, its file size (in *kilobytes,* or KB) should be next to the file-name in your folder. If it's too big, you can preview the photo in a photo editing program (for example, Windows Live Photo Gallery) and crop it to a smaller size.

Note: In this chapter, I am showing you figures of the screens I see on a PC that runs Windows Vista. Depending on what operating system you use on your computer, your screens may look a little different. But don't fear — the steps are the same.

5. Click Open, and the picture you chose will begin to make its merry way through the Web to Facebook automatically. (Nice, huh?) As shown in **Figure 5-7**, my photo has uploaded to Facebook.

6. If you don't like the photo you selected, you can always change it later in the Edit My Profile area. (You can find the link to this area under your picture on your Profile page.) To go with a different photograph, simply move your mouse over the top of the photo until you see the words *Change Picture.*

7. If you don't already have any photos you like, you can take a picture from your computer Web camera (if you have one). Click Take a Photo with Your Webcam on the

Set Your Profile Picture window (refer to Figure 5-7).

Figure 5-7

8. A window appears, as shown in **Figure 5-8**, asking your permission for Facebook to access your camera and microphone. Click the option button next to Allow.

9. Assuming that your webcam is pointing in the right direction, you will now see your image (as you sit at your computer) in the Take a Profile Picture window. Well, you kind of see it. If you want your computer to remember that you grant access to your camera at any time to Facebook, you must click the check box next to Remember. If you don't want to grant blanket access,

that's okay, too — I don't (refer to Figure 5-8). So click Close, and there you are, in all your glory.

10. You may now pose for your picture. When you're satisfied with how your picture appears, click the small camera icon at the bottom of your image.

Click this option to take your picture.

Figure 5-8

11. Facebook has now taken your picture! If you're happy with it (or as happy as you can be at the moment), click the Save Picture button and your photo will upload to your Facebook profile. (Remember, you can always swap out this picture later.)

Fill Out Other Profile Information

1. After the four steps in the Facebook profile-building process are completed (or skipped, based on your choices), you come to a page that lists the tasks you need to complete to finish posting your profile. At this point, you have a chance to put together the descriptive part of your personal profile. You decide what and how much you share: Make your profile as revealing as you like, or (for a little privacy) as vague. You can get all the privacy you want for your account in the Privacy Settings area under the Account drop-down menu on the left side of every page.

2. Edit the content in your Basic Information section. You've already entered your school and employment info, along with your gender and birth date. Now, under the Basic Information section, you have an opportunity to add your current city of residence, hometown (if different), relationship status, political and religious views, and favorite quotations.

    Remember that everything in the Basic Information area is optional.

3. Whatever you choose to share, filling in the blanks is simple. Here are the items to consider:

   • **Birthday**. Having the month and day listed is very important. Facebook notifies your Facebook friends about your birthday. They will come to your page and overwhelm you with birthday wishes. So you need to have something here.

   You do have options should you not want to show your birth year (whether real or bogus). You can show your whole birth date, your birth

129

date without the year, or no birthday at all. Check out **Figure 5-9** to see your choices.

- **Family Members**. If you have any family members on Facebook whom you want to link to, click the drop-down menu and select the appropriate relationship for that person. You can then type their name in the box to the right, and you get a link to their profile page on yours (once they confirm to Facebook that you really are related). Pretty cool.

- **Relationship Status**. You can leave the relationship space blank, or you have an opportunity to be far more specific (or not) than you might ever have imagined. Besides the boring old *Single* and *Married,* the choices on the drop-down menu also include *In a Relationship, Engaged, In An Open Relationship, Widowed,* and even *It's Complicated* (which things often are, but note that this term is rather ambiguous and some people may misconstrue it).

  If you indicate that you're in a relationship of some sort, you can then decide whether to list your anniversary date — either for others or simply to remind yourself.

- **Interested In**. You can list whether you're interested in Men or Women and just what you're Looking For from Facebook: Friendship, Dating, A Relationship, Networking — or leave all these boxes unchecked.

Choose how your birthday will appear.

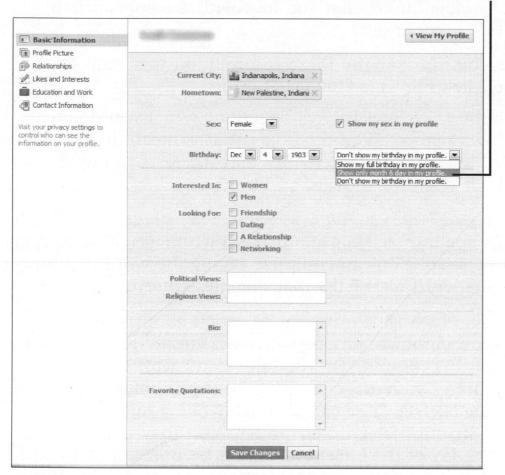

Figure 5-9

- **Political and Religious Views**. In the Political window, you can type in the name of a political party, or a comment that seems funny. In Religion, type in the name of your faith if you wish.

- **Bio**. People want to know a little about you, so type in a brief biography here.

- **Favorite Quotations**. People's favorite

quotations say a lot about them. Type in a few quotes that you love with the appropriate attributions.

4. After you input all the Basic Information you want to enter, click the Save Changes button.

5. Click the Likes and Interests section. When you do, a window opens with empty boxes that you can fill up with everything from your Activities and Interests to favorite music, TV shows, movies, and books.

When you begin to type in each box, suggestions (with proper spelling) appear in a drop-down menu, as shown in **Figure 5-10**. You can complete typing the word or simply click the word on the list that matches your intent.

 The idea isn't to reveal so much about yourself that you eliminate any mystery. It's simply to give others on Facebook a semi-definitive and representative picture of yourself, enough so your personality comes to the surface. You can also delay filling in this information until later if you prefer. You may decide to get the lay of the Facebook land a bit more prior to adding more personal information. Or you might decide never to reveal this stuff at all. It's really entirely up to you.

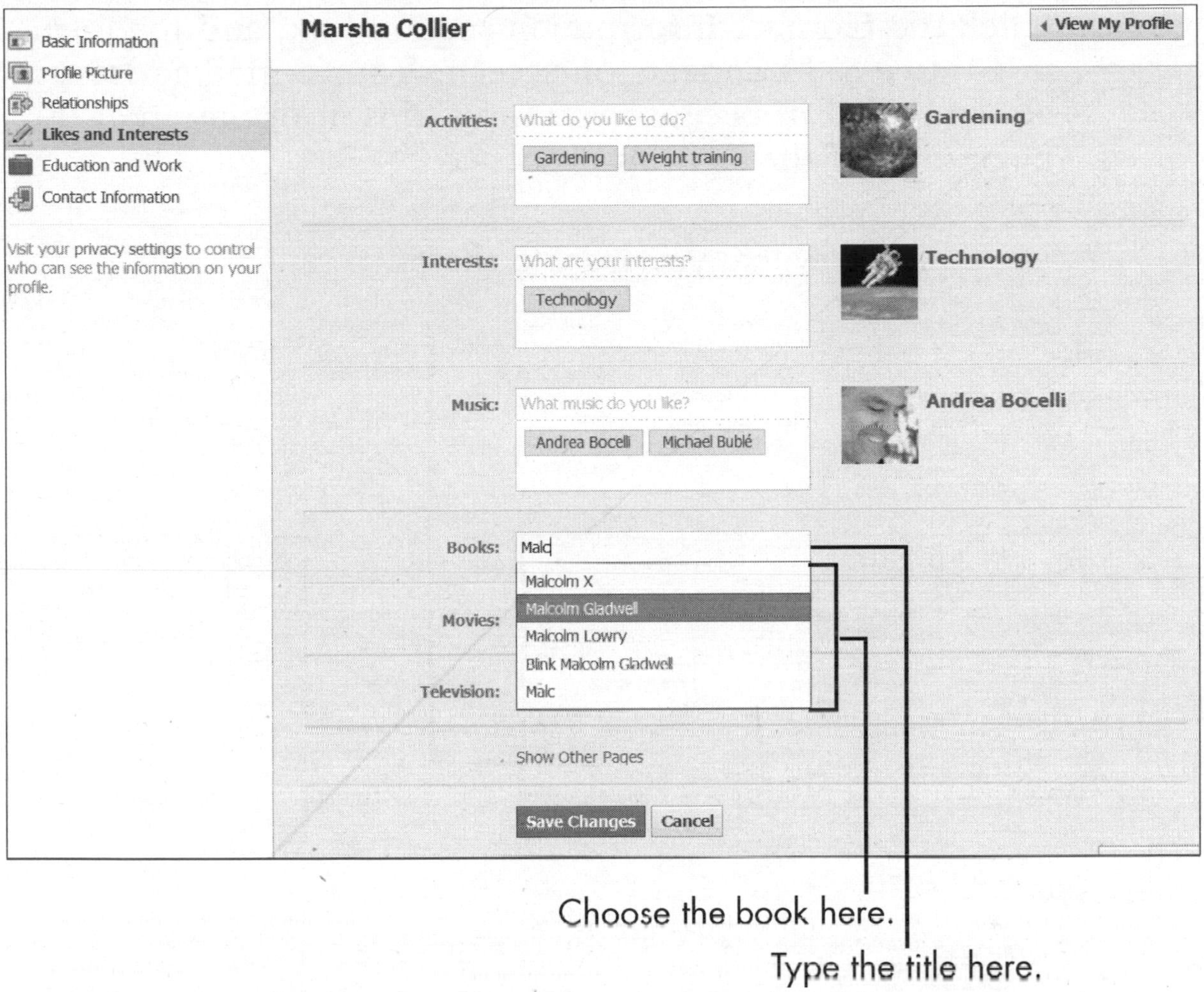

Marsha Collier

◀ View My Profile

Basic Information
Profile Picture
Relationships
Likes and Interests
Education and Work
Contact Information

Visit your privacy settings to control who can see the information on your profile.

Activities: | What do you like to do?

Gardening   Weight training

Gardening

Interests: | What are your interests?

Technology

Technology

Music: | What music do you like?

Andrea Bocelli   Michael Bublé

Andrea Bocelli

Books: | Malc

Malcolm X
Malcolm Gladwell
Malcolm Lowry
Blink Malcolm Gladwell
Malc

Movies:

Television:

Show Other Pages

Save Changes   **Cancel**

Choose the book here.

Type the title here.

Figure 5-10

6. Next click the Education and Work section link. This section affords you the chance to elaborate on your high-school and college info, as well as what you do (or did) for a living.

The benefit of including this information is that many people search for Facebook friends by schools or workplaces, and an old school chum may find you by performing such a search.

7. Click the Contact Information section link, and the form in **Figure 5-11** appears on-screen. Your e-mail address is already filled in because you input this information at the beginning of the sign-up process.

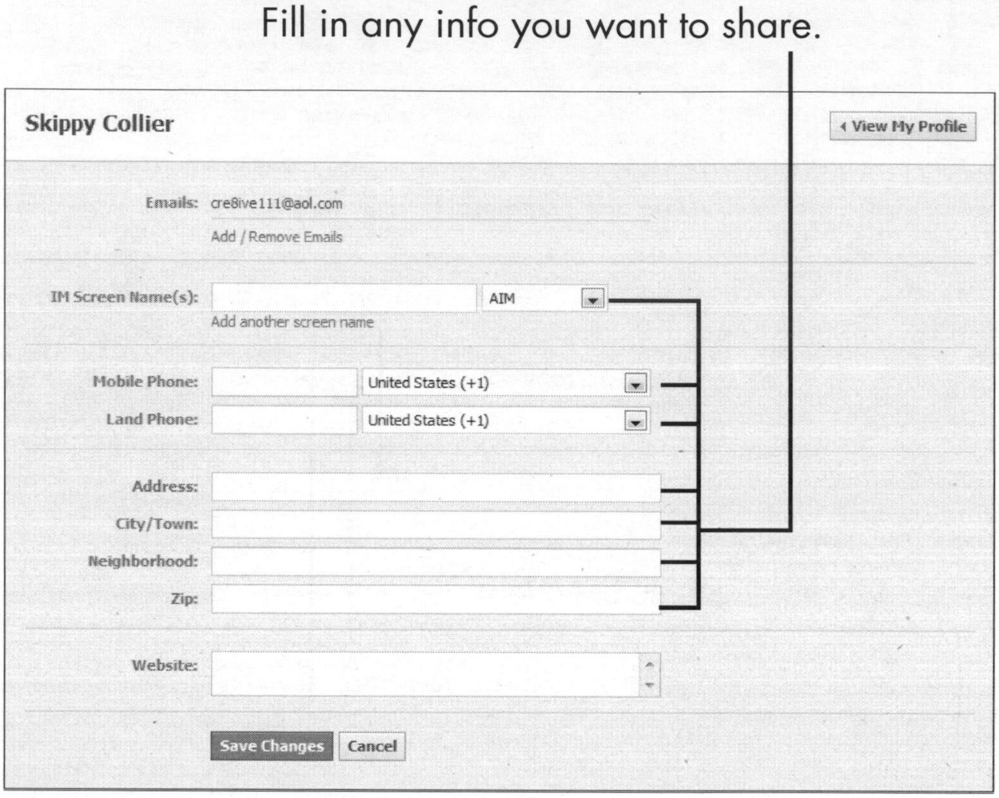

Fill in any info you want to share.

Figure 5-11

At this point, you can type in any contact information you want your Facebook friends to see, including your

- **IM (instant message) screen name.** Also, you can choose the IM service you use from the associated drop-down list.

- **Mobile phone and land line numbers.**

- **Address and ZIP code.**

 This is where sharing gets sticky for me. I may make friends on Facebook that I don't want to have my home address and phone number. For the sake of my security, I leave that blank. If I want someone to have that information, they can always send me an e-mail to request it.

- **Website URL.** If you have a blog or a Twitter page, type the URL in here.

Go Back to Edit Your Profile Later

1. When you have your information in place, you may decide to make additions and changes. You can always return to edit your profile information by clicking the Edit My Profile link below your profile photo on your profile page. (Get to your profile page by signing in to Facebook and clicking the Profile link near the top right of any page.)

 Remember that any Basic Information you enter about yourself — along with your name and friend list — is always visible and available to everyone in the Facebook community.

2. Most other profile info is invisible to everyone, but information that may be considered sensitive is available only to those whom you have befriended, based on your settings. And that's where the privacy and security settings come in. At any time, you can adjust your privacy settings for contact and profile information by clicking the Account link near the top right of any Facebook page and then choosing Privacy Settings from the resulting menu (see **Figure 5-12**). See Chapter 6 for a more complete look at choosing your privacy settings.

Figure 5-12

Chapter 6

Preparing to Share Info

On Facebook, there are three basic levels of privacy: *Friends, Friends of Friends,* and *Everyone*. You consistently hold the key to how much, or how little, information about yourself you allow to be accessed on the site. The personal information you choose to share is apart from the publicly available information — such as your name, profile picture, current city, gender, networks, friend list, and pages — that helps friends find and connect with you.

On Facebook, your privacy and security settings work as locks that control access to what's revealed about you, and to whom. In this chapter, I show you how to access and edit your privacy and security settings at any time. The idea behind these settings is to give you full control of your Facebook experience.

Use these settings so you don't have to worry about your personal information falling into the wrong hands — or having prying eyes access something about you that (for whatever reason) you don't want just anybody to know. You are in charge — and can filter who views your information to increase your feelings of security and privacy online.

Then, with your information secure, you can move on to the fun stuff! This chapter also shows you how to make the most of your Facebook pages, by posting updates and photos, and getting into the conversation. Let's get the tough stuff out of the way first.

Get Your Privacy and Security Settings in Place

1. To start the process of choosing your privacy and security settings, look at the top right of the screen on your Facebook page and locate the word *Account*. When you click the down arrow next to Account, a drop-down menu appears, as shown in **Figure 6-1**.

Figure 6-1

 Because Facebook (like any Web site) develops and morphs with new features every day, I recommend that you check out the Facebook blog, `http://blog.facebook.com` often. Facebook staffers (and the founder Jeff Zuckerberg) post updates and information on an almost daily basis.

2. Click Privacy Settings in the drop-down menu to go to the Privacy Settings page, which gives you a few options. The privacy settings enable you to control who can see your profile information, contact information, application and Web-site data, and searches. Also, you can control who can interact with you on Facebook through the Block List. You click each section name to get to the settings for that section. **Figure 6-2** shows my Choose Your Privacy Settings page. Notice that when you land on the page, you will see Facebook's recommended settings.

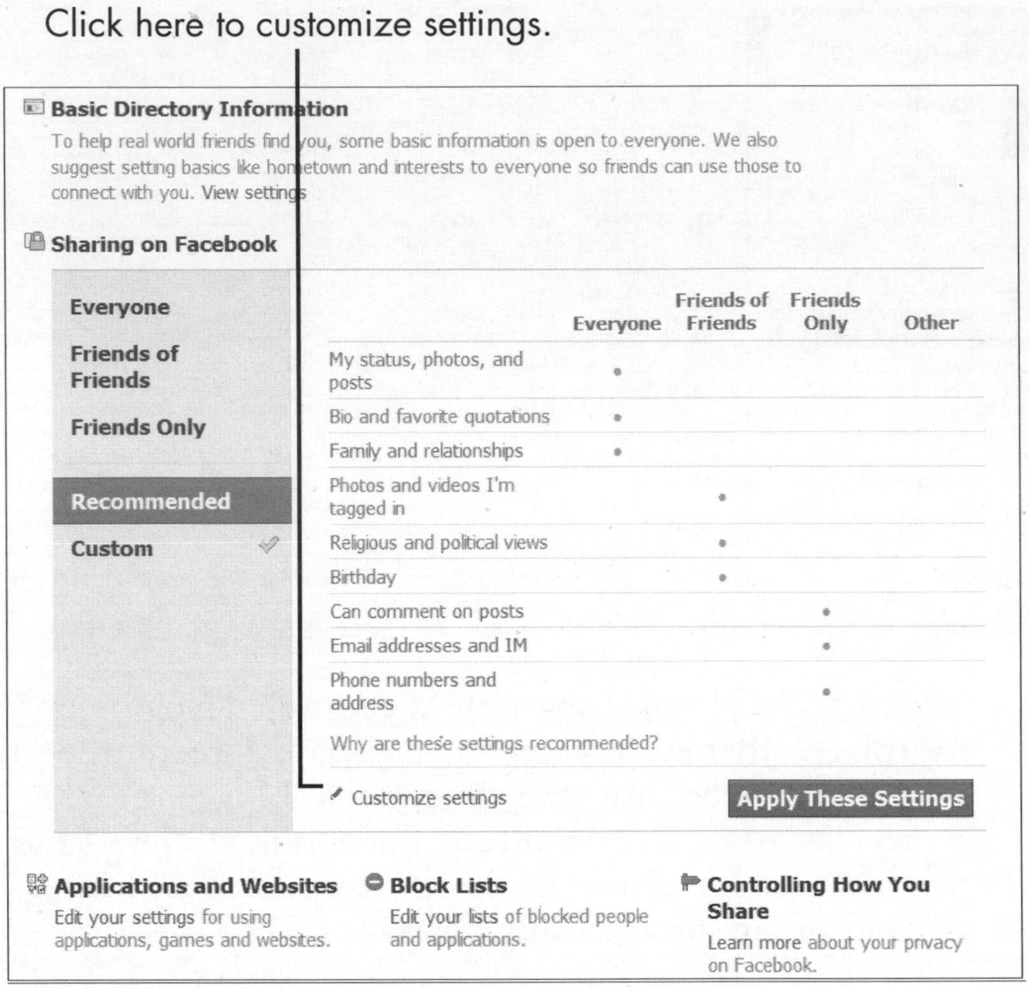

Click here to customize settings.

Figure 6-2

3. Click the Customize Settings link to make any changes to the defaults. You come to the Choose Your Privacy Settings: Customize Settings page which covers your profile and contact information settings. In each section, simply click the button at the end of a sub-category and choose a setting from the drop-down list. The standard settings are Everyone, Friends of Friends, Friends Only, or Customize. **Note:** If you have a special situation — for example, if you've joined a Facebook network — you may see other options in this list.

Here's a little more about each section of the Privacy Settings:

- **Things I Share:** Here you control who sees everything from your chosen personal information to your date of birth to your family and relationships, education, Web site, work info, photos, friends, and posted comments. When you choose the Customize option, a separate box pops up where you can make your profile information available to only you or to certain people (whom you specify). You can also choose to block certain people from seeing this information.

- **Things Others Share:** Part of the fun of Facebook is that other members can post comments, pictures, and video. If another member tags you in a posted item, it will also appear on your wall. Here's the area where you decide who can post (and comment) on your wall and who can view photos of you.

- **Contact Information:** Here's where you decide whom to allow access to your instant message (IM) screen name, phone numbers, home address, and e-mail addresses.

4. Click the Back to Privacy button to return to the main Choose Your Privacy Settings page where you find links to the other areas you may want to customize. They are

- **Applications and Websites:** In this section, you put into place controls on what your friends can share about you when they're using applications and Web sites on Facebook. You can also block certain applications from accessing

141

your information and contacting you; such applications include games, causes, and surveys. If you simply don't want to be bothered, you can choose to ignore application invites from specific friends.

On this page, you will also be able to edit Public Search. This privacy setting controls who can see your name or profile information as search results on Facebook. This setting also indicates whether to allow search engines such as Google to access your publicly available information. Click the Edit Settings button and then click See Preview, as I did in **Figure 6-3**, to view what your results might look like when someone finds you from a search engine.

Figure 6-3

- **Block Lists:** Click the Edit Your Lists link under Block Lists. If there are some folks you'd really rather not interact with on Facebook, this setting allows you to block them from access. Simply type in each name and/or e-mail address you want to block, and then click the Block this User button.

Meet Your Facebook Home Page

1. You have two pages on Facebook. You can select the one you want to view by clicking either Home or Profile in the upper-right corner of any Facebook page. Clicking Home brings you to your personal home page; **Figure 6-4** shows mine. Your home page has links for just about anything you want to do or see on Facebook. In the center of the page is a column for News Feeds, featuring your Top News.

Toolbar links are here.

Updates from friends are here.

Activities are here.

Figure 6-4

2. The Top News selection shows the updates your friends have posted that are getting the most attention with replies. Showing these posts is the default setting for this page. You may click Most Recent (at the top right of the News Feed column) if you'd like to see each post from each of your friends, in the order of posting.

3. You also have other sections with links to information and activities on the right side of this page. Click the links

(scroll down the page) to find how many requests are pending in each category — or simply to explore all that's available on Facebook. The home page sections include

- **Events:** In the upper-right corner is the Events heading. Under this section, you see links to upcoming events (in chronological order) that you've been invited to. You also see a list of your friends' upcoming birthdays, as shown in **Figure 6-5**. By clicking a name, you can go to each friend's page and wish him or her a happy birthday by putting a comment in the status box.

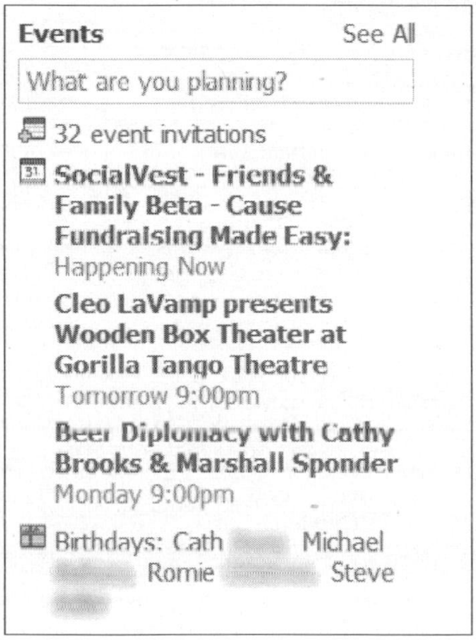

Events   See All

What are you planning?

📧 32 event invitations

📅 **SocialVest - Friends & Family Beta - Cause Fundraising Made Easy:**
Happening Now

Cleo LaVamp presents Wooden Box Theater at Gorilla Tango Theatre
Tomorrow 9:00pm

Beer Diplomacy with Cathy Brooks & Marshall Sponder
Monday 9:00pm

🎂 Birthdays: Cath   Michael   Romie   Steve

Figure 6-5

- **Requests:** Farther down the right-hand column (below an advertisement) you may find friend requests and suggestions (based on your current friends). The requests are those you receive from your friends, including new friend requests, new group invitations, page suggestions (someone thinks you'd like that page), and other requests.

145

- **Toolbar links:** On the left side (under a thumbnail of your profile picture, as shown in **Figure 6-6**), you see links to take you to your personal destinations on Facebook, as well as a link to Friends Online. (If you are offline — not open for chat as described in Chapter 7 — Facebook prompts you to Go Online.)

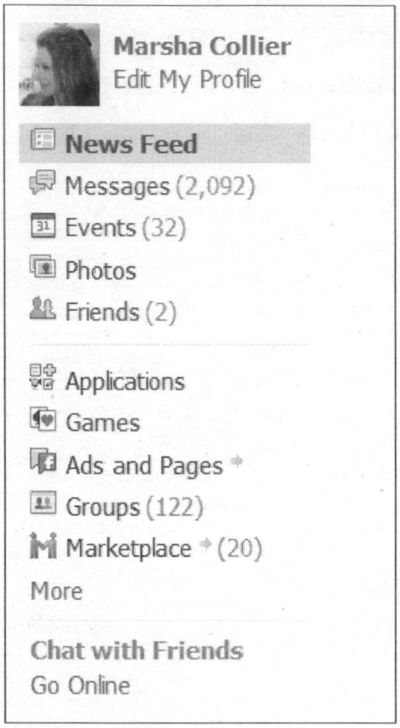

Marsha Collier
Edit My Profile

▣ **News Feed**
▣ Messages (2,092)
▣ Events (32)
▣ Photos
▣ Friends (2)

▣ Applications
▣ Games
▣ Ads and Pages *
▣ Groups (122)
▣ Marketplace * (20)
More

Chat with Friends
Go Online

Figure 6-6

Review the Profile Everyone Sees

1. Click Profile at the top-right of any Facebook page, and you arrive on the page showing your public profile. **Figure 6-7** shows mine. The page, as you see it, is exactly the way it looks to your friends when they visit your page. Notice that there are three tabs just below your name at the top of the page. Three tabs are just the start; you can always add more as you become a Facebook denizen.

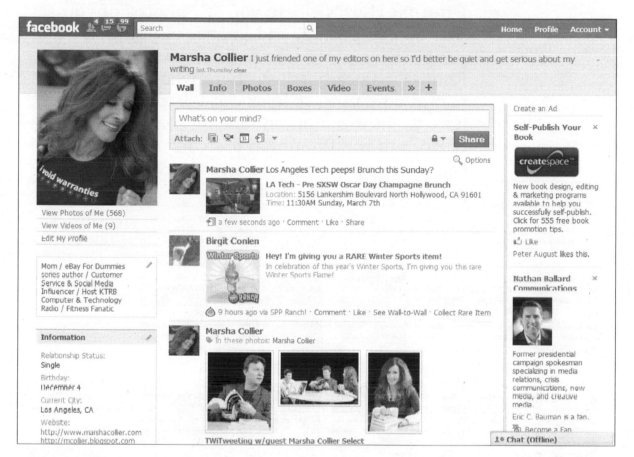

Figure 6-7

- **Wall:** This is the default view where you see posts (messages) that your friends have left for you (such as Happy Birthday messages), items you have posted to your page, and status updates that you have posted.

- **Info:** When someone clicks this tab, what appears is the profile information you put in and approved for public display while setting up your page (see Chapter 5). On this tab, your friends can see everything that you indicated was for their eyes only.

- **Photos:** Here's where you see photos of you that you've posted, and images of you that other people have posted, as shown in **Figure 6-8**. Photos magically appear here when a friend tags you in a picture. (Check out Chapter 9 for the how-to information on tagging photos.) At the bottom of the Photo tab are your albums. You can, for example, set up an album with specific photos of an event to display.

Figure 6-8

2. You may add additional tabs to your Profile page by clicking the + (plus) button on the end of your tabs. When you do, a drop-down menu presents options to add tabs for Links, Events, Notes, and Video. Choose an option, and it's added as the next tab on your Profile page.

Update Your Status

1. Here's where the fun really begins. In the thin, long rectangular box that appears at the top of either of your Facebook pages, type in your *status* — some words about what's going on with you at the moment. Inside the status-update box, you see the question *What's on your mind?* To answer the question — called *posting* — click inside the box and type any message you wish.

 Most people use the update feature to let people know what they're doing at that given moment — so often you see quick notes such as "Baking a cake for my in-laws" or "Going to work out on the treadmill."

2. If you're posting your update from your Profile page, you can also attach videos, photos, events, or links to interesting pages on the Web. Below the status update box is the word *Attach* and a row of icons representing the items you may want to attach to your comment. Just click the icon for the item you want to attach. After you type in your status update, follow these steps to attach a Web site link to it:

   1. *Click the rightmost icon (a thumbtack holding up a piece of paper) next to the word* Attach. Another text box appears under the status-update box.

   2. *Navigate in another browser tab to the Web site you want to share and select its URL by highlighting it in your*

browser's address bar. Then copy it by pressing Ctrl + C on your keyboard.

3. *Paste the URL into the Link box section by clicking in the new text box and pressing Ctrl + V on your keyboard.* A mini-version of your linked page will appear below the link box.

4. *Click the Attach button at the end of the link box.* The link will then be highlighted in your status as an active link, as shown in **Figure 6-9**.

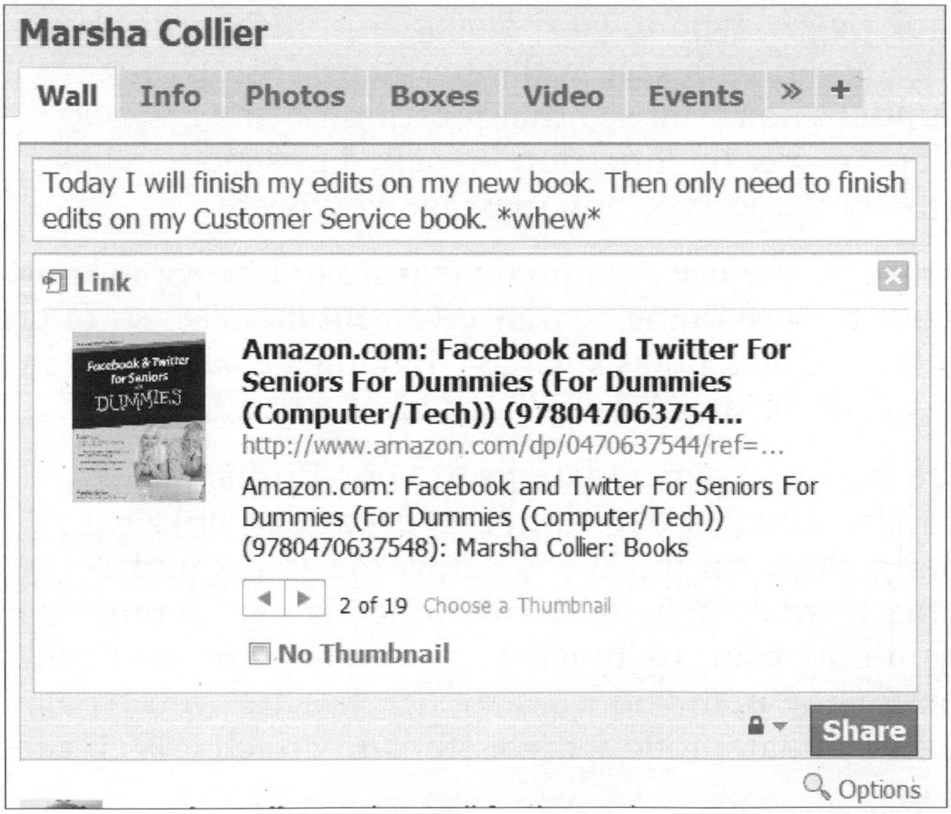

Marsha Collier

| Wall | Info | Photos | Boxes | Video | Events | » | + |

Today I will finish my edits on my new book. Then only need to finish edits on my Customer Service book. *whew*

🔗 Link ❌

Amazon.com: Facebook and Twitter For Seniors For Dummies (For Dummies (Computer/Tech)) (978047063754...
http://www.amazon.com/dp/0470637544/ref=...
Amazon.com: Facebook and Twitter For Seniors For Dummies (For Dummies (Computer/Tech)) (9780470637548): Marsha Collier: Books

◀ ▶ 2 of 19 Choose a Thumbnail

☐ No Thumbnail

🔒 ▾ **Share**

🔍 Options

Figure 6-9

3. When you're done typing the message (and attaching a photo, video, or link) click the Share button at the bottom right of the status-update section.

The words you typed in your status update (if you did not attach a link or photo) will appear beside your name at the top of your Facebook Profile page. This is what keeps people attuned to what you're up to, and makes them feel like they're plugged into your daily activities.

 You cannot post a link, photo, or event as part of your status update (which appears next to your name at the top of your Profile page). Those posts are limited to text only, and attachments show up only on your wall.

Delete a Status Update or Other Post

1. Removing the current status update from your Profile page is one of the simpler tasks to perform on Facebook. You can move your cursor to the spot beside your current status update and click the Clear link. Or you can write a new status update, click the Share button, and the old one will disappear from the top of the page.

2. If you wish to remove a previous update, move your cursor to the far right of any post that's listed on your Profile page *feed* (the middle column). Click the Remove link that appears when you put your mouse pointer over the post, as shown in **Figure 6-10**.

Click to remove any post.

Figure 6-10

Add a Photo to Your Wall

1. To post a photo to your Facebook wall, locate the word *Attach* and the row of icons right under the status update text box where you see the question *What's on your mind?*

2. Next to the word *Attach,* move your cursor over the first icon — the Photos icon — and click. Doing this click brings up three links: Upload a Photo from Your Drive, Take a Photo with a Webcam, and Create an Album with Many Photos. The procedure is the same as loading a photo for your Profile page.

3. Click Upload a Photo, and you see a box that prompts you to browse for a photo (an image file) on your computer or to upload an image via e-mail. Click the Browse button to look for a picture on your computer. After you find a photo, click that photo to select it. Then you can put it up on your Facebook wall by clicking the Share button at the bottom of the status-update box.

Share a YouTube Video on Facebook

1. So you just watched a video on YouTube and you can't

wait to show it to all your friends. Well, it turns out that Facebook is the perfect place to show a video to the maximum number of friends in the minimum amount of time. Start out by going to YouTube (www.youtube.com) and clicking the video you want to share. Beneath the screen that's showing the actual video, you should see a Share button. Click it, and you get several buttons you can click to share the video on various social networking sites, including Twitter, MySpace, StumbleUpon, and (you guessed it) Facebook.

2. Click the Facebook button, and you're prompted to add a message in a rectangular text box (similar to the status update space). Type in your message, click the Share button at bottom right, and voila! You've posted a video to your Facebook wall.

 You can also copy the URL of your video, and then paste it into a status update, as you would when posting any link. See this chapter's earlier task, "Update Your Status" for the steps.

 If you want to upload a video of your own that you have on your computer, you can post it the same way you upload a photo. Just be sure to click the icon of the teeny movie camera in the Attach area.

Post an Event to Your Wall

1. To post an event on your Profile page for your friends and fans to see, locate the spot just below the rectangular status update text box. Move your cursor over the Event icon (the third icon after the word *Attach,* featuring a square with a number inside it) and click.

2. Two long, rectangular text boxes appear: One says *Title,* and the other says *Location.* You also see the label *Time*

that features drop-down lists for choosing a date and time for your event. (See **Figure 6-11**.) Type the name of your event in the Title text box and the place where your event will happen in the Location text box. Then use the drop-down menus to set any day and month of the year, as well as all times on the half-hour.

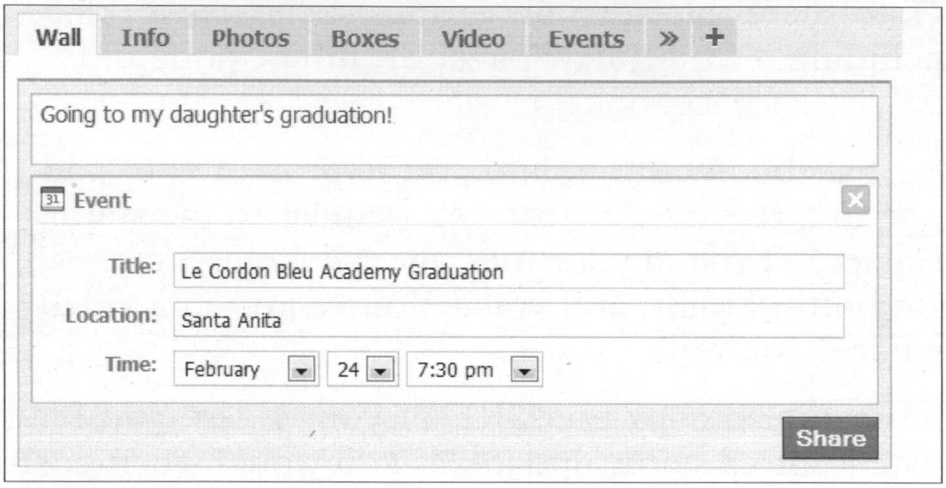

Figure 6-11

3. Of course, the rectangular status-update box is still at the top. Type the comment you want to post or add a description of your event (for example *Come One, Come All!*).When you're finished, click Share and your event will be listed on your Facebook page for all to see.

Chapter 7

Connecting with Friends and Family

Now that your Facebook Profile page is all set up and people can see who you are, it would make sense to have some friends online to connect with. Facebook can be a lonely place if you don't make friends, so in this chapter, I help you find lots of friends: old and new.

So put on your thinking cap. Think of the various offline connections you have — aside from the people in your daily life (and your family) — think back to friends from previous jobs, church, schools, and maybe even summer camp. (I'm friends on Facebook with the girl who use to pick on me mercilessly when I was a kid; she's not half bad now!)

Ready? This is going to be fun.

Make the Navigation Bar Your First Stop

1. Whenever you visit Facebook, you see a blue bar at the top of the page. This Navigation bar, as shown in **Figure 7-1**, appears on all Facebook pages. The Navigation bar does just what its name implies: It allows you to navigate to different pages on Facebook quickly. From here, you can get a brief view of what's going on with your Facebook account. At the top left are small red squares over icons that may have white numbers in them.

See requests, messages, and notifications here.
facebook
1
14
98
Search
Home
Profile
Account

Figure 7-1

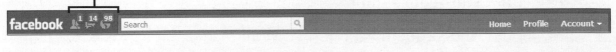

2. Check out the activities available from the Navigation bar. From Figure 7-1, I can see that I have one friend request, 14 new messages and 98 Notifications. Clicking these icons will do different things (keep in mind that anything you can do by clicking these icons you can also do from your home page):

- **Friend Requests:** When you click here, you'll see a drop-down menu showing the people who have requested your friendship online. You may click on their names to go directly to their profiles.

- **Messages:** You have this many messages from other Facebook members in your message area. You may view previews of their messages here, and click to go directly to each message.

- **Notifications:** If someone has posted a note on your wall, commented on a post of yours, commented on a picture you're in, it's a notification. Click here and you'll get a drop-down menu like the one in **Figure 7-2**.

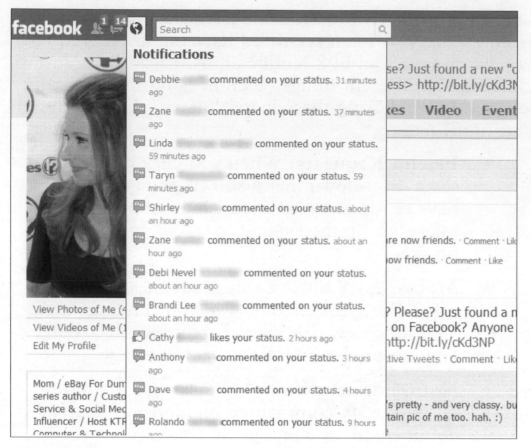

Figure 7-2

3. Are you looking for something on Facebook? A friend, your local coffee shop (if it has a fan page, it may post coupons), your favorite movie or author? Try out the Facebook search feature. Just start typing the name or topic in the Search box, and a drop-down list appears. As you type the words, Facebook uses the drop-down list to suggest a name (or topic) that matches what you are typing. If you see what you're looking for, click that name or phrase. If the name doesn't show up, click See More Results at the bottom of the drop-down list and search from there.

If you don't see a See More Results link at the bottom of the menu, odds are there's no match on Facebook. You can still try to search by clicking the little magnifying glass in the Search box.

4. Clicking the Home link takes you to your Home page, the hub for your news feed and all your invitations and (most important) the organization area on the left side of the screen. This area gives you access to other Facebook activities, including photos and your friends. (Later sections in this chapter cover these activities.)

5. Clicking the Profile link takes you to your Profile page. From there, you can see what your friends have posted on your wall as well as edit any information on the page.

6. Next is the Account link — unless you haven't signed up any friends on Facebook — in that case, you will see the words *Find Friends* before the Account link. (Read the next section, where I help you with finding friends.) Once you've gotten connected to a few friends, what you see here is only a link to your Account.

Click the Account link and arrive at your account area where you set your preferences to control how you operate on Facebook — including how private you want to be. (I cover the details in Chapter 6.)

Find a Friend with Facebook Search

1. Think of a small group of your friends and write down a list. Then sign in to your Facebook account; you'll land on your Home page. From here, you have two ways of finding people; start by using the Search box. Type one of your friend's names in the Search box, as I've done in **Figure** 7-3. Just as when you're searching for anything on Facebook, a drop-down list appears — this one with

159

semi-matching names.

If you're not sure how to spell your friend's name, just type in as many characters of it as you think may be right. Facebook will pick up the slack. Alternatively, you can type in your friend's last known e-mail address, but people change e-mail addresses so often these days, that it might not be valid anymore.

Figure 7-3

2. If your friend is not on the suggested list, click the See More Results link. You'll then see a page (or many pages) with results that match what you've typed in. You should be able to find your friend if he or she is a member of Facebook.

3. Remember that I said there were two ways to find friends? Look on the left side of your home page. See the Information area? Click the Friends link. The main area

of the resulting page (shown in **Figure 7-4**) fills up with a list of Facebook members who want to be your friends. Also on this page, you can click the Find Friends link (that appears below your friends-to-be) and find friends using your e-mail account. Type in your e-mail password, and Facebook imports your contacts automatically.

This Facebook feature is called Friend Finder. It's perfectly safe and Facebook does not store your password. But even so, I don't like it; here are some reasons why:

- I'm a stickler for privacy and do not wish to share my online contact lists with anyone.

- Friend Finder makes automatic connections based on the e-mail addresses in your address book. Facebook says: "We *may* use the e-mail addresses you upload through this importer to help you connect with friends, including using this information to generate Suggestions for you and your contacts on Facebook. If you don't want us to store this information, visit this page." Then you have to go to that page and make your preference known.

 Making suggestions for you and your e-mail contacts may sound like a fair deal. But when you click the link to read the deeper details, you're told that once you import your contacts, you must manually remove each one you don't want — one at a time. Facebook adds a caveat: "Note that it may take some time before your name will be completely removed from Suggestions."

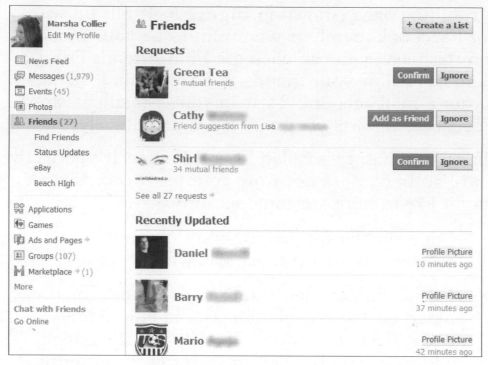

Figure 7-4

4. If the features of Friend Finder are fine with you, feel free to add your online contact list. I can tell you that Facebook won't lie, but be sure you read every message before agreeing to any Facebook activity.

Other links at the left show you which friends have recently made changes to their Profile pages. The changes they have made are highlighted to the right of their names.

Send a Friend Request

1. When you find someone on Facebook you'd like to add as a friend, doing so is a pretty simple task. After clicking the link to your prospective friend's Profile page, you may see an Add as Friend box next to the name.

2. Click the Add as Friend button and a window pops up, asking you to confirm your friend request. This window lets you send or cancel the request, and gives you the option of entering a personal message.

3. You then have to fill in a Captcha code. (See **Figure 7-5** for an example and Chapter 5 for an explanation of what this does and how it works.) Fill in the words in the code and click the Send Request button.

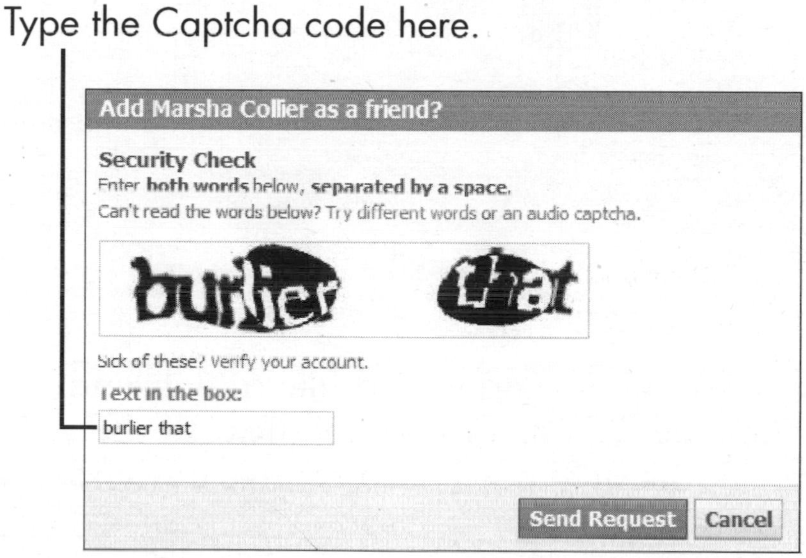

Type the Captcha code here.

Figure 7-5

4. The window that opens contains pictures of potential friends that are friends of your newly requested friend (see **Figure 7-6**).

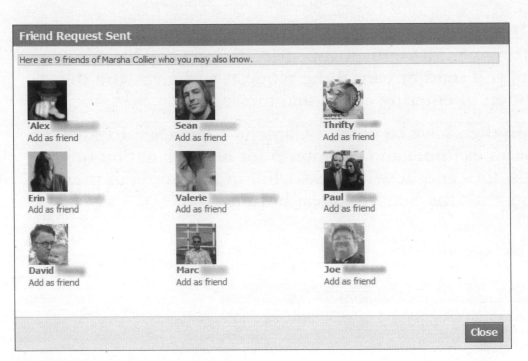

Figure 7-6

5. If you see anyone you know and would like to befriend on Facebook, click the Add as Friend link next to the person's picture and he or she will also receive a friend request.

 Once you send your requests, a friend request is posted to each recipient's Facebook notifications. Your prospective new friends also receive an e-mail notice with an easy link they can click to respond.

Find Friends in Other Friend Lists

1. Odds are that the friends you have on Facebook are connected to people you may know. Would you like to make those people your friends on Facebook, too? It's easy. Facebook Profile pages have Friends boxes you can find on the left side of the screen (unless the member has

164

chosen to block the box from view). If you have Facebook friends in common, you'll see a Mutual Friends box — and below that, a Friends box, as shown in **Figure** 7-7.

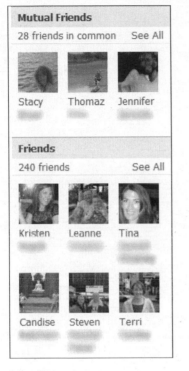

Figure 7-7

2. By clicking the friend-count number or the See All link, you can view all of your friend's connections in a new window (see **Figure** 7-8). And you can categorize your view by seeing Everyone, Mutual Friends, or Browse.

3. You can search through the list (looking for a specific person) in two ways: by typing the person's name in the search box and clicking the magnifying glass, or by scrolling down the list and viewing each friend individually. When someone is not already your friend on Facebook, to the right of each entry is an Add as Friend link that you can click to send a friend request.

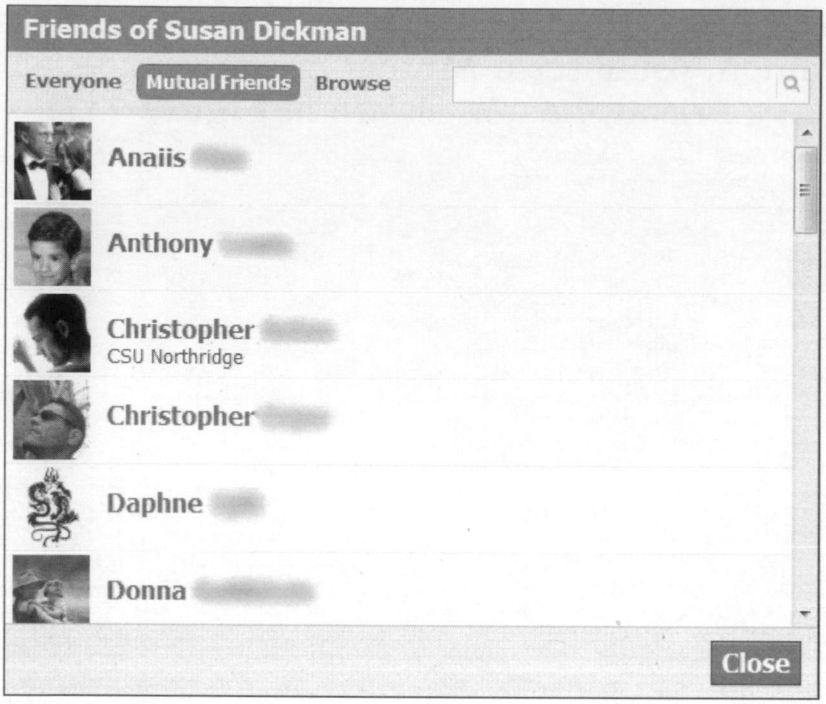

Friends of Susan Dickman

Everyone | **Mutual Friends** | Browse

Anaiis

Anthony

Christopher
CSU Northridge

Christopher

Daphne

Donna

Close

Figure 7-8

Respond to a Friend Request

1. When people know you're a Facebook member, someone is going to want to be your friend on Facebook. There are two ways you will be notified of a friend request: You get a notification via e-mail, or you find out when you log in to your Facebook home page. If you receive your notification via e-mail, just click the link contained in the message and you go directly to the request.

2. When you log in to Facebook, your home page offers you three different places to see whether you have any friend requests. **Figure 7-9** shows you two of them.

   • **The first place to check is in your Requests area on the right side of your home page.**

You find an icon that looks like a person's silhouette with a +1 overlapping it. Next to that icon is the number of friend requests you have. To access them, click the text link that says *Friend Requests*.

Friend requests show up in these two places.

Figure 7-9

- **Another place to check is a button in your tool bar at the top left of your page.** The button resembles the silhouette of two people. If you have a new friend request, you'll see a small red box with a number in it, overlapping the icon. To access your requests, click on icon.

- **The final place that offers links to your friend notifications is on your left-side toolbar.** You'll see the same silhouette icon from your top tool bar beside the word *Friends*. A number in parenthesis indicates the number of friend requests you have waiting. Click Friends, and Facebook takes you to your requests.

3. When you access your friend requests, you see your potential friend's photo and name. You also see whether you have any mutual friends with this person (and how many). By clicking the Mutual Friends link under the potential friend's name, you can see the friends you have in common.

4. To respond to a friend request, click one of the two buttons to the right of your potential friend's name. One button reads *Confirm* and one reads *Ignore*. Clicking those buttons allow you to add a friend or to ignore the request quietly.

 When you ignore a friend request, an e-mail isn't sent to the person who placed the request. That person will not know that you chose to ignore him or her, except for the fact that you didn't accept the request. Oops?

Connect with a Facebook Network

1. Facebook gives you the chance to become part of a network. *Networks* (in Facebook-speak) are a group of people who have similar hometowns, backgrounds, or interests. This feature allows you to easily connect with your current or past coworkers or classmates and helps you to be easily identified. To start the simple task of joining a network, choose Account⇨Account Settings from the top navigation bar.

2. When you arrive at your My Account page, select the Networks tab on the menu bar, as shown in **Figure 7-10**.

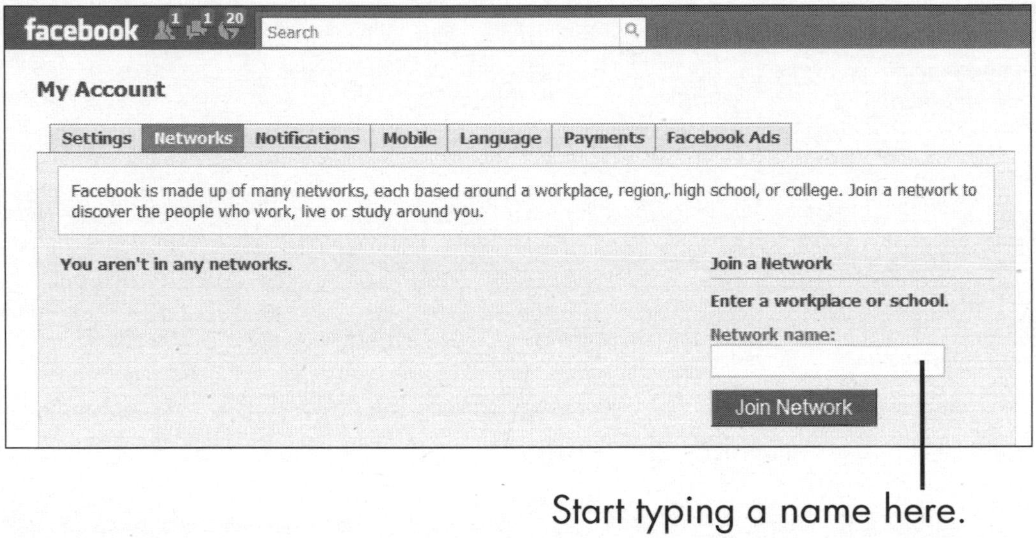

facebook 👤¹ 📧¹ 🚩²⁰ | Search 🔍 |

My Account

| Settings | **Networks** | Notifications | Mobile | Language | Payments | Facebook Ads |

Facebook is made up of many networks, each based around a workplace, region, high school, or college. Join a network to discover the people who work, live or study around you.

You aren't in any networks.

Join a Network

Enter a workplace or school.

Network name:

[   ]

Join Network

Start typing a name here.

Figure 7-10

3. On this tab, you have the option to join a network. Enter a city, workplace, school, or region in the Network Name text box. The auto-fill feature shows you the names of networks that match what you're typing. I typed *Los Angeles* because I live and worked there, and got the results shown in **Figure 7-11**. My old employer popped up — and, if I were still working there, I could select that entry to become part of the Los Angeles Daily News network.

 When you select an employer network, you are often asked for your e-mail address so they can confirm your employment.

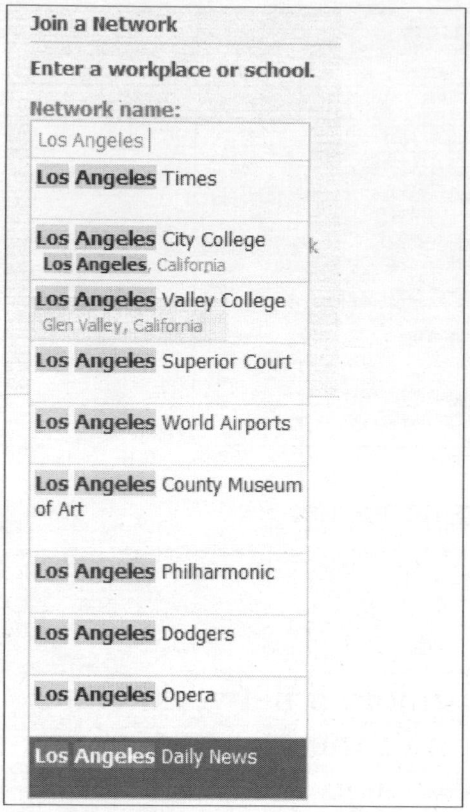

Join a Network

Enter a workplace or school.

Network name:

Los Angeles

Los Angeles Times

Los Angeles City College
Los Angeles, California

Los Angeles Valley College
Glen Valley, California

Los Angeles Superior Court

Los Angeles World Airports

Los Angeles County Museum of Art

Los Angeles Philharmonic

Los Angeles Dodgers

Los Angeles Opera

Los Angeles Daily News

Figure 7-11

4. After you fill in any required information, click the Join Network button. Facebook sends your request, and all you have to do is await confirmation.

Send Private Messages to Friends

1. Facebook has a feature that enables you to send private messages to your friends. Think of it like Facebook e-mail, only your personal e-mail address is not revealed. Even better, you can e-mail those whose e-mail addresses you don't know. One way to send a message to a friend is to click the Messages link on the left side of your home page. Facebook takes you to your Messages page, as shown in **Figure 7-12**.

2. Click the New Message button in the top-right corner of this page, and a blank message form opens on your screen, as shown in **Figure 7-13**. Alternatively, you can visit a friend's Facebook Profile page. In the left-side tool box, you should see the Send *(Friend's Name)* a Message link. Click it, and you get the same blank message form.

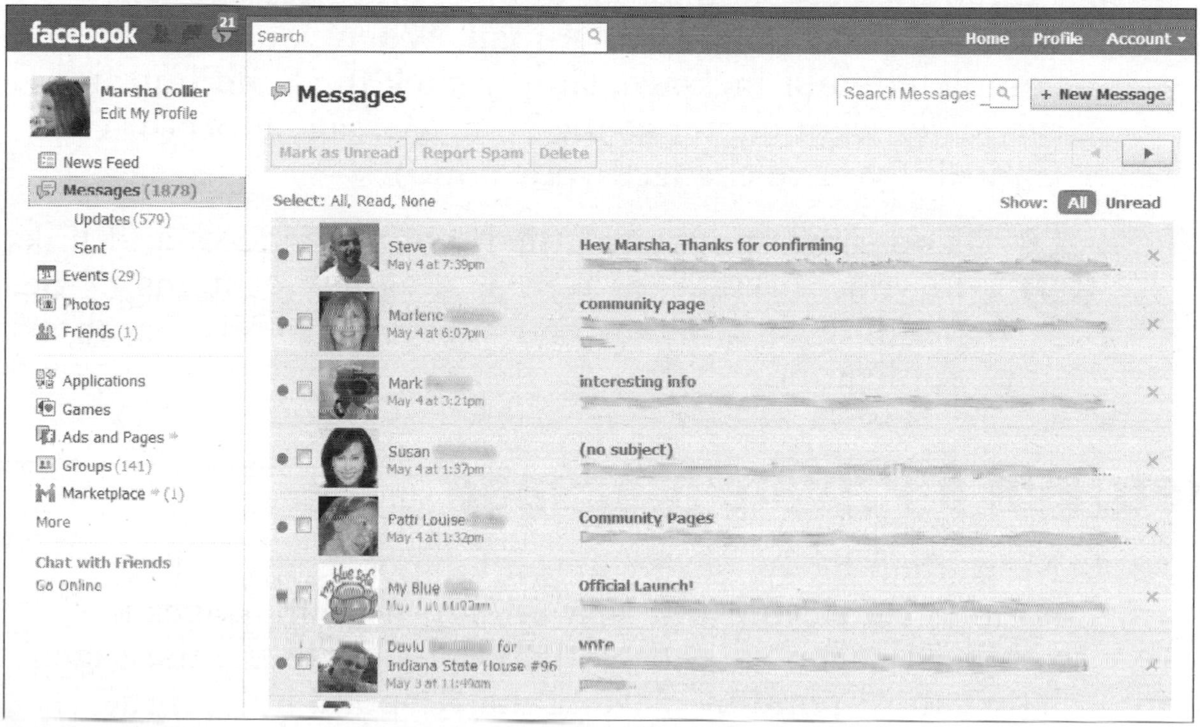

Figure 7-12

Figure 7-13

3. In the blank message form (refer to Figure 7-13), address the message by typing your friend's name into the To box. Facebook begins to auto fill names from your friend list as you type. When you find the correct friend, select the name by either clicking it or highlighting it and pressing Enter.

4. For all messages, fill in the Subject and Message text boxes as you would for an e-mail. When you have completed your message, simply click the Send button in the lower-right corner of the New Message form (or click Cancel if you've changed your mind).

 You have options to attach photos, videos, and links to your message, as well as a variety of items — depending on whether you subscribe to any Facebook applications.

Retrieve a Private Message

1. More than likely, once you send a message, you'll get a reply. Retrieving and answering private messages is simple. Facebook sends you an e-mail with the message. You can respond by clicking the Respond link on the message.

2. But as with most Facebook tasks, you also have two places on the site where you can retrieve a private message:

   • Click the button (that resembles two conversation bubbles) in the toolbar on the top left of your home page, and a drop-down list with a snap shot of your current messages opens (see **Figure 7-14**). Click to select the message you wish to read from the list and you see the full message.

As you may notice, Figure 7-14 (at the bottom) says that I have 1,876 unread messages. That's not really true. The tabulation only changes if you access your messages through your home page. I access mine from links in the e-mail that Facebook sends me.

- Click the Messages link on the left side of your home page, and Facebook takes you to your Messages page. It's like your e-mail Inbox. To read a message, simply click it and the full message opens.

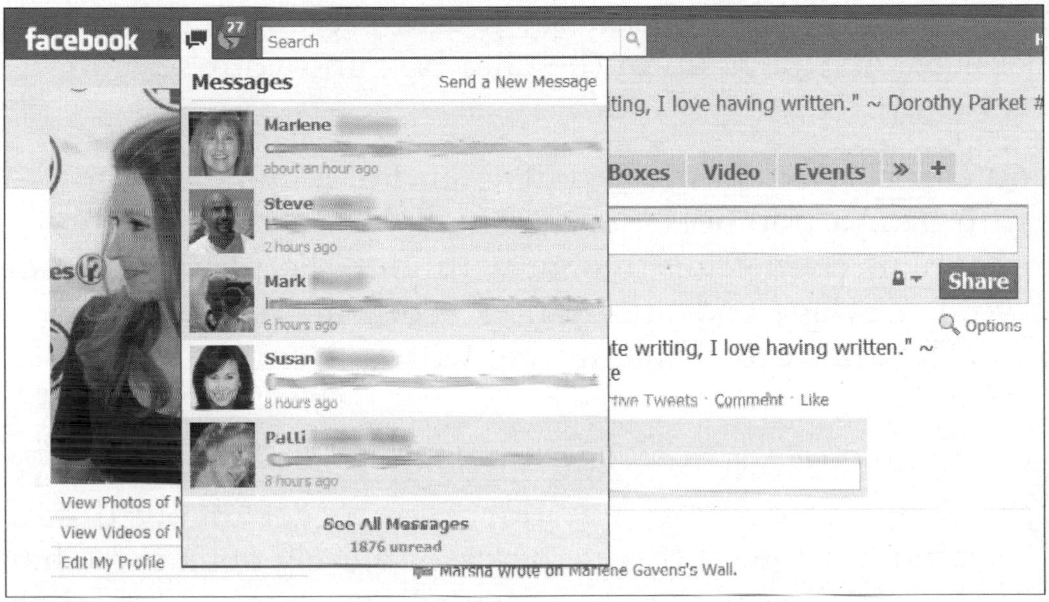

Figure 7-14

Chat with Your Friends

1. You've heard about Instant Messengers (IMs), right? Like AOL Instant Messenger? Well, a *chat session* is Facebook's version of the instant message service. It allows you to chat with friends who are online at the same time you are. To see the friends you have online you can check in two places:

- On the left side of your home page, beneath your messages, you see a Friends Online area.

- At the lower-right corner of your home page, you see a Chat box. Click it, and you see a scrollable list of all your friends who are currently online.

2. If you see someone online that you'd like to speak to and want to start a chat session, click the name of the friend. A chat box opens at the bottom of your screen. After the box opens, type in your message and press Enter. Your message then pops up in the chat box and your session has begun.

3. You can also be on the receiving end of a chat session. If you hear a pop noise, and a small window opens, someone is requesting to chat with you. To respond, type in your message and press Enter. Your message will pop up in the chat box. I'm chatting with a friend in **Figure 7-15**.

 If you're just breezing through Facebook and have things to do, you may not want to get involved in a chat session. If this is the case, merely click the Chat link in the lower right of your home page. Then click Options⇨Go Offline at the top of the chat box that opens. (See **Figure 7-16**.) You will become invisible to all, and you'll be free to go about your Facebook chores undisturbed.

Chat messages show up here.

Figure 7-15

Click here if you don't want to chat.

Figure 7-16

Post Messages on a Friend's Wall

1. On your Facebook home page, you'll see notations from your friends' walls. They are put there either with a status update from the person whose wall it is, or by one of their friends posting a message. To post a message on a friend's wall, go to your friend's Facebook Profile page. Make sure you are on your friend's wall by selecting the Wall tab from the toolbar below their name and above the text box. The text box is filled with a prompt that reads *Write something* in grayed-out letters.

2. To post your message, simply type it in the message box, as I did in **Figure 7-17**. If you'd like to add an attachment to your message, like a photo, a link to a page on the Web, a video, or a Facebook gift, click the appropriate link and add it. (Find more about attachments in Chapter 8.)

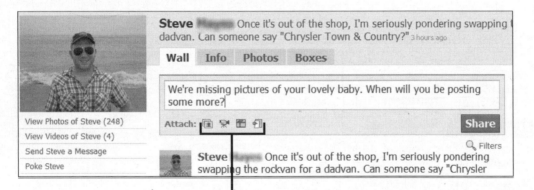

Click a link to include a photo, video, gift, or link.

Figure 7-17

3. When you're done with your message and attachments, click the Share button on the right side under the message box. Voila! Your message is now on display for your

176

friend and potentially all visitors to their page.

If you want to refer to another friend in your posted message, before you type in his or her name, type the @ sign (the symbol for *at*). Then begin to type in the person's name. When the name pops up in the drop-down menu of friends' names that appears (see **Figure 7-18**), click it to create a link to that friend in your post. Your post will then also appear on the linked friend's Profile page.

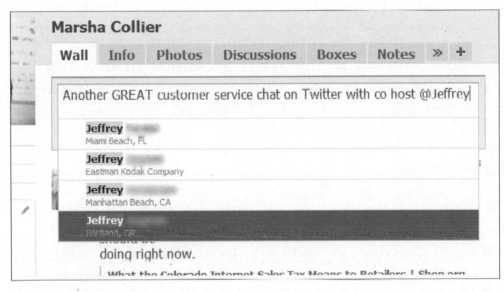

Figure 7-18

Comment on a Friend's Status

1. If you see a status message your friend has posted and you'd like to comment on it, it's as simple as 1, 2, 3. Click the Comment link under the status post. A window drops down with a blank box in which you can type your comment, as I've done in **Figure 7-19**.

177

Type your comment here.

Figure 7-19

2. Type your comment in the Write a Comment box and click the Comment button. Your response will be posted below your friend's posting for all to see.

Post a Note

1. Notes on Facebook are like mini-blog posts. They're displayed on the Notes tab of your Profile page. Posting a note is, in essence, posting an open letter to all your Facebook friends. You can access your notes by clicking the Notes tab on your Profile page or by clicking More and then Notes and My Notes on the left side of your home page.

2. On the resulting Notes page, click the Write a Note or Write a New Note button (whichever you see). You arrive at a Write a Note page, which provides you with a template to write your note. Fill in the note's title and body in the Title and Body boxes, and your note is essentially ready to be posted.

3. You may tag friends in your note by listing them in the box at the right. That way they receive a message from

178

Facebook, inviting them to read the note — a very helpful tool if you want multiple individuals to be notified of the posting. If you don't tag anyone in your note but still want your friends to know about it, you can notify your friends by posting the note to your wall.

4. As with private messages, you have the option to attach photos, videos, and links.

 Before you publish the note to Facebook, you can set the Note's degree of privacy. Making an adjustment here (as in **Figure 7-20**) allows you to decide who can view the note: just your friends, everyone, friends of friends, or people you specify in a customized setting.

5. After you complete your note, you may preview, save, discard, or publish it. To publish, click the Publish button at the bottom of the page.

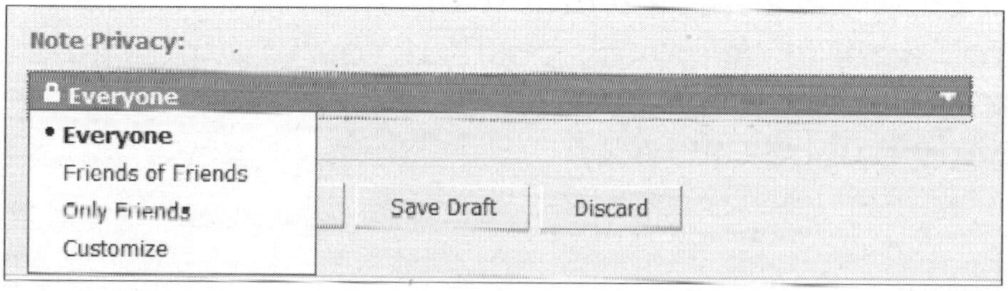

Note Privacy:

🔒 Everyone

• **Everyone**
Friends of Friends
Only Friends
Customize

Save Draft   Discard

Figure 7-20

Remove Messages from Your Wall

1. There may be a time when someone posts a message on your wall that might be too personal, or you don't want others to see. Facebook gives you the option to delete the post. (Your friend may never know that's happened unless he or she comes back to your Profile page.) To delete a post, find the post on your Profile page. Move your cursor over the right side of the post and a Remove button appears, as shown in **Figure 7-21**.

 If, out of courtesy, you want to let your friend know why you removed their post, you can send them a Private Message to explain.

Figure 7-21

2. When you click Remove, a window opens and asks *Are you sure you want to delete this post?* If you're sure, click the Delete button and the post will be removed from your wall. Nobody will be the wiser.

Chapter 8

Adding Photos and Videos to Facebook

Since Facebook is all about sharing, it's up to you to share! Putting up photos of you, your family (that includes pets), and your friends is fun — and it gives your Facebook friends a chance to interact with you.

I figure you've uploaded an image to your Profile page already, but what I'm talking about in this chapter is setting up online photo albums.

So let's get started!

181

Upload a Photo to Your Account

1. As with most Facebook tasks, you have more than one way to post a photo. The easiest and best way to post a *single* photo is to post it directly to your Profile page. Start by signing in to your Facebook account and navigating to your Profile page (click Profile in the upper-right corner).

2. Type a message about the photo in the Wall posting box that says *What's on your mind?*

3. Below your message, find the icon for uploading a photo (it looks like a little stack of photo prints), as I've done in **Figure 8-1**. Clicking that icon changes the window.

Click here to add photos.

Figure 8-1

4. The new window gives you three choices: Upload a Photo from your computer, Take a Photo with a webcam, or Create an Album with many photos. Here's how those choices work:

1. *To use a photo already on your computer, click the Upload a Photo link.* Your window changes to a window like the one shown in **Figure 8-2**, with a browse button to select a photo from your computer's hard drive. Click Browse and a dialog box opens; from here, you can look for a photo on your computer's hard drive. Find the photo you want to upload and double-click it to select it. Click Open. The photo opens and uploads while the dialog box closes, and you see the location of your photo in the text box next to Browse. To post the photo, click Share.

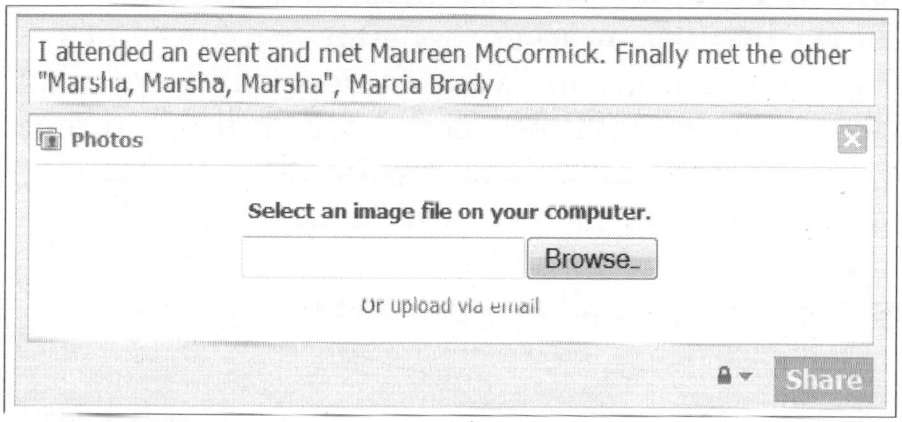

I attended an event and met Maureen McCormick. Finally met the other "Marsha, Marsha, Marsha", Marcia Brady

🖼 Photos   ☒

Select an image file on your computer.

_____ [Browse_]

Or upload via email

🔒 ▾ [Share]

Figure 8-2

Before clicking Share when you're uploading photos to Facebook, you have some privacy options to choose. **Figure 8-3** shows the options that appear when you click the arrow next to the small lock at the bottom of the posting box. Click the appropriate privacy option, and then click Share.

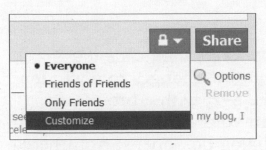

Figure 8-3

2. *If you have a webcam, click Take a Photo.* If you're using a laptop computer, the webcam is most likely built in at the top of your screen. Clicking this option activates your camera automatically — and a warning appears (as shown in **Figure 8-4**). You must give the Adobe Flash Player permission to access your camera. Click the Allow radio button and your camera will have permission for this one time. You'll see yourself in the camera — smile! Or hide behind your cat (see **Figure 8-5**) if you want a cat picture, and click the small camera icon at the bottom of the screen. After selecting your privacy setting (I allow everyone to see) click Share.

Figure 8-4

Choose who can see your photo.

Figure 8-5

3. *If you're ready to work with a batch of photos on Facebook, click Create an Album.* I discuss this fairly complex task in the next section.

Create a Photo Album

1. Facebook has many ways to get to the page where you can create photo albums. Here are the two easiest:

1. *Select the Photos tab on your Profile page.* The resulting page, as shown in **Figure 8-6**, brings you to all the

photos of you that you currently have on Facebook. At the top right, click the *Create a Photo Album* link, and you arrive at the Create Album page.

Figure 8-6

2. *Go to your Home page and, from the toolbar at the left, click Photos (as I've done in **Figure 8-7**).* This shows you a page with the most recent photos that your friends have uploaded. In the upper-right corner is a link to *+Upload Photos.* You might expect it to open a page for uploading single images, but instead, it opens the *Create Album* page.

2. On the Create Album page, give your album a name, type in the location where the photos were taken, put in a description of the photos in the album, and select your privacy setting (for who can see the album).

186

Figure 8-7

3. Click the link to Select Photos. A window opens, showing you the contents of your computer. You can navigate around your computer by clicking the folders to find where your photos reside.

4. After you find the proper folder, you can begin selecting photos for your album. If you want to use all of the images in a folder, click Select All. If you want to select just a few, click the check boxes for individual thumbnails, one at a time, to select them for upload.

5. Once you've finished picking the images, click Use Selected Photos. This brings you back to the Create Album page (see **Figure 8-8**). Before clicking Create Album, notice a box that has a check mark that says *Publish Automatically.*

- If you leave the check mark where it is, your photos show up on Facebook pages immediately. You can edit the album later with captions and tags if you want.

- Uncheck this box if you'd rather preview the photos and edit them before they appear on Facebook.

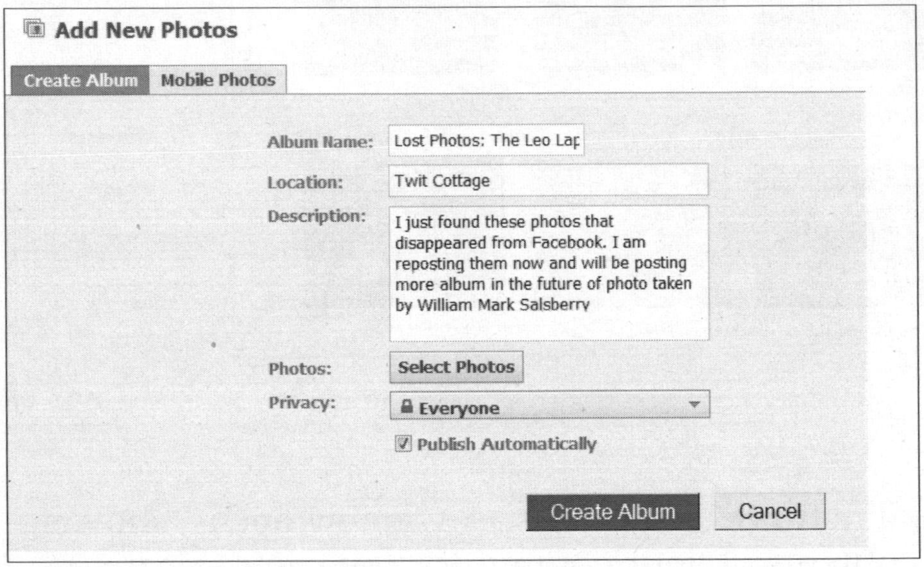

Figure 8-8

6. You can edit the album by going to your profile and clicking the Photos tab. Scroll down the page and you'll see your album (or albums), as in **Figure 8-9**.

Marsha's Albums 31 Photo Albums
View Comments | Album Privacy   1 2 3 4 5 Next Last

Lost Photos: Leo
Laporte Show
6 photos

Posterous Photos
1 photo

140conf Meetup
22 photos

Wall Photos
25 photos

Profile Pictures
12 photos

Figure 8-9

7. Click the album you want to edit and you'll be brought to a page with thumbnail versions of your pictures. Click the link above the thumbnails to Edit Photos, and you're brought to the Edit page.

   Note: If you haven't published the photos, you see a notice at the top of the page. **Figure 8-10** shows you the Edit Album page. First go through the photos, tag the pictures (more on tagging later), write captions and delete any you would rather not use. When you're done, go to the bottom of the page, and click Save Changes.

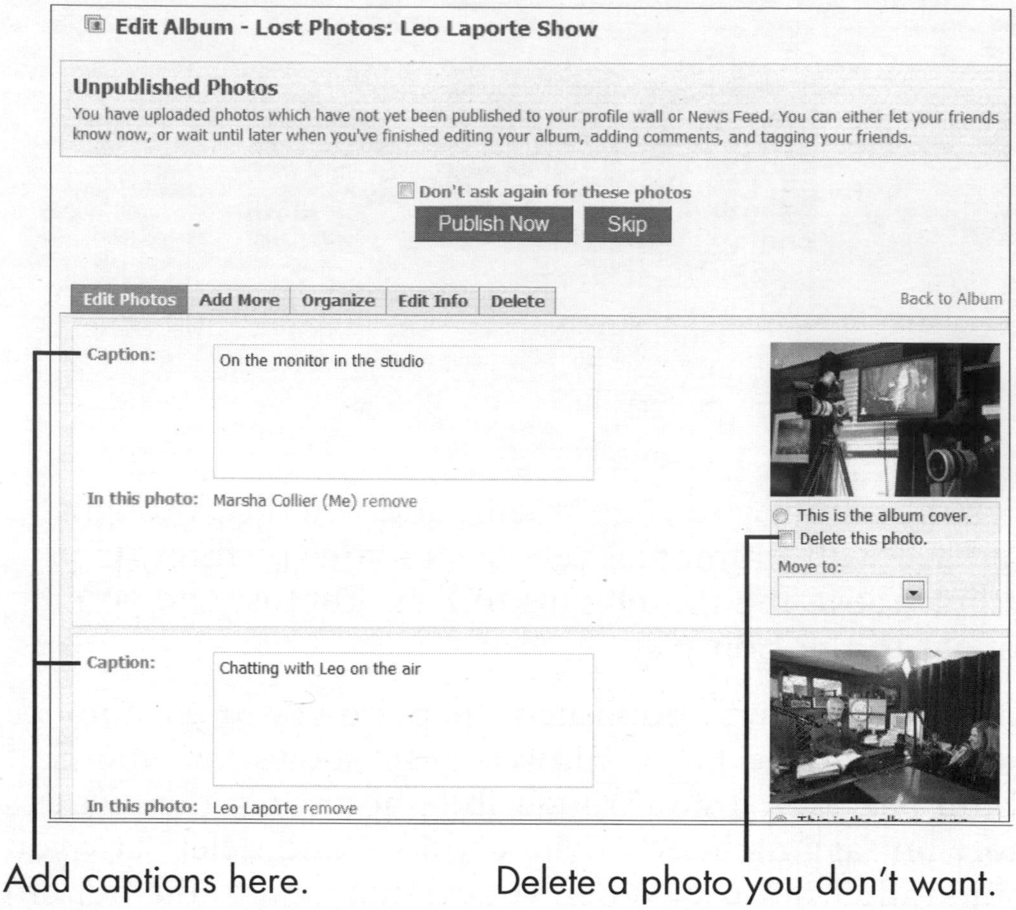

Edit Album - Lost Photos: Leo Laporte Show

Unpublished Photos
You have uploaded photos which have not yet been published to your profile wall or News Feed. You can either let your friends know now, or wait until later when you've finished editing your album, adding comments, and tagging your friends.

☐ Don't ask again for these photos

[Publish Now]   [Skip]

| **Edit Photos** | Add More | Organize | Edit Info | Delete | | Back to Album |

Caption: On the monitor in the studio

In this photo: Marsha Collier (Me) remove

○ This is the album cover.
☐ Delete this photo.
Move to:

Caption: Chatting with Leo on the air

In this photo: Leo Laporte remove

Add captions here.   Delete a photo you don't want.

Figure 8-10

8. Your photos will now show up on your Profile page; if you've tagged friends in the photos, those pictures appear on your friends' Profile pages.

Tag Photos

1. No matter where you find photos of you or one of your friends on Facebook, you'll be able to tag them. *Tagging* is the Facebook phrase for adding the names of friends to photo information. Tagging a friend makes his or her name appear when someone puts a mouse pointer over

the tagged friend's image. Tagging also links the photo to the appropriate profile. Whenever friends are tagged in a photo, that photo appears on their individual walls and becomes a permanent part of their Photos areas.

 When you or anyone on Facebook is tagged, the *tagee* receives an e-mail notifying him or her of the new-found fame. Then the tagee can get online and look at the picture.

2. When you see a photo of you or one of your friends on Facebook, click it and you arrive at the Photos page. If no one has been tagged in the picture, no linkable names will appear below it.

3. At the lower right, below the photo, click the Tag This Photo link, as I did in **Figure 8-11**.

Figure 8-11

4. Move your cursor, and click it on the face of one of your friends. A box will come up, framing the face; so will a list of your friends, so you can select a name to put in the tag.

5. Start typing in your friend's name (or your name if the photo is of you), and Facebook narrows the selection as you type. (You can also use the scroll bar next to the names to find the right one. I found my friend's name in **Figure 8-12**.)

Figure 8-12

6. When you've found the person in the photo, click to put a check in the box next to his or her name; then click Tag. Bingo! The name of the person you tagged is now at the bottom of the photo — and the photo has been posted to your tagged friend's Profile page.

192

7. If you have more than one friend in the picture, repeat Steps 1–5 given here until you've tagged everyone. When you've tagged all the friends in the picture, click the Done Tagging button above the picture.

 You must be friends with someone on Facebook in order to tag him or her in a photo. If you see a photo with a person you know — but aren't Facebook friends with (yet) — send that person a Friend invitation. After your friend accepts, you can then add a tag to the photo.

8. As people view the photo, they'll see the tagged names at the bottom. If they move their mouse pointers over the picture, the person's name pops up (as in **Figure 8-13**).

Names pop up in a tagged picture.

Figure 8-13

193

Untag Yourself in a Photo

1. You may get an e-mail and find that one of your friends has tagged you in a photo on Facebook. Excited, you log on to your Profile page . . . and groan. Have no fear. If you find a photo that a friend has taken of you that doesn't quite meet your standards, you can do something about it. Click the photo, and Facebook takes you to the photo's page. Below the photo, next to your name (as in **Figure 8-14**), is a Remove Tag link.

Photos of You

Photo 339 of 455   Photos of Me   Previous Next

Photo is (CC) Jonathan Dingman

In this photo: Yvette   Marsha Collier (photos | remove tag)

From the album:
BCCF Charity Event in Santa
Barbara by Jonathan Dingman

Click here to untag a picture, if you want.

Figure 8-14

2. Click the Remove Tag link. The photo goes into the Facebook ether and will never be associated with your

profile again. The photo does remain in your friend's album, but someone would have to view the album to see you. Once you've untagged yourself in a photo, no one but you can tag you in that particular photo again.

 If you've accidentally tagged the wrong person in a photo, you can undo your error by clicking the Remove Tag link.

Delete a Photo

1. If you upload a photo by mistake — or simply decide you'd rather not put that photo-taken-with-your-ex online — you can remove it. You can delete only the photos that you, personally, have uploaded.

 If you want to disassociate yourself from a photo that someone else uploaded, you'll have to settle for untagging yourself (see the previous task in this chapter).

2. Under the photo, on the photo page, you'll find a list of commands, as shown in **Figure 8-15**. Click the Delete This Photo link, and (poof) the photo is gone from your Facebook page.

From your album:
Operation Smile Gala

Share

Tag This Photo
Edit This Photo
Delete This Photo
Make Profile Picture

Figure 8-15

Upload a Video to Facebook

1. This isn't rocket science. If you've uploaded a photo, you can upload a video. Go to your Facebook Home page and click the Photos link on the left side toolbar.

2. The newly posted photos of your friends appear on the resulting page. When you're through admiring them, look at the top left, and next to the Upload Photos button, you should see an Upload Video button, as shown in **Figure 8-16**.

Figure 8-16

3. Click the button, and you arrive at the Create a New Video page. This page, shown in **Figure 8-17**, works similarly to the Upload a Photo page. The difference is that when you click the Browse button, a standard search window opens on your computer.

196

Click here to browse for a video.

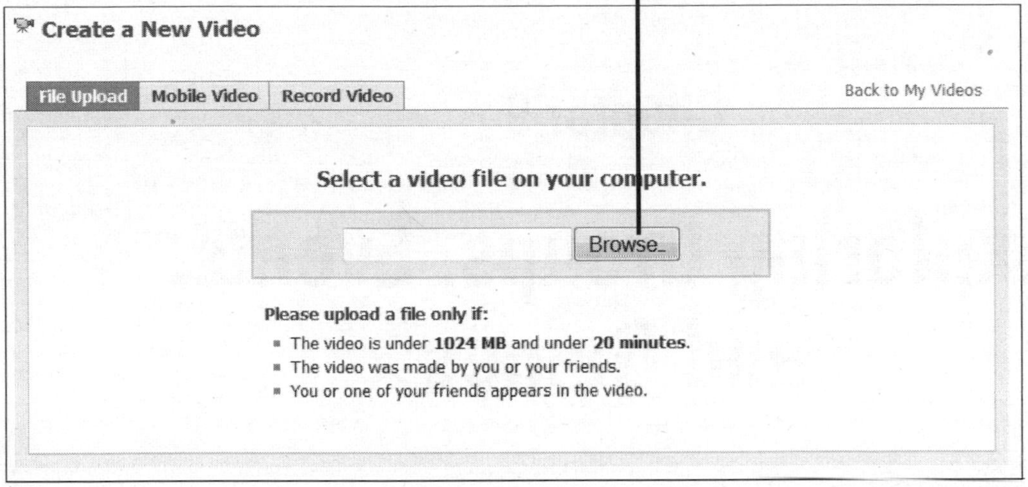

```
✺ Create a New Video

┌─────────────┬──────────────┬──────────────┐
│ File Upload │ Mobile Video │ Record Video │          Back to My Videos
└─────────────┴──────────────┴──────────────┘

              Select a video file on your computer.

        ┌──────────────────────┬─────────────┐
        │                      │   Browse.   │
        └──────────────────────┴─────────────┘

        Please upload a file only if:
        ▪ The video is under 1024 MB and under 20 minutes.
        ▪ The video was made by you or your friends.
        ▪ You or one of your friends appears in the video.
```

Figure 8-17

4. Browse your computer's folders, find the video file you want to upload, and click to select it. The upload begins immediately.

5. After the upload finishes, the video will be on your Facebook page, ready for you to tag and caption.

Chapter 9

Exploring Groups, Events, and Games

If you thought your teen years were a busy time, just wait. Being a member of Facebook means that you're about to have a whole new group of friends to combine with your old ones. Best of all? You'll meet people who have interests just like yours. You'll have the opportunity to attend chats and join groups — and you don't even have to get out of your pajamas.

Is there something you really like? A series of books, films, or products? Look for a related page on Facebook; many businesses are joining up on Facebook. Even California Cat Center, where I board my cats, has a Facebook page. (I visit their page to check out the cute photos of their feline guests.)

And here are some other instances of Facebook member involvement:

➤ When Kashi products stopped manufacturing my favorite shake mix, unhappy customers started a Facebook group to protest!

➤ Someone came up with the idea that Betty White should host *Saturday Night Live* and started a Facebook group. They had a great idea. After spreading the word through wall posts and messages, over 500,000 people joined. Eighty-eight-year-old Betty hosted the 2010 Mother's Day show, and SNL had the highest ratings in over 18 months! All because of a Facebook group.

Other ways to enjoy community action are to play games and use Facebook applications (or *apps*). To many members, these are the best parts of Facebook. Be advised: Games and other apps can burn a lot of time, but they are a lot of fun. And they're social — you can involve your online friends in your game.

So what are you waiting for? Check out the info in this chapter and get active with a Facebook group, game, or app — you can even start your own group or plan an event!

Find Your Favorite Things on Facebook

1. If you're planning on navigating your way around Facebook, you're going to be up close and personal with that little search box at the top of the page. To look at some of the magic it can perform, type the *keyword* that best describes the topic you're looking for in the search box at the top of the page. Following on the idea of looking for people who love small animals, for this example, (see **Figure 9-1**), I typed *Cats*.

Facebook finds pages with *Cats* in the name and puts them in a drop-down menu. As Figure 9-1 shows, you get a few interesting hits, and the top seven results are shown. If you want to check out any of the results at this point, just click the name, and you're brought to that page.

Figure 9-1

2. Click the See More Results link at the bottom of the drop-down menu. You arrive at the Facebook All Results page. As **Figure 9-2** shows, you can get some great hits — but clicking the View All Page Results link would net 22,000 pages (as noted in the upper-right corner). That might be too much to browse through.

 If you look below All Results at the top left, you see a navigation area with links to Posts by Friends and Web Results that also include your search term. Both areas have links to view more; you see only the top results on this page.

3. In the left navigation area, click Pages. Facebook takes you to a page with more results, but they're almost as confusing. Notice a little box at the top that reads *Show: All Page Types*? Click the down arrow next to the box, and a drop-down menu appears. You now have choices to help narrow down your search. In **Figure 9-3**, I selected *Non-Profit*.

Cats	**Search**		

Q All Results	⚑ **Pages**		About 22,000 Results
👤 People		Name: **cats**	Like
⚑ Pages		Type: Pets	
👥 Groups		Fans: 447,774 people like this.	
➕ Applications			
31 Events		Name: **Laughing at Cats**	Like
💿 Web Results		Type: Website	
🗊 Posts by Friends		Fans: 59,960 people like this.	
🗊 Posts by Everyone			
		Name: **Cats**	Like
		Type: Pets	
		Fans: 10,582 people like this.	
			View All Page Results ▸

Figure 9-2

201

Make selections to narrow your results.

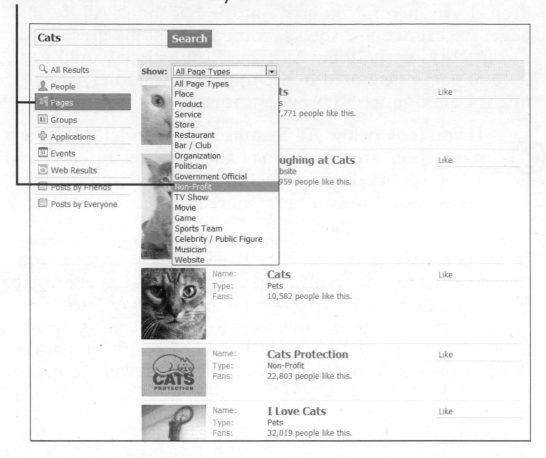

Figure 9-3

4. The resulting page nets pared-down results, as shown in
Figure 9-4, because the search is now limited to Non-
Profit Pages. Next to each page listing is a Like link on
the far right. Don't jump willy-nilly into just any group
that has a nice title and a cute picture. Click the title of a
page and check it out before you choose to join; that way,
you see what the page is really all about and who's behind
it. (I clicked a couple in the example just given, and they
weren't my cup of tea at all.)

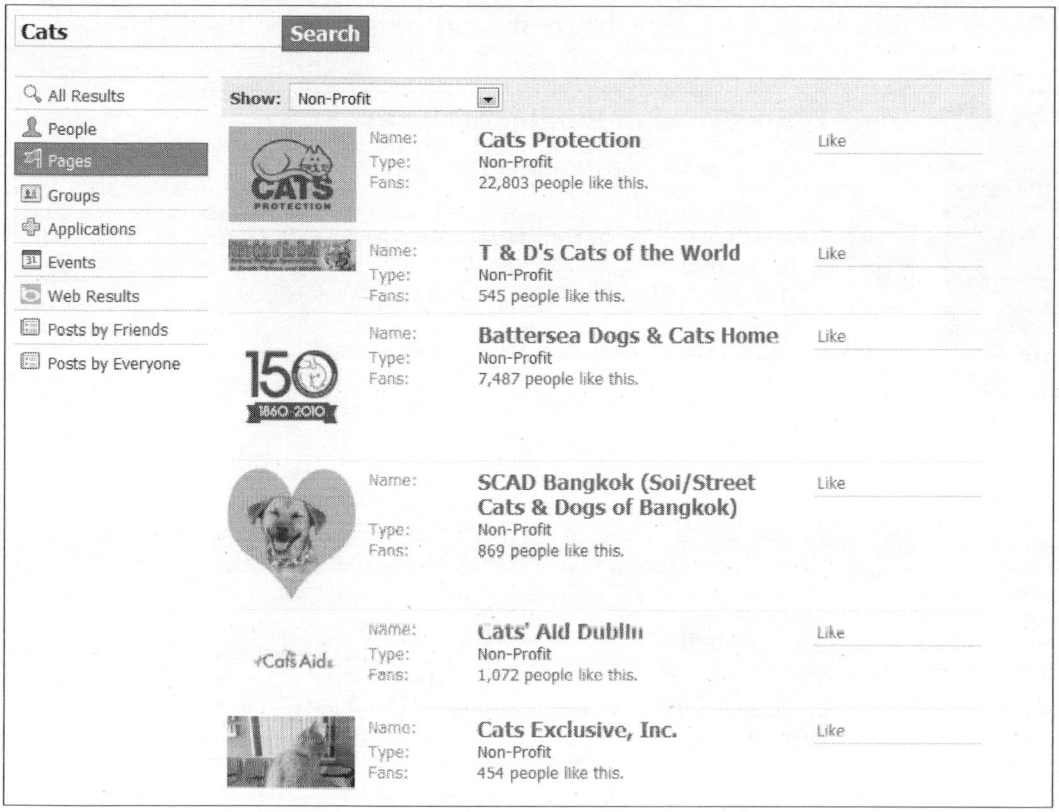

Figure 9-4

5. Clicking on the title takes you to the page. In **Figure 9-5,** you can see I clicked on a charming page from a veterinarian. After reviewing the page, I clicked Like and became a member.

Animal Care Center of Huntington Beach 👍 Like

Wall Info Photos Discussions Reviews Twitter »

🔍 Filters

Animal Care Center of Huntington Beach WHOO HOO! My Tanner's spleen mass and liver biopsy
came back benign! Par-tay (and my clients dog who's spleen came out same
day had a benign splenic mass and liver biopsy too!) Life is good.
Very, very good.
4 hours ago

👍 8 people like this.

Kirsten ▓▓▓▓▓ Thanks so much for taking such amazing care of Badger, he is feeling so much better and is a happy puppy now!

Add to My Page's Favorites
Suggest to Friends

A full service animal hospital serving Huntington Beach, Fountain Valley, Costa Mesa, Newport Beach and surrounding Orange County. We treat dogs, cats AND exotics!

Information

Figure 9-5

 If you'd rather just not look at the top 10 results, but don't want to trudge through all 22,000; add another keyword in your search terms. Typing another keyword in the box can help you refine your search. Also, you can click each link in the left navigation area to further narrow your results.

Join a Facebook Group

As a member of Facebook, you'll no doubt want to connect with people who have common likes — and doing that through groups is quick and easy! Here's how:

1. Find a group through search. To find a group you are interested in, you can search for your keywords as I describe in the preceding section. Then just click the Groups link on the left after you receive your search results.

Click a group title that suits your fancy and check it out. If you think you've found one that you'd like to join, click the Join link on the top of the group's page. In **Figure 9-6,** you can see the Join link. After looking at many pages, I could see this was one I liked enough that it was worth joining.

To join the group, click here.

Figure 9-6

 Some Facebook groups are private. In this case, you need to click the Request to Join link on the Group page and await confirmation. Confirmation will come to your through e-mail and Facebook messages. Some groups require an invitation in order to join. The only way you will be able to join these groups is if a group administrator invites you and gives you access.

2. Receive a group request from one of your Facebook friends. You receive a notification via e-mail — or one that shows up in the Requests box on the right side of your home page, or by clicking the Groups link found in the toolbar on the left side of your home page (as in **Figure 9-**7). Clicking either of those two links will display your group requests from Facebook.

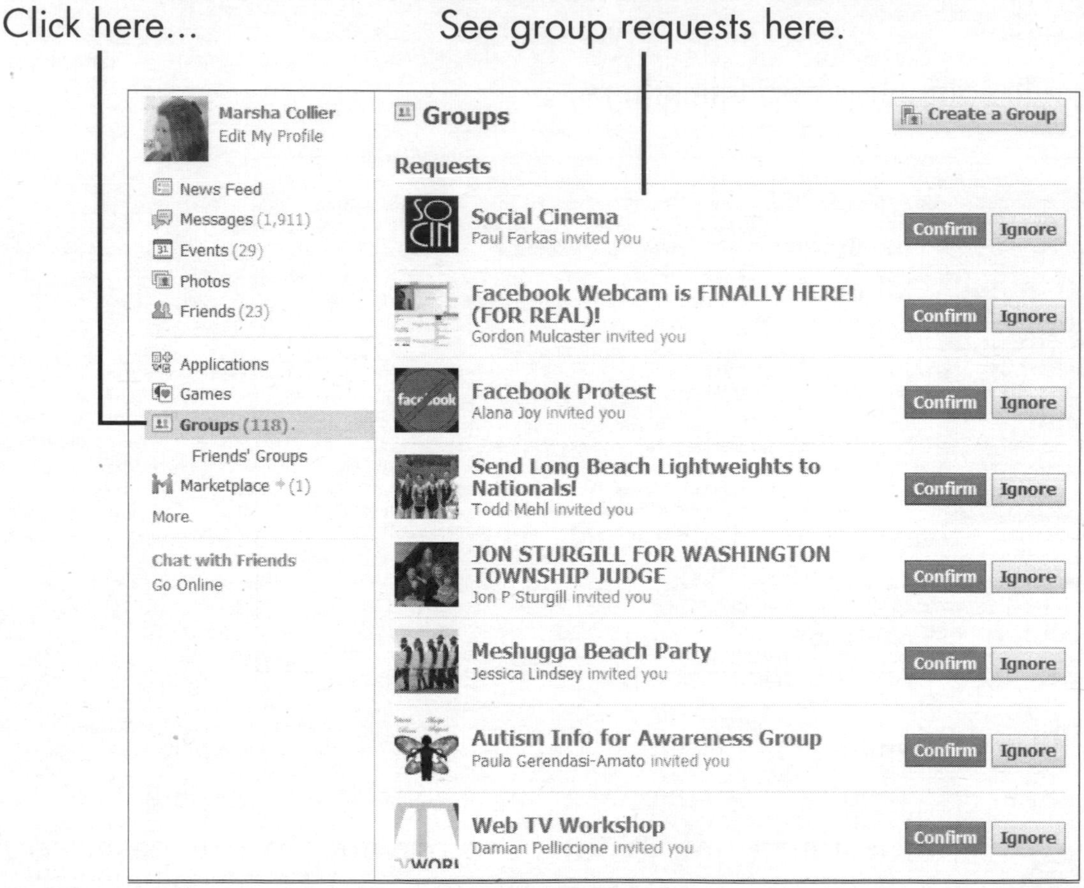

Click here...   See group requests here.

Figure 9-7

Although Facebook sends e-mails with group requests, it's best to go to your Facebook page to check the groups. E-mails are notorious for carrying spam or even computer viruses, and clicking their enclosed links can be a risky proposition. Most e-mails you get from Facebook are benign, but think twice if you get a warning that the link you are about to click is taking you to a page outside of Facebook.

3. Respond to a group request as you would to a friend request. You can click the Confirm button to join, but I find it best to click the group's name first, to check out the page and see what it's all about. After clicking through and checking out the group, I respond to an invitation in **Figure 9-8** by clicking the Respond to Group Invitation button at the top of the page.

4. A box opens on the page. **Figure 9-9** shows the three choices you find there.

Click here to respond.

Figure 9-8

See your choices here.

Add group membership?

Do you want to join The Perils of Cyber-Dating?

Join | Ignore | Cancel

Figure 9-9

- **Join.** Click here and voila! You're a card-carrying member of the group. (Okay, there's no card, but it's fun to think of it that way.)

- **Ignore.** When you select Ignore, the notification disappears from your pages. The person who invited you won't be notified, so don't worry. If (say) you're really not a morning person and don't want to join your neighbor's "Good Morning Coffee" group, you can always say you never saw the e-mail. (Your unaccepted invitation will still appear in your neighbor's group's Not Yet Replied invitation area.)

- **Cancel.** Click here and you can decide later (or never). But note that the group request will still appear in your list.

Start a Facebook Group

1. Want to plan a family reunion? Perhaps you might be interested in starting a new group on Facebook based on your hobby? You can do it. Start by clicking the Groups link found in the navigation bar on the left side of your home page. (You may have to click the More link first.) You'll be brought to your Groups page.

2. Click the Create a Group button on the upper-right side of your page, as shown in **Figure 9-10**. You're taken to the Create a Group form page.

Figure 9-10

3. Fill in the form. Facebook requires you to fill in text boxes labeled *Group Name, Description,* and *Group Type.* To select your group type, click the arrow next to the Select Category drop-down list (as in **Figure 9-11**). Optionally, you can fill in contact information and news about the group.

4. When you've filled out the page (you can always edit it later), click Create Group and your group will be live on Facebook.

Fill in a name and description.   Choose a group category here.

Step 1: Group Info

Group Name:
(required)   Cigars & Magic

Description:
(required)   This is a group for cigar lovers that love magic...
                 or, magicians that love cigars! Join, pull up a chair,
                 light a nice stogie, pull out the cards & coins and
                 let's have a "smoky" session. Let's talk about
                 cigars, magic, tricks, food, drink and things that
                 make life fun!

Group Type:
(required)   Select Category: Select Type:
                 Select Category:
Recent News: Business
                 Common Interest
                 Entertainment & Arts
                 Geography
                 Internet & Technology
                 Just for Fun
                 Music
Office: Organizations
                 Sports & Recreation
Email: Student Groups

Website:

Street:

City/Town:

                 Create Group   Cancel

Figure 9-11

 Be aware! Facebook has a rule about groups: "Groups
that attack a specific person or group of people (e.g.
racist, sexist, or other hate groups) will not be toler-
ated. Creating such a group will result in the immediate termination of your Facebook account."

5. You can edit your page and settings at any time by
clicking the little pencil icon next to the word Edit that
appears (only to you) on the sections of your group page.
In **Figure 9-12**, I'm editing the Group information.
Figure 9-13 shows the editing commands I need to
change the group's profile picture.

Information	✎ Edit Box
	Edit Information

Category:
Entertainment & Arts -
Performing Arts

Description:
This is a group for cigar lovers
that love magic... or, magicians
that love cigars! Join, pull up a
chair, light a nice stogie, pull
out the cards & coins and let's
have a "smoky" session. Let's
talk about cigars, magic, tricks,
food, drink and things that
make life fun!

Privacy Type:
Open: All content is public.

30% Cuban
M
n:
30

Experience:
Ecuadorian

See More

Yesterday

👍 Tony Blak

Figure 9-12

✎ Edit your Profile Picture

⬆ Upload a Picture

📷 Take a Picture

✎ Edit Thumbnail

✗ Remove your
Picture

Tom Frank
night while
and I don't
w/ friends.

Alec Bradley
and potatoe
of big-ring

See More

Yesterday a

👍 Tony Blake

Figure 9-13

Communicate with Group Members

When you set up a group on Facebook, you are usually the group administrator (*admin,* for short) by default. As the group administrator, you will be able to adjust the privacy settings, edit information, and add a group profile photo. It's just like setting up your own Facebook page. Think of your group page the same as your regular Profile page; it's not any different — except when it comes to communicating with members:

➤ If you're the admin of your group (the Big Kahuna, the person who created the group and runs it), you can post messages to the group's wall just as you can on any Facebook Wall, as shown in **Figure 9-14**. Your message posts on the page so any member who visits will see it.

➤ If you are merely a member of a group, the only way you can connect with other members is by posting to their individual walls or sending each of them a message through Facebook.

Post your message to the group wall.

Figure 9-14

But the magic of groups is that admins can send blanket communications to all members. Below the group photo is an area of links where Facebook allows you unique controls. (Only the admins can see these.)

➡ **Message All Members.** Clicking this link will take you to a page that looks like any other Facebook message page. The only difference is that when you click *Send,* the message will go to all the members of your Group.

➡ **Promote Group with Ad.** If you'd like to buy a Facebook ad to promote your group, here's your chance!

➡ **Edit Group Settings.** This takes you to an Administration page where you decide about privacy settings, page setup, and general information.

➡ **Edit Members.** This takes you to a Member Administration page where you can view all your members and choose officers or other admins. **Figure 9-15** shows you the available tabs and options.

Figure 9-15

➡ **Invite people to join.** This link takes you to a page that shows all your Facebook personal friends. You may select as many or as few as you want and invite them to join your group.

➤ **Create Group Event.** Want to have a meeting? A party? Admins only can click here and go to the Create an Event page. **Figure 9-16** shows you how this procedure differs from a regular Facebook event invitation. You have three options:

a. *Open:* Anyone can see this Event and its information. Anyone can RSVP or invite others to this Event.

b. *Closed:* Anyone can see this Event, but its content is only shown to guests. People need to be invited or request invitations to be able to RSVP.

c. *Secret:* Only people who are invited can see this Event and details. People will need to be invited and to RSVP.

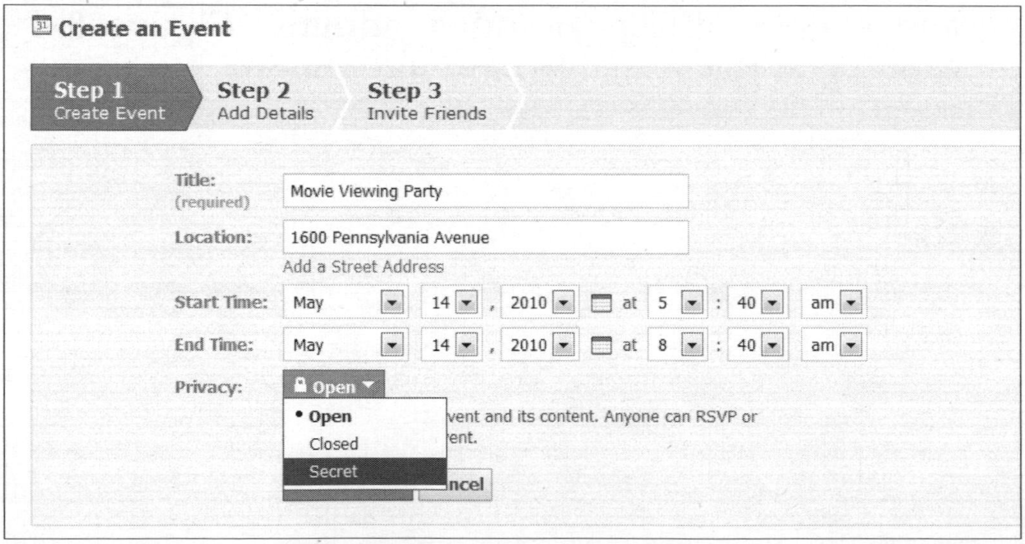

Figure 9-16

Create an Event Invitation

1. Are you planning a party? Facebook is a good way to send out invitations. Any Facebook member can create an event and invite all their friends. Start by going to your Facebook Home page and clicking the Events tab found in the toolbar on the left side of the screen (as in **Figure 9-17**). In the upper-right corner of your Events page, you'll see the Create an Event button.

Click here to see events.

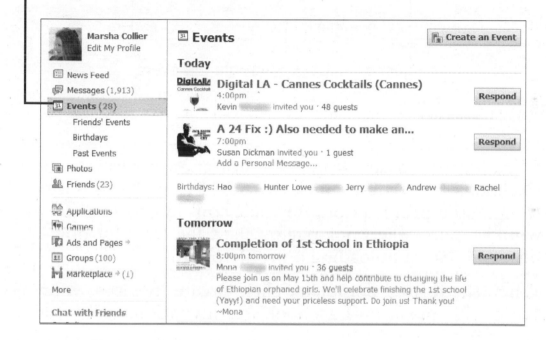

Figure 9-17

2. Clicking the Create an Event button takes you to the Create an Event page, as shown in **Figure 9-18**. Fill out the when, what, and where of the event.

215

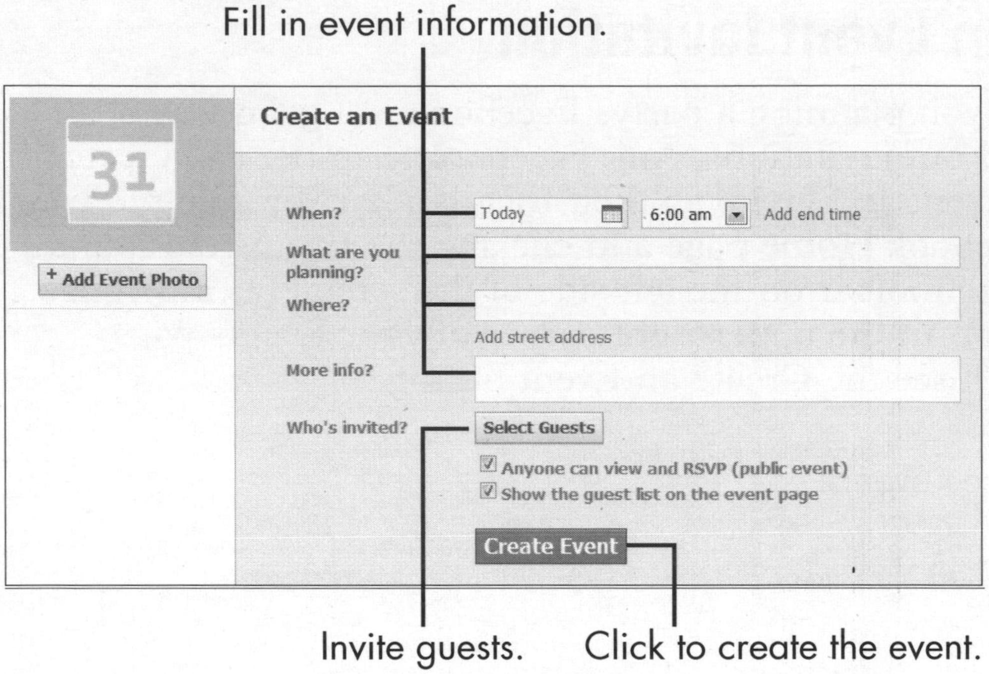

Fill in event information.

Create an Event

When? | Today | 6:00 am | Add end time

What are you planning?

Where?

Add street address

More info?

Who's invited? | Select Guests

☑ Anyone can view and RSVP (public event)
☑ Show the guest list on the event page

Create Event

+ Add Event Photo

31

Invite guests.   Click to create the event.

Figure 9-18

3. Click Select Guests to prepare your guest list from your Facebook friends list. Click the Add Event Photo button to upload a profile photo for the event, just as you would on any Facebook page. (See Chapter 5 for how-to instructions on uploading a profile photo.)

4. When the form is complete, click Create Event — your event will appear on Facebook and invitations will be sent to the friends you selected.

 As the event administrator, you can adjust the event's privacy settings, invite more people, edit the guest list, cancel the event, edit the event, and send messages to your guests.

Review Upcoming Events

1. To review your upcoming events, click the Events link in the links on the left side of your homepage. You're taken to your Events page, where you can view all your upcoming events in chronological order. When you click the Events link, you open a drop-down sub-menu with selections for Friends' Events, Birthdays, and Past Events.

 Viewing Friends' Events can be convenient if you would like to see what your friends are up to — and if the events are public, you may be able to figure out some plans for your next Friday night.

2. Your events are listed on the Events page (refer to Figure 9-17) and you have the chance to respond to the invitations right there. I always recommend that you take a moment and click the title of the event so you can find out exactly what's planned and where the event is. If you know all those details and are in a hurry, you can click the Respond button next to the event.

3. A small window like the one in **Figure 9-19** appears. There you can let the organizer know whether you'll be attending. Optionally, you can write a short note to go along with your RSVP. You can also change your mind at any time (assuming it's okay with the host) and change your RSVP directly on the Event page.

Click an RSVP option here.

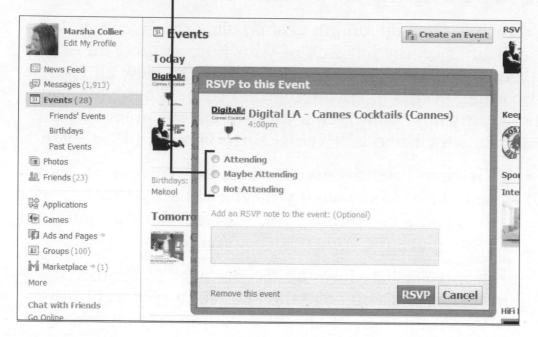

Figure 9-19

Export an Event to Another Calendar

1. If you don't rely on Facebook as your main event
calendar, it's a good idea to use the Export feature to
send your Facebook Events into whatever calendar you
use. Facebook supports lots of applications, including
Microsoft Outlook and Apple iCal. Facebook also claims
that it can export to Google Calendar, but I've never been
able to make that feature work consistently.

 Your Events section shows you all the events you've
been invited to. Rather than merely clicking the Respond button, click the event's title to see all the details.

2. When you're on the Event invitation page, you can export the event by clicking the Export button found above the RSVP box on the right side of the Event page (as shown in **Figure 9-20**). A pop-up window will appear, giving you the option to export, download the appointment to your computer, or send yourself an e-mail with the event details.

Choose where to send this event.

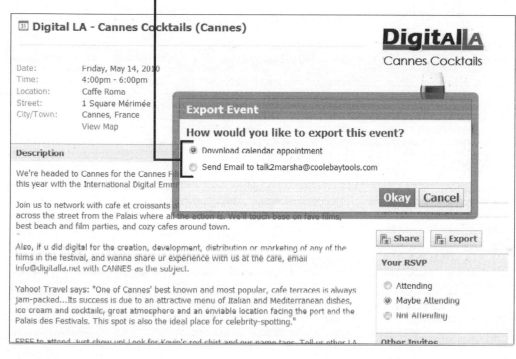

Figure 9-20

Have Some Fun with Games and Applications

Your first exposure to Facebook's games or applications (apps) happens when you see posts from some of your friends like those shown in **Figure 9-21**. Facebook has loads of games and applications. Applications are a little different from games, since they don't require as many hours to have fun with them.

Figure 9-21

Facebook's many applications enable you to do almost anything you can imagine — send gifts, take quizzes, throw snowballs — you name it! A popular type of app centers around taking quizzes. You can find a quiz on everything from how to determine "What Sex and the City character you are" to "Which color best suits your personality." Another very popular application lets you make up your own quizzes to send to your friends.

 Playing with a quiz application lets your friends see that you have taken the quiz by posting your results to your news feed. Potentially, your friends will play along with you.

The most popular games on Facebook are currently the products of Zynga, the creators of Farmville, Mafia Wars, Fishville, Texas HoldEm Poker, and numerous other games. When you find a game (or an application) you'd like to participate in, you must give permission for Facebook to allow the game to have access to your account, as shown in **Figure 9-22**. If you want to play, this access is a requirement. So stick to the most popular, time tested games.

♣ **Allow Access?**

Allowing FarmVille access will let it pull your profile information, photos, your friends' info, and other content that it requires to work.

FarmVille   ★★★☆
Howdy Ya'll! Come on down to the Farm today and play with your friends. We got plenty of land for everyone. Come and see what everyone is hootin' and hollerin' about.

[Allow] or Leave Application

By using FarmVille, you agree to the FarmVille Terms of Service.   Report Application

Figure 9-22

Browse Facebook Apps and Games

1. To browse apps on Facebook, go to your home page and click the Applications link in the toolbar on the left. When you get to your Applications page (as shown in **Figure 9-23**), you can see two sections in the middle column: Your Applications (if you've signed up for any) and Friends' Applications (those most recently used). On the right side of the page are links to Facebook's featured applications.

2. To see all the available applications, you simply browse Facebook's Applications Directory. But finding this directory through a Facebook search is a little tricky, so just type **www.facebook.com/apps/directory.php** in your browser's address bar. Press Enter, and you see a page similar to the one shown in **Figure 9-24**. Click the On Facebook link in the left side toolbar, and you see a page similar to the one in **Figure 9-25**.

Figure 9-23

Click here for apps on Facebook.

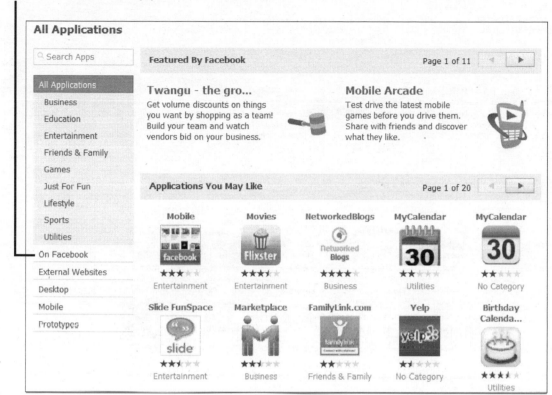

Figure 9-24

Click an app category here.

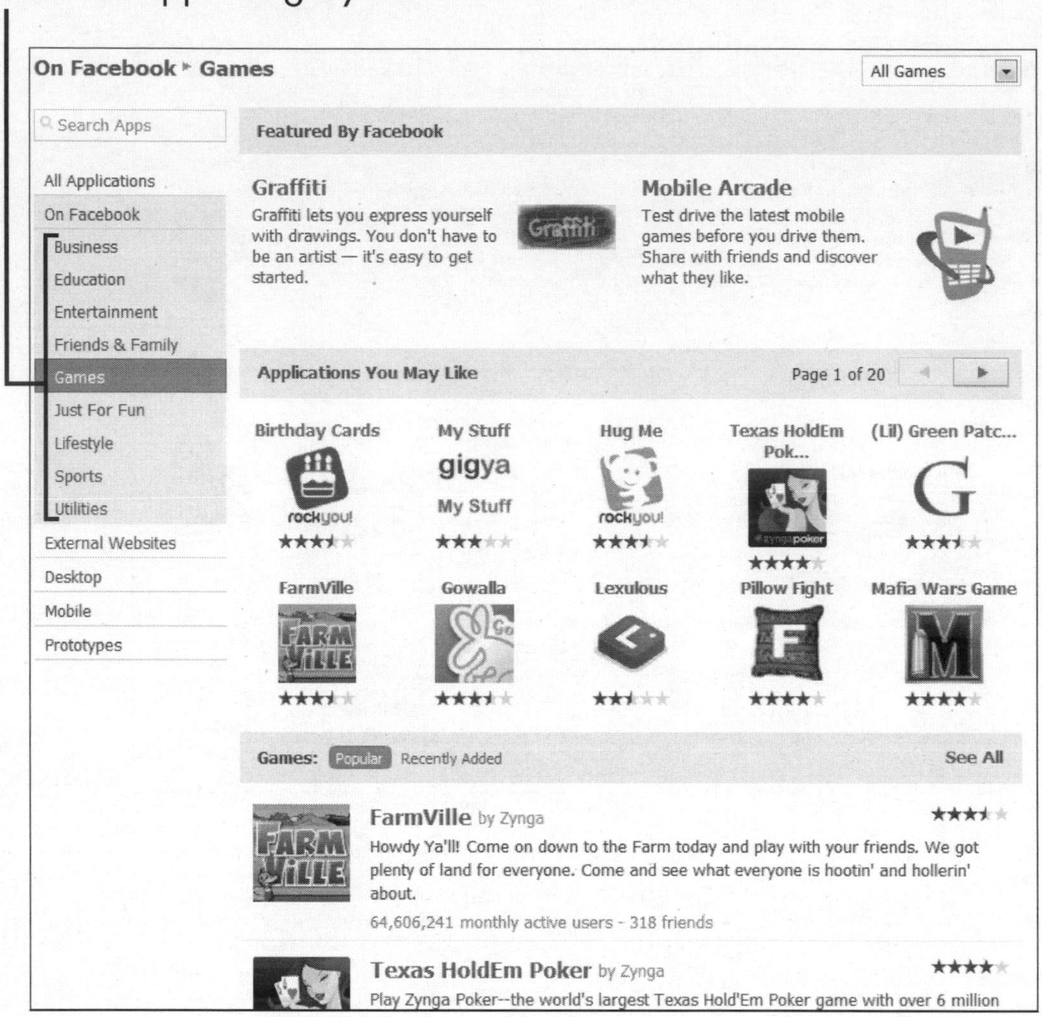

Figure 9-25

3. The resulting On Facebook Applications Directory has a number of category links on the left side toolbar. By clicking these links you will find specific types of applications, for example, Games and Utilities. Click a link, and you see featured items and application recommendations in that category. Browse through and you'll be sure to find an application to suit your needs.

4. To specifically find games on Facebook, click the Games link in the left toolbar. You'll see game icons, and a list of the currently most popular. When you see a game you'd like to play, click its name and you arrive on that game's Facebook page. Click the blue Go To Application button on the left side of the page under the large game icon, as shown in **Figure 9-26**.

Click here to get started with the chosen app.

Figure 9-26

Currently, millions of people play these top games:

➤ **Farmville:** 64,004,337 players. Ever wanted to have

a farm? Now you can without getting your hands dirty! Farmville allows you to build and cultivate your own. The game comes complete with your own plot of land and lots of opportunities to grow your farm through planting, harvesting, gifting, and building.

➤ **Texas HoldEm Poker:** 28,561,070 players. Fancy yourself a poker star? This is the top poker game in the world. Play online with your friends and see who's got the best poker face, or meet some new people. The game also runs weekly tournaments. (By the way, your winnings are virtual — no cash payouts.)

➤ **Treasure Isle:** 21,635,321 players. Become an adventurer without leaving your computer. On Treasure Isle, you visit strange places, dig for rare and valuable treasure with your friends, and decorate your very own island.

➤ **Café World:** 20,690,157 players. Become a restaurateur and run your own restaurant. Choose your menu from dozens of dishes to cook, then slice, chop, sauté, and bake your way to success. You can decorate your Café and hire friends.

➤ **Mafia Wars:** 18,935,023 players. Did you love Al Pacino in *The Godfather*? You might just have fun playing Mafia Wars, the wildly popular crime game. Build alliances, amass property, and fight mobs of enemies in games of power and deception.

Part III

And Now, It's Twitter Time

The 5th Wave   By Rich Tennant

"I'd respond to this person's comment on Twitter, but I'm a former Marine, Bernard, and a Marine never retweets."

Chapter 10

A Beginner's Guide to Twitter

I really enjoy the time I spend on Twitter. I can visit the site at any hour and find a friend to chat with. It may not be someone I've met in real life, but someone I've met on Twitter with whom I have fun. People on Twitter come from all walks of life, and you can make friends with people of all ages.

Keep in mind that Twitter is not just about posting pithy

229

thoughts online; it's all about having conversations. The second-best part of Twitter is that by listening (reading other people's posts, or *Tweets,* as they're nick-named), you learn all sorts of interesting things. Most news events appear on Twitter before you hear about them on radio or television.

Twitter users love to spread information of all sorts. When you find your niche, you'll see what fun participating on the site can be.

Your posts on Twitter are limited to 140 characters. (When you send text messages on your phone, you're allowed 160 characters.) Figuring out how to abbreviate your thoughts and get your message into such a short sentence will definitely exercise your brain; it can take a bit of thinking!

In this chapter, I help you get started with Twitter — by registering, setting up an account and profile page, deciding what notices you want to receive, and getting familiar with Twitter shorthand. Are you ready? Let's sign up and start making new friends!

Register with Twitter

1. As with all interactive Web sites, you can't play until you sign up and agree to the rules. So type **www.twitter.com** in your browser's address bar, press Enter, and you'll come to a page similar to the one in **Figure 10-1**.

Click here to register with Twitter.

Figure 10-1

2. Before you start to click things, take a look at the Twitter Web page. You find a list of topics that are currently popular (trending) on the site. Don't worry if you aren't interested in any topics you see here. With over 75 million users, I'm sure that a few will have interests similar to yours! You also see some of the famous Twtterati who use the service (on the left), as well as a scroll of top tweets from the current timeline.

3. To start your registration, click the button that says Get Started, Join Today, or Sign Up. The greeting changes from minute to minute, but you get the drift, right? You're presented with a page prompting you to enter some information that identifies you to Twitter, as follows:

1. *Type in your full, real name so that your friends can find you if they look for you in Twitter search.* (Chapter 11 tells you more about searching on Twitter.)

2. *Come up with a catchy username for use on Twitter.*

 Your username can be a nickname or your real name, whichever you prefer. If you choose a nickname, it can be a name that reflects one of your hobbies, or a special interest you may have. Get creative! But remember: Your username cannot have any spaces or symbols, just letters and/or numbers. If your selected username is already in use on the site, Twitter will let you know, as shown in **Figure 10-2**.

3. *Select a password and type it in the Password text box.*

Twitter will let you know the security strength of your password after you type it in.

 You may want to check out the information on picking a password in Chapter 3 to make sure you select a secure password.

4. *Type in your e-mail address.*

This information will not be shown to anyone; Twitter uses it to send you a confirmation e-mail message and (after you're active on the site) to send you any notifications you've requested.

Fill in your information.

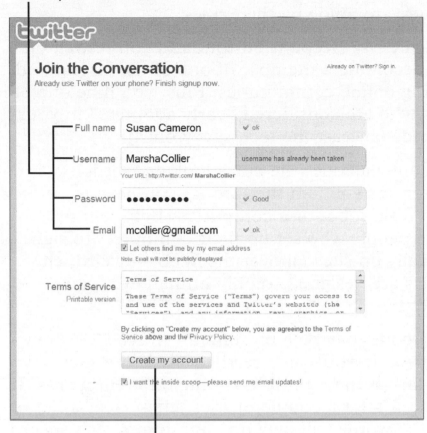

Click here to create your account.

Figure 10-2

4. Click to check the box labeled Let Others Find Me by My Email Address. Do this if you want your friends to be able to type your e-mail address into a Twitter search to find you. If that's an option you don't want, just uncheck it (if it's checked by default), and leave it without the check mark.

5. Read and agree to the Terms of Service. Every Web site has Terms of Service (TOS), which are basically the rules that everyone participating on the site has to follow. Read them and print them out if you want. Even if you don't

do that, know that opening your account on Twitter means you agree to abide by their rules.

6. Click the Create My Account button, and you're well on your way to becoming a member of one of the largest and fastest-growing online communities. Plus, you'll be one of the cool kids who are considered "early adopters" in your group of friends (at least the tech-savvy ones)!

7. Tackle the Captcha code (the crazy looking words). Before Twitter lets you join the throng, you have to prove you aren't a robot or a computer. (Believe it or not, there are people who set up their computers to sign up automatically on sites all over the Web — weird, eh? Captcha codes are designed so only human eyes can figure them out.)

The Captcha code may be a bit difficult to read, as shown in **Figure 10-3**. If you can't read it, click the Get Two New Words link at the right to try some different words. If you can't read it after a couple of tries, click Hear a Set of Words, and the words will play on your computer's speakers. The code words are random and may not make sense. But when you've figured out the words for the Captcha test, type them in the box as prompted and click the Finish button.

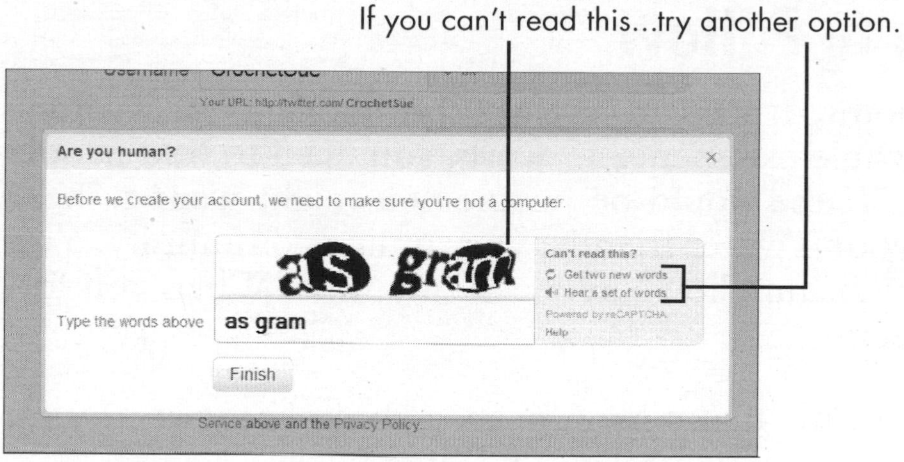

If you can't read this...try another option.

Figure 10-3

8. Clicking Finish brings you to a topic page, similar to the one shown in **Figure 10-4**. Move on to the next section, which instructs you about how to find folks to follow on Twitter.

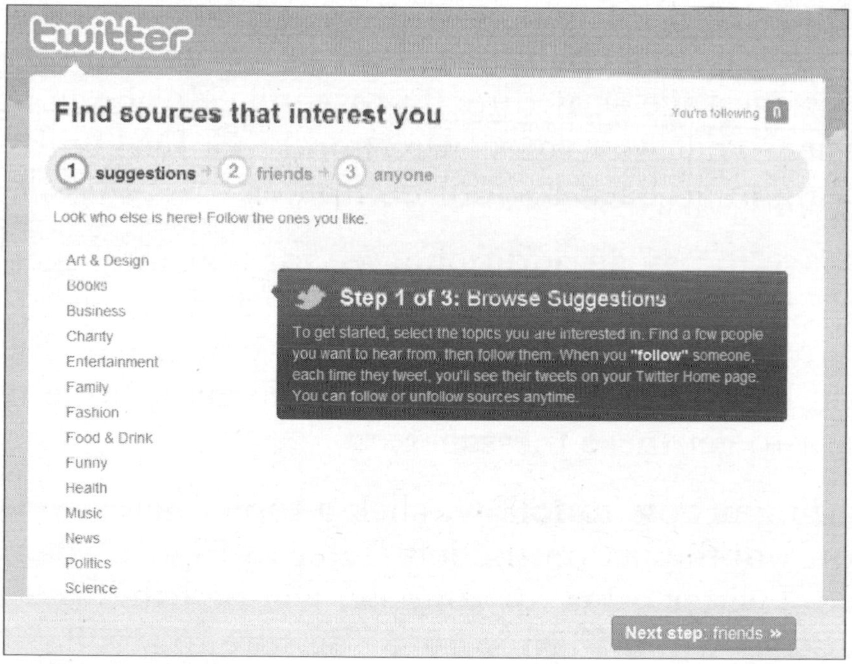

Figure 10-4

Find People to Follow

At this point, I need to explain the workings of Twitter. For the whole experience to work, you need to find people to *follow*. These would be people you might want to hear from — your Twitter friends, your online community. You can follow or unfollow anyone at any time. When you follow someone

➥ Each time that person posts a comment (tweet), you will see it on your Twitter home page.

➥ The folks you follow may follow you back, and if they do, they'll see *your* comments on *their* pages.

➥ You can send a Direct Message (or DM) to someone you're following. A DM is like a text message that you send on your cell phone. It's a private message between you and the recipient. It does not appear in the public stream of tweets. In the "Set Up Notices" section later in this chapter, I show you how you can have this message sent directly to your cell phone if you desire. That way you can respond to a DM without having to go back to your computer.

 If you have to pay an additional fee for text messages on your mobile-phone plan, sending and receiving too many direct messages could get expensive. Be sure you have a full data plan on your smartphone if you want to get these messages.

1. To begin finding people to follow, click a topic that interests you from the list on the left (refer to Figure 10-4). Suggested Twitter users (or sources) will be listed to the right, as shown in **Figure 10-5**. Be sure to scroll down the page so you see the full list; you can click more

at the bottom to see more.

2. If you see someone and think that you might be interested in hearing what that person has to say, follow him or her by clicking the Follow button to the right of the name.

3. Repeat Steps 1 and 2 (click another category and scroll though the names) to find more people to follow. When you feel like you have enough people selected, click the Next Step: Friends button at the bottom right.

 Know that you can always search for more people to add to your Follow list after you're fully set up on the site — so don't feel pressured to keep looking for people to follow as you're getting started.

Click a topic here...to find people to follow here.

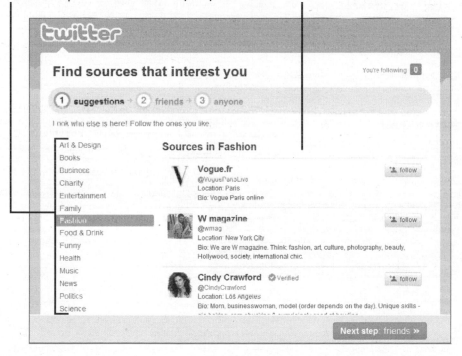

Figure 10-5

4. The next page you see, as in **Figure 10-6**, lists Web-

based e-mail services Gmail, Yahoo!, and AOL. You can use these to find (and follow) people from your e-mail lists who are already on Twitter. If you use one of these services and want to search Twitter for your e-mail buddies, you can click the name of the e-mail service and type your user ID and password when prompted (this is safe to do because Twitter doesn't store your password).

 Personally, I'd skip this step. You might want to be a bit more settled and secure with your participation on Twitter before you involve your real-world friends. (The point of this book is to make *you* the expert!)

5. Click the Next Step: Others button. On the resulting page, you see an empty text box. If you have a friend who's already on Twitter, type his or her name in the text box and click Search.

Find friends on Twitter through an online service.

Find sources that interest you

You're following 1

(1) suggestions → (2) friends → (3) anyone

Many of your friends and colleagues already use Twitter. Find and follow them.

Find your contacts from

M Gmail
Y Yahoo
AOL

Step 2 of 3: Find your friends

Scan your email address book or contacts to discover which of your friends are already using Twitter. Select an email service from the list to the left. Follow any of the friends you find to add their Tweets to your Home **timeline**.

« Previous step: suggestions

Next step: others »

Figure 10-6

If you don't know anyone to follow, just type in my name **MarshaCollier**. When my Twitter result comes up on-screen (as it does in **Figure 10-7**), click the Follow button and we'll be connected. (Don't forget to say "Hi" once we're connected — I show you how to do that in Chapter 11.)

6. When you're finished typing in people's names and following them (remember, you can do this all later after you've gotten the lay of Twitter-land), click the Next step: You're Done button. You're now on your Twitter home page where you see the most recent tweets from the people you followed (check out **Figure 10-8**). If you haven't followed anyone, your page will look pretty blank.

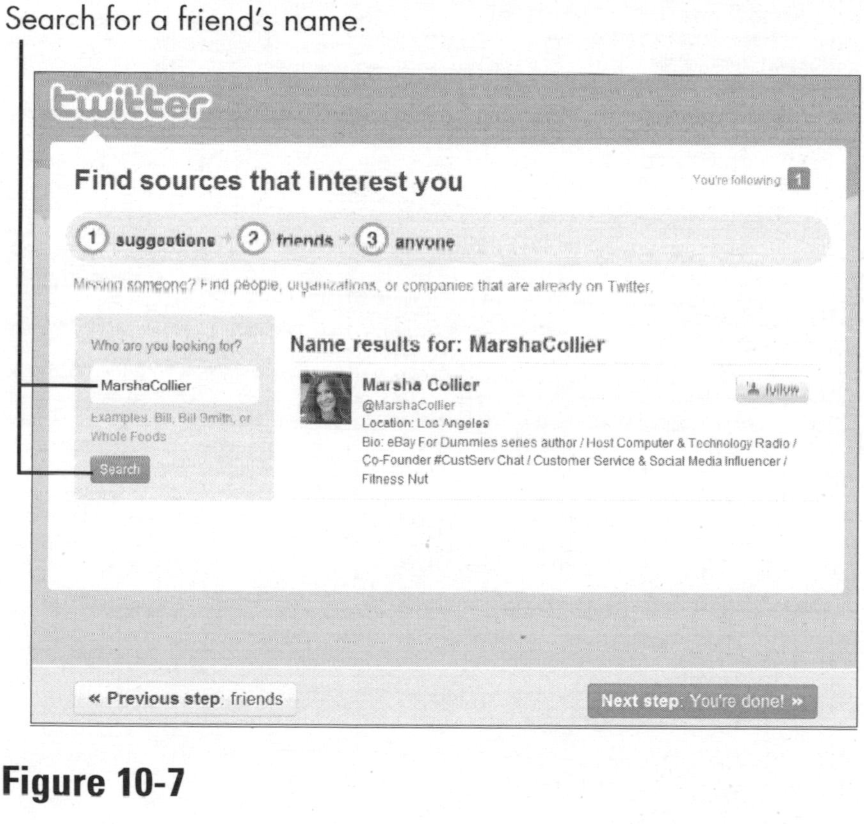

Search for a friend's name.

Figure 10-7

7. While you've been doing all this following, Twitter sent an e-mail message to the e-mail address you provided when you filled out the sign-up form. Open your e-mail program and look for the message. You'll see an e-mail like the one shown in **Figure 10-9**. Click the link in the e-mail, or copy it (by highlighting the link and pressing the Ctrl+C) and paste it (by clicking in your browser's address line and pressing Ctrl+V) into your browser.

You are now an official member of Twitter; congratulations!

See tweets from the people you follow here.

Figure 10-8

Click here to confirm your Twitter account.

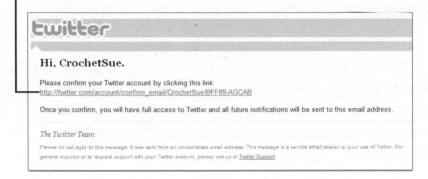

Figure 10-9

Adjust Your Account Settings

1. Click the Settings link on the top right side of your Twitter home page. The information that you input when you signed up is filled in on this page. Scroll down so that you can add some additional important data.

 As an official member of Twitter, you'll need to let other Twitter members know who you are. People follow other people who interest them on Twitter, and identifying yourself as an interesting, charming person will add a lot to the time you spend on Twitter.

2. Choose a language. English is filled in as the default (and I assume you speak English since you're reading this book). If you'd prefer a different language, click the down arrow on the Language text box and select another language from the drop-down menu.

3. Check for your correct time zone. GMT (Greenwich Mean Time) will be filled in. If you don't live in the United Kingdom (where Greenwich is, the last I looked),

241

I suggest that you click the down arrow and select the time zone where you live from the drop-down menu.

4. Click the Add a Location to Your Tweets check box (a check mark appears in the box) and (not surprisingly) you add the location you're tweeting from to your tweets. This is an optional setting, and you don't have to check this. By not revealing your exact location, you can maintain a semblance of privacy. (I usually don't put a check by this setting; I prefer not to reveal my exact location.)

5. If you click to check the Protect My Tweets check box, your tweets will not appear in the public Twitter timeline. Checking this option kind of defeats the purpose of Twitter; you're on the site to be part of the giant conversation.

 If you protect your tweets, there's a chance that people won't follow you back when you follow them. People like to know what they're getting into when they follow someone — and if they can't see your tweets, they may be concerned that you may not be the kind of person they'd want to follow. Twitter is all about *transparency*.

6. After you fill out the balance of your account information, click Save. You'll have to retype your password to save your account settings.

If you've forgotten your password, click the Forgot Your Password link and Twitter sends you a reminder by e-mail so you can reset your password. Click the link in the e-mail message or copy the link into your browser. You arrive at a page where you can change your password, as shown in **Figure 10-10**. Type in your new password twice (the second time is to verify your typing) and click the Change button.

Type a password twice to change it.

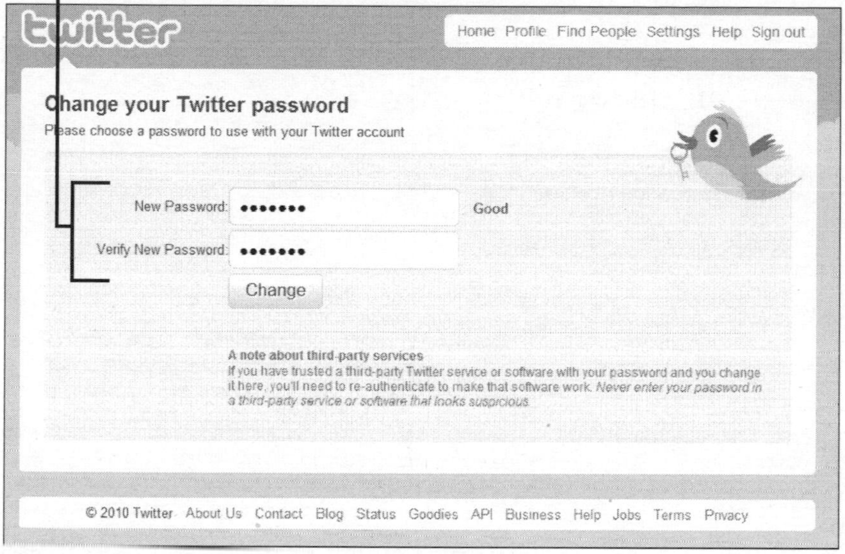

twitter
Home Profile Find People Settings Help Sign out
Change your Twitter password
Please choose a password to use with your Twitter account
New Password: •••••••
Good
Verify New Password: •••••••
Change
A note about third-party services
If you have trusted a third-party Twitter service or software with your password and you change it here, you'll need to re-authenticate to make that software work. Never enter your password in a third-party service or software that looks suspicious.
© 2010 Twitter About Us Contact Blog Status Goodies API Business Help Jobs Terms Privacy

Figure 10-10

To change your password at any time, just click the Settings link at the top right of your Twitter home page and, on the resulting Settings page, click the Password link that appears above your settings.

7. At this point, your pals at Twitter are so revved up to have you aboard that they send you a welcoming e-mail message. **Figure 10-11** shows you a sample of what the message looks like.

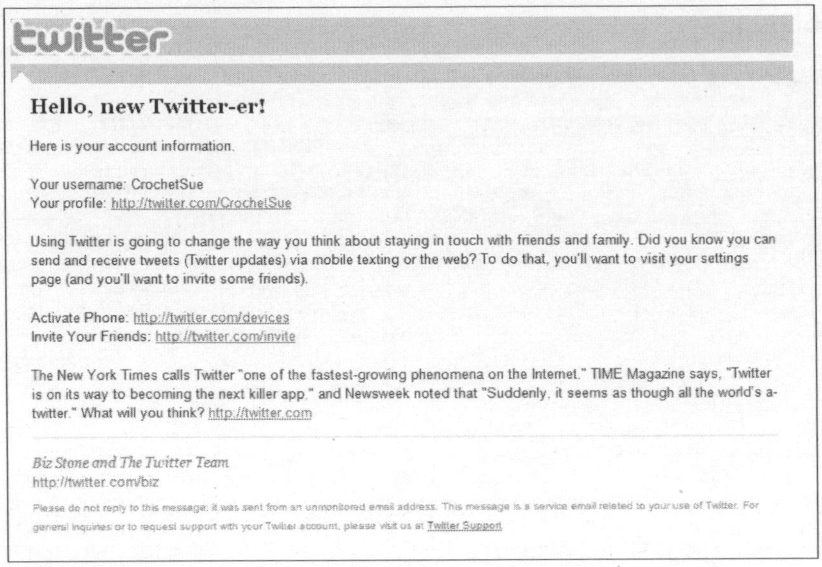

Hello, new Twitter-er!

Here is your account information.

Your username: CrochetSue
Your profile: http://twitter.com/CrochetSue

Using Twitter is going to change the way you think about staying in touch with friends and family. Did you know you can send and receive tweets (Twitter updates) via mobile texting or the web? To do that, you'll want to visit your settings page (and you'll want to invite some friends).

Activate Phone: http://twitter.com/devices
Invite Your Friends: http://twitter.com/invite

The New York Times calls Twitter "one of the fastest-growing phenomena on the Internet." TIME Magazine says, "Twitter is on its way to becoming the next killer app." and Newsweek noted that "Suddenly, it seems as though all the world's a-twitter." What will you think? http://twitter.com

Biz Stone and The Twitter Team
http://twitter.com/biz

Please do not reply to this message; it was sent from an unmonitored email address. This message is a service email related to your use of Twitter. For general inquiries or to request support with your Twitter account, please visit us at Twitter Support.

Figure 10-11

Open your e-mail. On it, you find that Twitter notifies you of a few things:

- **Your username**. I entered *CrochetSue* as my sample username when I first signed up, and there it is!

- **The URL** (Internet address) of your Twitter profile. You can include this in your e-mails to let your friends know where they can find you on Twitter.

- **A link to activate your phone**. If you'd like to receive Twitter notifications on your smartphone, you can click this link to input your cell phone number. Activating your phone will also allow you to send tweets from your cell phone. FYI: You text your messages to Twitter at 40404.

- **An Invite Your Friends link**. Click this link and you arrive on a page where you can type in the e-mail addresses of people you'd like to have join you on Twitter. Twitter will send them an e-mail message on your behalf, inviting them to join. I recommend that you ask your friends whether they'd like to join Twitter before you send those e-mails. Some people feel that invitation e-mails are an intrusion.

Upload Your Avatar

1. Get to your Twitter home page by browsing to www .twitter.com, signing in (if you're not already), and clicking the Home link near the top of the page. Your home page probably looks pretty darned bare before you install the bells and whistles. In the place where your photo should go is a small Twitter bird icon, which looks nothing like you! So get ready to make your page look like it belongs to a Twitter pro.

2. Click the Settings link in the toolbar at the top-right of the page and then click the Profile link on the Settings page (see **Figure 10-12**). You're now at the Profile Settings page, and your first order of business is to upload an image to serve as your avatar on Twitter.

Figure 10-12

 Nope, we're not revisiting James Cameron's epic 3D film *Avatar*. In tech-speak, an *avatar* is an image that

245

represents you online. On Twitter, it means a picture of you. People want to see a picture when they go to follow someone new, so they have some idea of who they're becoming friends with. Some people use pictures of their dogs or the logos for their businesses as avatars, but if you're on Twitter to make friends, I suggest posting a flattering image of yourself.

3. To upload your photo, click the Browse button to open a dialog box where you can look for a photo on your computer.

4. In the dialog box, find the folder on your computer where you store your photos and select a photo by clicking it so that the name of the photo appears in the File Name box. Click Open after you select your picture, and you return to the Twitter Profile setup. (The photo you select can be no more than 700K in size, and can be in either jpg, gif, or png format.) The filename and location on your computer appears in the picture box. Voilá!

5. As long as you're on this page, it's time to fill in your bio. In keeping with the brevity of the site, you have 160 characters to describe yourself. You can change this description at any time, so just put in a little information about yourself for now. You can compare your bio to those of the people you meet on Twitter and refine it as you go.

6. Click Save at the bottom of the page, and your settings are saved. You return to the Profile settings page, and you see the picture you just uploaded next to your name (where the Twitterbird used to be). If you select the wrong photo accidentally, don't fret. Just go through the upload process again by repeating Steps 2 and 3, and then clicking Save again.

Select a Theme for Your Profile Page

1. Now it's time to gussy up your page. You're probably not quite ready to design a custom background (such as the one I have on my MarshaCollier Twitter profile page), so Twitter gives you a choice of 20 decorative backgrounds (or *themes*) to use on your page. From the main Settings page, click the Design link.

2. On the resulting Design settings page, you find the 20 different themes that Twitter offers their members to start. Click any of the theme images and your page background changes automatically to the one you selected. **Figure 10-13** shows that I selected a theme with birds (second from the left in the bottom row).

3. Keep selecting themes until you find a background you like — and then click the Save Changes button at the bottom of the page.

 You'll also notice some other options at the bottom of the page to change the background image and design colors. These are advanced settings; it's best to play with them after you've been using Twitter for a while.

If you'd like to get a fancy background for your Twitter page in the future, check out these sites for *free* backgrounds and instructions:

➤ www.custombackgroundsfortwitter.com

➤ www.twitbacks.com

➤ www.twitterbackgrounds.org

➤ www.colourlovers.com/themeleon/twitter

Click a theme to choose it.

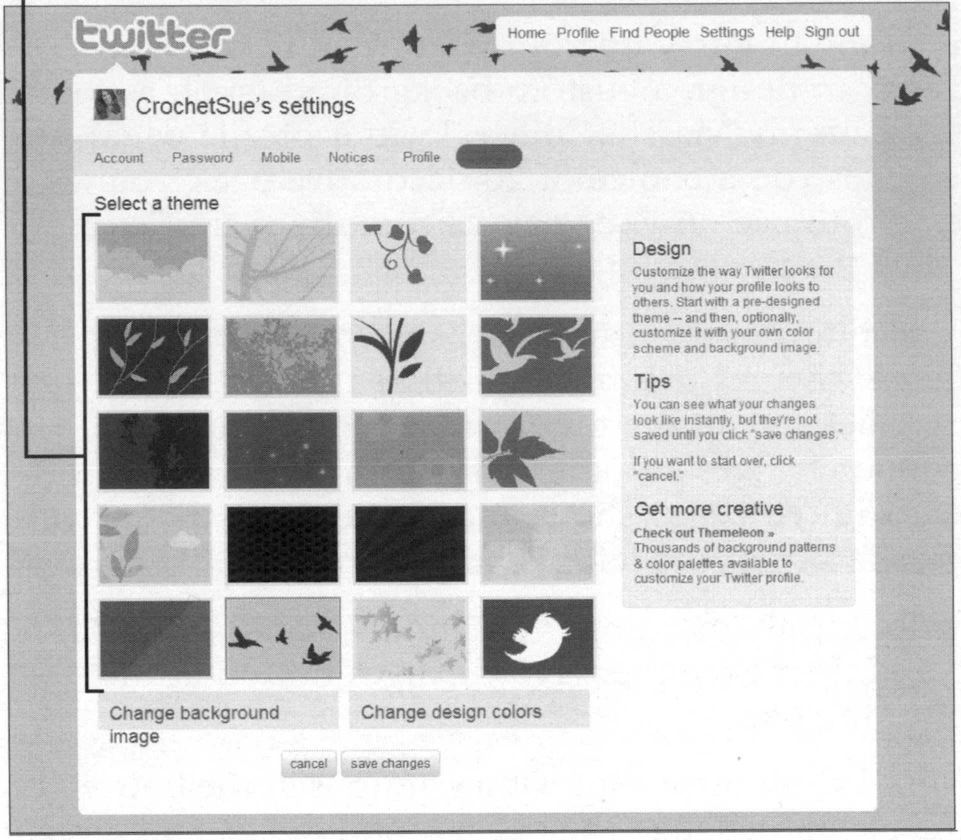

Figure 10-13

Set Up Notices

1. On your Twitter Settings page, you see a link for Notices. Click Notices, and you find an area where you can customize how you'd like to be notified when a particular action occurs on your Twitter account.

2. Read the descriptions and click the check box only next to the notices you want to receive. Twitter will send you an e-mail communication when the following things happen:

- **Someone starts following you.** If someone

finds you and decides to follow you (I explain how all that happens in Chapter 11), Twitter sends you an e-mail telling you so. If you don't want this e-mail notification, be sure there is no check mark in the box next to New Follower E-mails.

- **You receive a new direct message (DM).** Here's where you decide whether you want your direct messages sent to your cell phone. If you don't want the text messages on your phone (especially if you don't have an unlimited data plan), click to remove the check mark from the box next to Direct Text E-mails.

 Even if you uncheck this box, you still receive DMs to your registered e-mail address. You won't miss a thing. The fun of Twitter, though, is that all the conversation happens in real time. Unless you're checking your e-mail regularly, you won't be in on the immediacy of the experience.

- **Twitter has a newsletter to share.** Occasionally, Twitter's founders and bigwigs like to reach out to users to explain new features on the site, or to let you know about changes in the rules (the Terms of Service, or TOS for short). You really need to know about this stuff, so leave the check in the box next to E-mail Newsletter.

Know Twitter Shorthand

When you decide you'd like to send tweets from your smartphone — or even if you're tweeting on the Web — Twitter has some shorthand commands that can facilitate (shorten) your Twitter messaging experience.

249

When a direct message (DM) comes to your phone from Twitter, it has a return numeric shortcut of 40404. You can reply to 40404 to tweet, to send a direct message, or perform some other valuable Twitter actions. If you merely send a text message to 40404 without preceding it with one of the commands listed in **Table 10-1**, your text will simply appear as a Tweet in your Twitter stream.

Table 10-1 shows some shorthand commands you can use to direct an action other than simply posting to your Twitter stream. (I used my Twitter username as an example in the table.)

Table 10-1	Twitter Smartphone Shorthand Commands	
Command	*How it looks*	*What it does*
FOLLOW *username*	FOLLOW marshacollier	Starts following marshacollier
UNFOLLOW *username*	UNFOLLOW marshacollier	Stops following marshacollier
ON/OFF	ON or OFF	Turns all Tweet notifications on or off
ON/OFF *username*	ON or OFF marshacollier	Turns Tweet notifications for a user on or off
GET *username*	GET marshacollier	Shows the last tweet from user
RT *username*	RT marshacollier	Retweets a user's latest tweet*
FAV *username*	FAV marshacollier	Puts a user's latest tweet on your list of

D *username yourmessage*	D marshacollier Hi how are you?	Sends a direct message to a user

* Find more about these functions in Chapter 11.

Chapter 11

Conversing on Twitter with Friends, Family, and More

When you register on Twitter, you get all sorts of suggestions about how to connect with people. As I suggest in Chapter 10, I think it's best to get familiar with the basic concepts of a new site before inviting all your friends to the party. I mean, after all, what kind of host or hostess can you be if you barely know the lay of the land yourself?

I hope you've checked out Twitter a bit. I must confess, it took me quite a while to really "get" it. But once I did, I wanted to invite all my friends — and if they weren't already on Twitter, I wanted them to join so I could share my new shiny toy!

In this chapter, I talk a little more about the finer details of communicating on Twitter. I give you guidelines about making hip tweets, show you how to retweet and accumulate favorite tweets, and give you some advice on what to tweet about.

Follow Basic Guidelines for Conversing

1. We're all adults here. I'm not going to tell you who to be friends with on Twitter, and I'm certainly not going to tell you what to tweet. There are a few conventions and standards that make Twitter interesting, so read on and you'll be twittering like a pro in no time.

   - **Don't just broadcast your ideas.** When you're on Twitter, you'll see that some people just continually broadcast their thoughts over the stream. *Broadcast media is so yesterday!* In 21st-century new media, it's all about conversation and engaging others. Your interaction is with real people — talk to them!

   - **Do tweet out ideas and comments.** Since it's all about conversation, give people something to reply to you about. Did you ruin a batch of cookies in the oven? If you're following other people who might be baking cookies, they'll commiserate with you. You have to buy new tires, and you're going through sticker shock? Certainly, in this economy, someone out there can relate.

   - **Reply to others.** When someone makes a comment that you're interested in, make a comment back! In **Figure 11-1**, I'm about to reply to the user @Greetums about her soup experience. You can also see my *Latest* (or last) tweet just below the What's Happening text box. I remarked to @Krystyl about how much I liked her new avatar (avatar = picture, remember?).

2. Starting any posting with the at-sign (@), followed by the name of the person you're sending it to, is like putting an address on the tweet: @Krystyl means this tweet is addressed to @Krystyl, as if we were in a conversation. Here's how to reply:

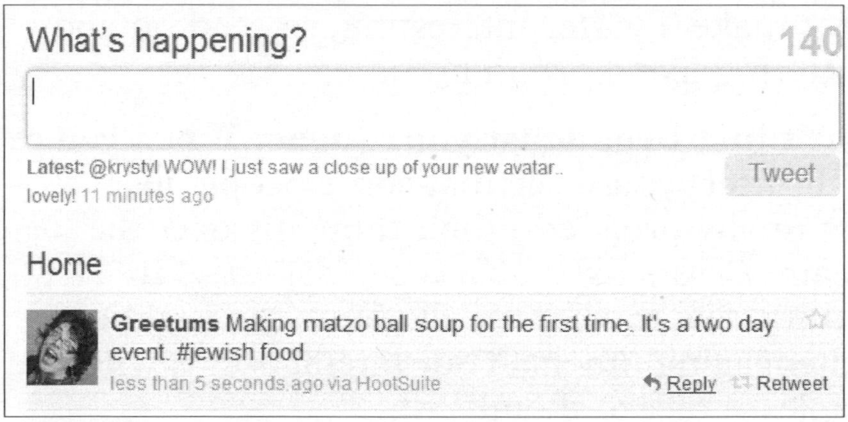

What's happening?	140

Latest: @krystyl WOW! I just saw a close up of your new avatar.. lovely! 11 minutes ago   Tweet

Home

Greetums Making matzo ball soup for the first time. It's a two day event. #jewish food
less than 5 seconds ago via HootSuite   ↩ Reply ⇄ Retweet

Figure 11-1

1. *When you mouse over the right side of a tweet on your Twitter page, the word* Reply *comes up out of nowhere.* When you click this Reply link (or *swoosh*), the tweeter's ID appears in the What's Happening text box with an at-sign (@) in front of it — for example, @Greetums. These are called @ (at) replies; they're visible to the person you addressed them to, and to the people who follow both of you.

2. *If you want all the people who follow you to see an @*

reply, embed it within your tweet. See the example in **Figure 11-2**, where I reply to @MakeItWork.

 Remember that @ replies are not private; the private messages you can send are called *Direct Messages*.

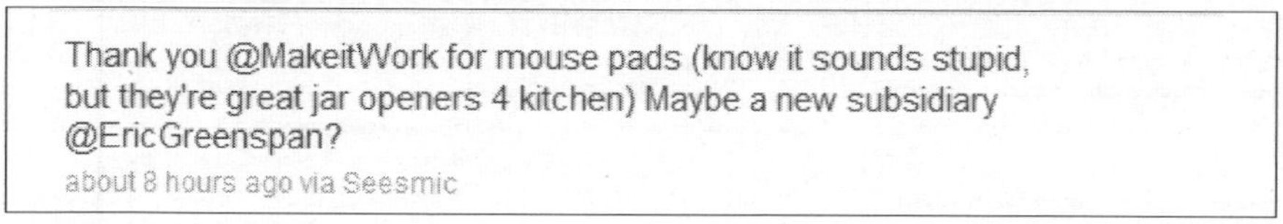

Thank you @MakeitWork for mouse pads (know it sounds stupid, but they're great jar openers 4 kitchen) Maybe a new subsidiary @EricGreenspan?
about 8 hours ago via Seesmic

Figure 11-2

3. *In **Figure 11-3**, notice how the message looks after I responded to @Greetums (even though I forgot about the soup).* When you send a tweet like this, the recipient will definitely recognize it as conversation and will most likely respond to you.

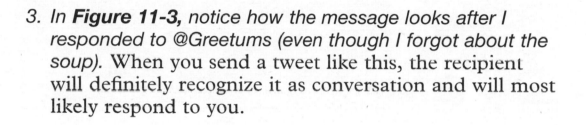
MarshaCollier @**Greetums** :) Your matzoh ball tweet just ended up in a screen shot of my upcoming book, Twitter & Facebook For Seniors
less than a minute ago from web

Figure 11-3

3. To see all your @ replies, click the link on the right side of your Twitter home page that has the @ and your ID next to it. **Figure 11-4** shows you what I mean.

Click on your home page for tweets that mention you.

Figure 11-4

Pass Along a Chosen Tweet

1. To make a statement on Twitter is to *tweet,* so to repeat a statement on Twitter is to *RE-tweet,* right? If you see a comment from someone you're following, you can retweet what they said to all your followers. That way, your followers who aren't following the person who made the pithy comment can have the chance to see it, too. (Twitter is all about sharing!)

2. You can retweet (RT) in two ways. You accomplish the classic RT when you copy and paste the original tweet in the What's Happening text box; then type the letters

RT before @ and the username of the original tweeter. **Figure 11-5**, shows a couple of interesting comments that I chose to retweet to the people who follow me.

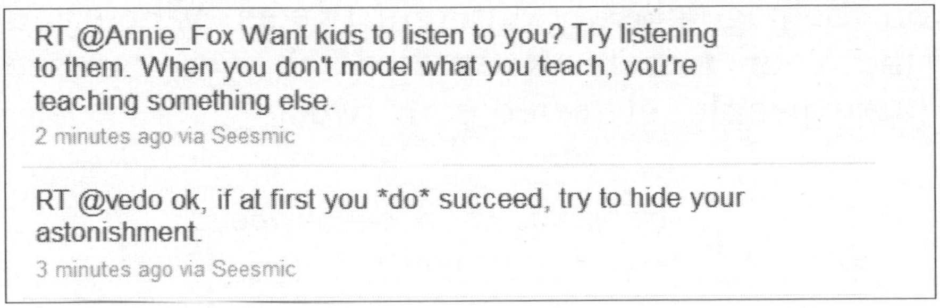

RT @Annie_Fox Want kids to listen to you? Try listening to them. When you don't model what you teach, you're teaching something else.
2 minutes ago via Seesmic

RT @vedo ok, if at first you *do* succeed, try to hide your astonishment.
3 minutes ago via Seesmic

Figure 11-5

3. The second (new improved) way to retweet is to find a tweet in your tweet stream (just as you did in the @ reply). Hover your mouse pointer over the right side of the tweet and the word *Retweet* will show up next to a little recycling symbol.

 Some people don't like this type of retweeting because they find it harder to tell whether it's a retweet. But it's the only format to use if the original Tweet is too long once you add the RT symbols. **Figure 11-6** shows the difference: Instead of the RT and @ symbol, a recycling icon appears next to my name.

The recycling icon shows up here.

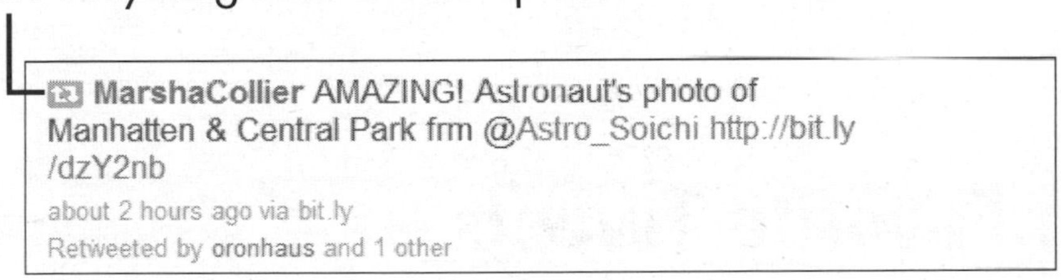

MarshaCollier AMAZING! Astronaut's photo of Manhatten & Central Park frm @Astro_Soichi http://bit.ly /dzY2nb
about 2 hours ago via bit.ly
Retweeted by oronhaus and 1 other

Figure 11-6

If you want to track which of your tweets get retweeted, click the Home link near the top right and go to your home page. On the right, click the Retweets link, and you see a page like the one in **Figure 11-7**. Three tabs on the page classify different tweets. When you click the Your Tweets, Retweeted tab, you can see how many people retweeted your tweet.

Click here to check out retweets.

Home Profile Find People Settings Help Sign out

What's happening?   140

Latest: @Annie_Fox Thanks! 10 minutes ago   Tweet

| Retweets By Others | Retweets By You | Your Tweets, Retweeted |

MarshaCollier RT @Annie_Fox Want kids to listen to you? Try listening to them. When you don't model what you teach, you're teaching something else.
43 minutes ago via Seesmic
Retweeted by 2 people

MarshaCollier RT @mzayfert "A hug is like a boomerang - you get it back right away." - Bil Keane #quote
about 1 hour ago via Seesmic
Retweeted by 1 person

MarshaCollier AMAZING! Astronaut's photo of Manhatten & Central Park frm @Astro_Soichi http://bit.ly/dzY2nb
about 2 hours ago via bit.ly

MarshaCollier
16,237 tweets

15,513 16,160 846
following followers listed

Twest·i·val
n. a way to take part in a global event that transforms lives.

Home
@MarshaCollier
Direct Messages   827
Favorites
Retweets

Search

Lists
custserv
friends
funny-twits

Figure 11-7

Favorite Your Favorite Tweets

1. When you see a tweet that strikes your fancy, or a tweet sent to you that makes you smile, Twitter lets you make it a Favorite. You can make any tweet (except a private Direct Message) a favorite. If you guide your mouse pointer over the tweet, just above where the Reply and Retweet appear on the right, you see a small outline of a star. Click the star, and it turns gold. After you click it, the tweet is saved to your Favorites page.

2. To find the favorites you've *favorited* (that's the Twitter term), click the Home link at the top of the page and go to your home page. The fourth link on the right is Favorites. If you click it, you arrive at the page that lists your favorite tweets. Check out **Figure 11-8**, and you'll see my recent favorites. Notice that all these tweets have a little gold star next to them.

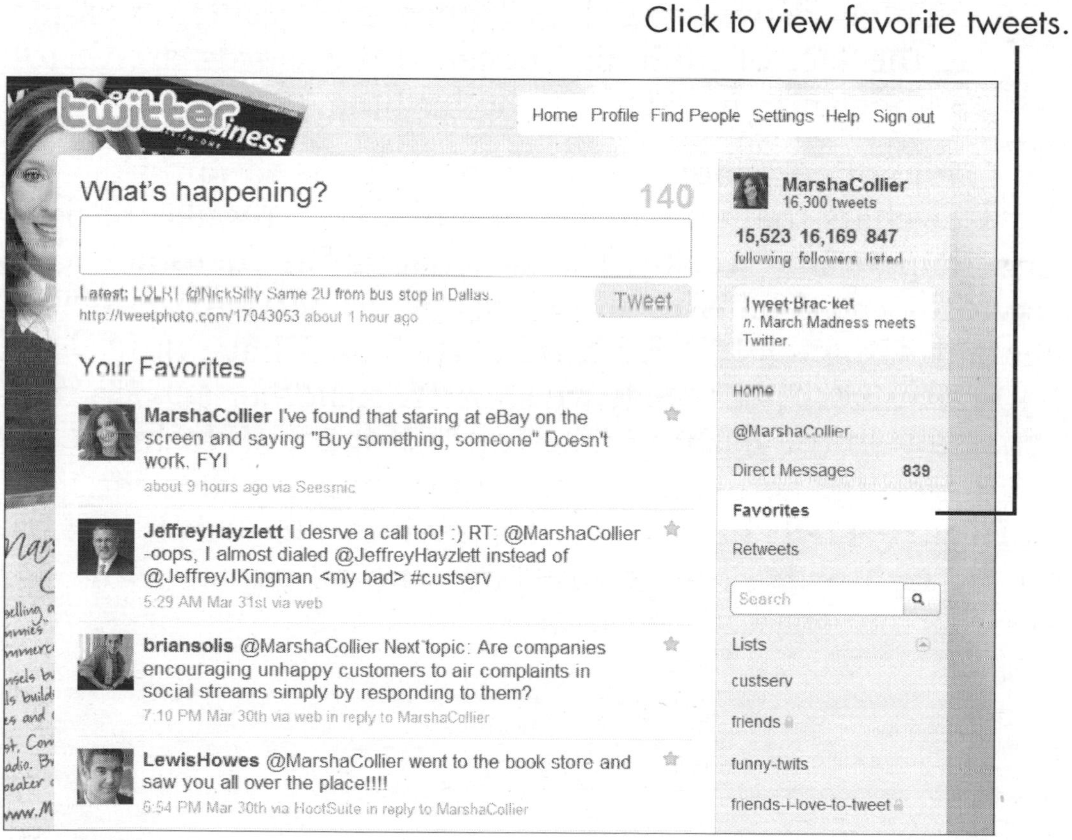

Click to view favorite tweets.

Figure 11-8

Search for Tweeted Topics

1. You can use *hashtags* — words with the pound sign (#) in front of them — in your tweets to simply identify single word topics or abbreviations of events. And you can search to find tweets about the topics or events that are identified this way. For example, if you regularly watch *American Idol* and want to find all tweets about the show, you can search for them by typing **#americanidol** in the search box at the right side of your home page and pressing Enter.

 Because a search is not case-sensitive, you could also type #AmericanIdol or #AMERICANIDOL and get the same results. What you won't get in your search results are tweets such as "*American* President Obama is the *idol* of millions" because the words aren't together and preceded by the hashtag.

2. You can append your tweets with hashtags to join in Twitter chats that take place on a planned, regular basis. I participate in a weekly Twitter chat about customer service. (Yes, I tell you all about how to participate in chats in Chapter 12.) Because participants have only 140 characters per tweet, we shorten *customer service* to *#custserv* so the hashtag takes up less space. (Hashtags get a message across in a much more concise manner.) In **Figure 11-9**, I typed **#custserv** into the search box on the right side of my home page and all tweets with #custserv showed up.

260

Type a topic here to search for tweets.

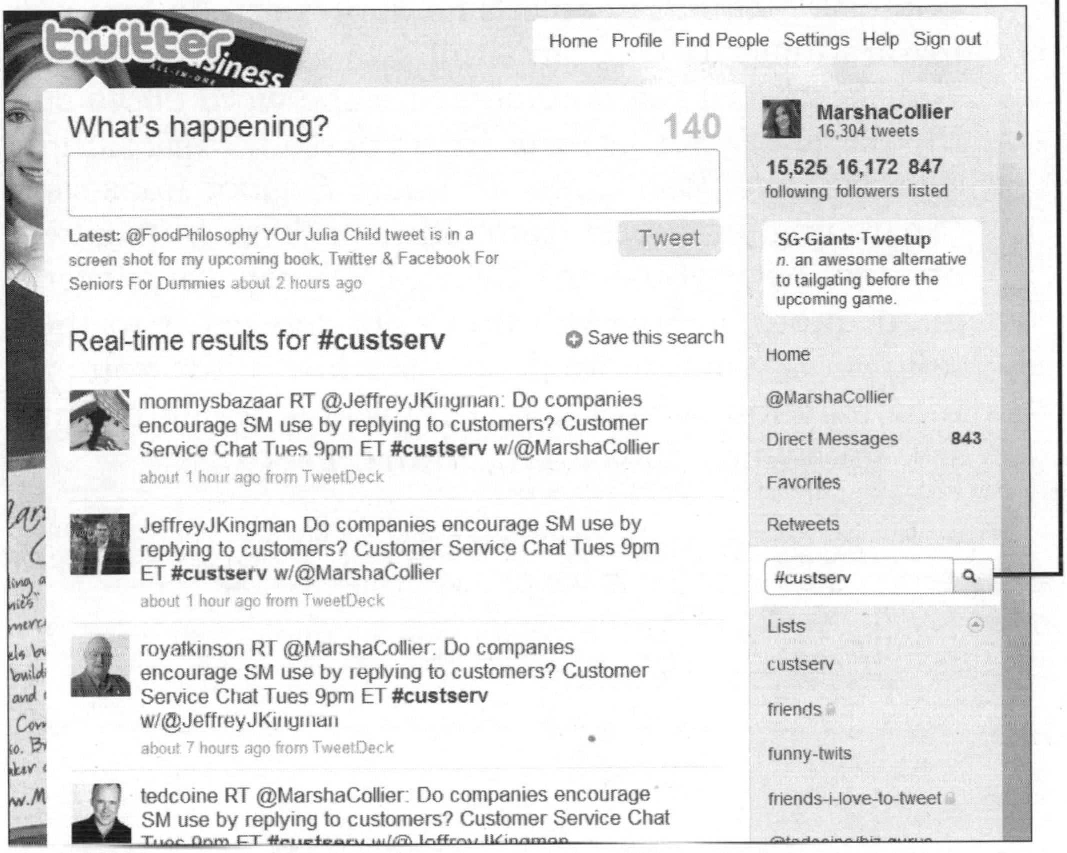

Figure 11-9

Know What to Tweet About

I know that when you're new on Twitter (you're called a *newbie*), you want to join in the fun but maybe you can't think of anything to tweet about. It's a frustrating feeling — know that I feel your pain. Even now, I often face the blank What's Happening text box with nothing in my head.

Check out this bullet list for some good ideas about common ways to start a Twitter conversation:

➤ **Share quotes.** People on Twitter just love to read quotes by famous people. The quotes can be funny or inspirational. If you can't think of any off the top of your head, just search Google for the word *quote* and the name of your favorite smart person. For example search *quote Joan Rivers* or *quote Eleanor Roosevelt*. (Searching for quotes from either of these women will no doubt net you some doozies!) When you tweet a good quote, people will no doubt retweet it to their followers. When more people see how pithy you are, they may follow you, too. I retweeted a quote that I saw on Twitter today (see **Figure 11-10**).

 LoriMoreno There is only one happiness in life, to love and be loved. ~George Sand #quote
10 minutes ago via SocialOomph

Figure 11-10

➤ **Ask questions.** If you are curious about something or just want to know what other people think about a subject, ask a question. In **Figure 11-11**, my friend @Lotay asked a question about the iPad. Notice, he used the word Poll and a hashtag preceding it. You don't have to use either. People will know what a question is! By the way, he got 18 responses.

 lotay #Poll: Will you buy an Apple iPad?
30 minutes ago from UberTwitter

Figure 11-11

→ **Share music.** Remember how much fun it used to be when you'd sit on the floor with your friends and play records? I love listening to Nina Simone, and in **Figure 11-12**, my friend Melissa tweeted out one of her songs. You can do that on Twitter (I do this often) by tweeting links to recorded music. When someone clicks the link in your tweet, he or she lands on a Web site that plays the music! In Chapter 15, I show you how to find and link to music.

MelissaRowley listening to "Nina Simone - Feeling Good"
♫ http://blip.fm/~o2lto
31 minutes ago via Blip.fm

Figure 11-12

→ **Share a funny "overheard."** What's an *overheard?* Have you ever been in the supermarket and overheard someone say something that makes you want to laugh out loud? That something is an overheard. When you post an overheard on Twitter, you abbreviate the words to just OH. In **Figure 11-13**, I think @Ed must have been listening to his buddies at the barbershop!

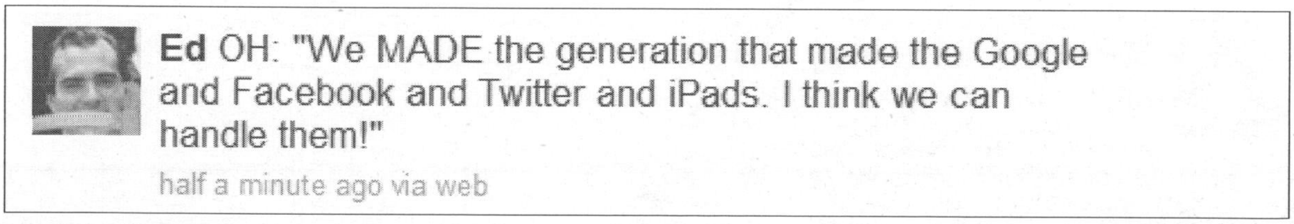

Ed OH: "We MADE the generation that made the Google and Facebook and Twitter and iPads. I think we can handle them!"
half a minute ago via web

Figure 11-13

➤ **Pass on a news story.** There are so many great articles on the Internet, and news stories come to mind almost immediately. Why not send out an interesting article to your friends? I love cooking, so when I saw the tweet in **Figure 11-14**, I clicked the link to see the story on Julia Child.

foodphilosophy Here's why I love her, FYI. Julia Child: Boutez en Avant http://bit.ly/dp5Z47

23 minutes ago via Tweetie

Figure 11-14

 You will notice that the link looks a little like gibberish. That's because the Web address for the story was shortened. In Chapter 13, I show you how to shorten long URLs for your tweets.

➤ **Show off your pictures.** Everyone on Twitter loves to share photos. In **Figure 11-15**, I tweeted a link to a picture of some lovely flowers in my garden on Easter. People on Twitter know that the link contains pictures because it points to the Twitpic Web site where people upload their photos. I tell you about Twitpic in Chapter 13.

MarshaCollier **Happy Easter** from my **garden**. http://twitpic.com/1d0ut8

about 5 hours ago from Seesmic

Figure 11-15

Chapter 12

Gathering Tools
of the Twitter Trade

Now that you're on Twitter and you're building a small group of friends, you'll see that you want to do even more. I'll bet you'd enjoy following even more people, right?

Some people feel that if they have a small group of friends, they can manage conversing easily — but sometimes it's okay to branch out and meet more. In this chapter, I show you how to make groups (lists) of different people so you can focus certain Twitter conversations on certain friends. And, I introduce a couple of applications that you can install on your computer and use to see everything that's going on — no matter how many people you follow.

Let's really call this chapter *Twitter — the Advanced Course.* But don't let that scare you. I show you some simple ways to enhance your tweeting experience. And you needn't spend any money on extra tools; I explain how to do just about anything you can on Twitter.

Search for Tweeps on WeFollow

1. I'm a big believer in "the more, the merrier." Although I don't always see everything that everyone on Twitter says, I always have the option to listen and reply to those who are not on my list of closest friends. So, if you're looking for that option, check out *WeFollow,* a user-powered directory of Twitter peeps (known as *Tweeps*). Not *everyone* is listed — only over 800,000 people.

 Considering that Twitter has over 8 million users, I feel this site gives me an idea of the more active and interesting ones. You can find not only celebrities, but also people who have common interests and share the kind of hobbies you like.

2. Type **www.wefollow.com** into your Web browser. When the page loads, you have a decision to make. **Figure 12-1** shows you the window you see. You can visit the site just to browse, or you can add yourself to the directory so that others will find you. I suggest that you just browse to start by clicking the Not Now, Just Browsing button. (Baby steps, right?)

3. When you land on the opening page shown in **Figure 12-2**, you'll see a lot of information. Several of the

more popular categories (of the thousands listed on the site) appear here — along with the people, in order of influence, who've been listed in each category (or *tag,* as it's also called).

 Some Twitter directories list users by number of followers. Okay, any monkey — with enough effort and time — can accumulate a following of thousands of people. The deal on Twitter is to find *influential* people. Influential Twitter users are ranked according to the interesting things they say (other people retweet their tweets), their interaction with others via @ conversations, and the fair amount of time they spend on the site to engage new people.

Click here to start out just browsing.

Figure 12-1

4. On the right of the opening page are two boxes you can use to find people you want to follow:

- **Top Tags:** The most popular tags (or categories) that people search through for people to follow on the site. To see more? Click the More Tags link at the bottom of the box.

- **Top Cities:** If you'd like to make more friends in your local area, use this list to see cities in order of their popularity on the site. If you don't see your city, click the More Cities link.

  When you click a city (I clicked New York, NY in **Figure 12-3**), you see a list of New York City Twitter users shown in the order of their influence on the site.

Check out the users in a category.   Type a keyword here to find a category.

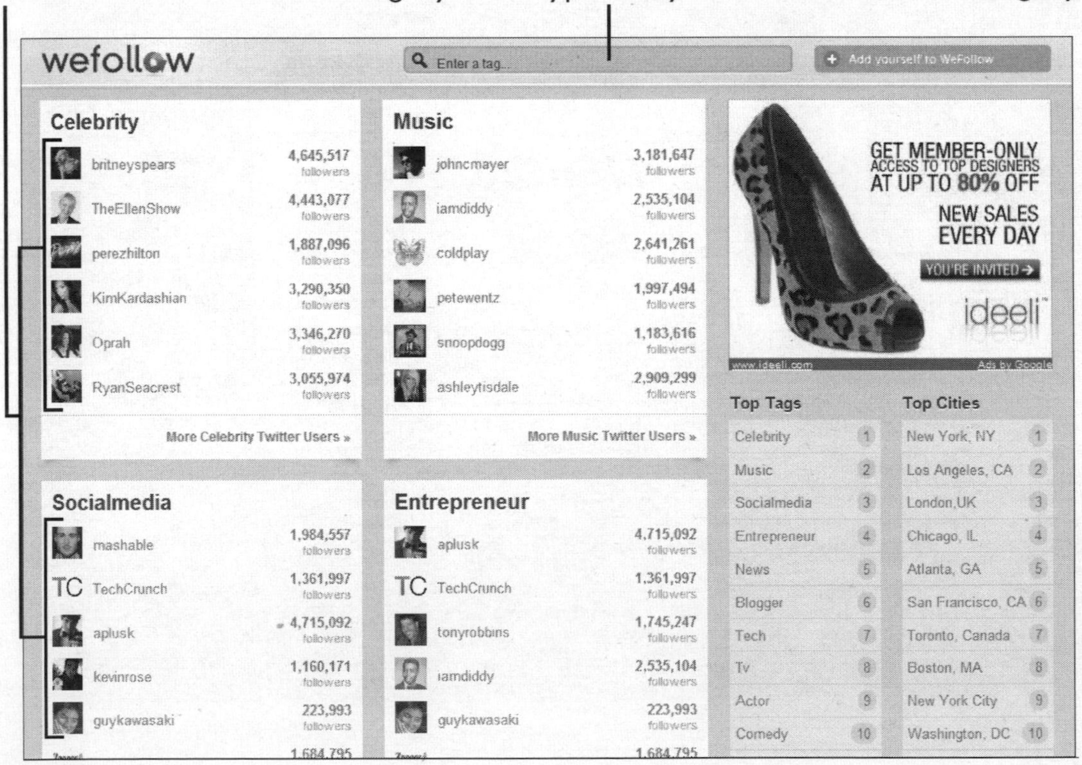

Figure 12-2

5. At the top of the page, you find a gray box that says *Enter a tag*. Here you can type in any subject you wish. As you type, a drop-down list appears and shows you categories that match what you're typing — and how many people are in the category. Click a category from this list to view its influential users.

I started typing eBay and discovered that the single tag *eBay* (rather than *ebayseller, ebaypowerseller,* and so on) showed the most people in the tags mentioning eBay. I clicked the eBay category — and was sent to a page of users (**Figure 12-4**), listed in order of influence, who have categorized themselves with the eBay tag. To find out more about any of these people, click a name.

wefollow

Enter a tag...

New York, NY 4,370 Users

Most Influential | Most Followers

#1 **themoment** 1,590,832 followers
Where Style Meets Culture

#2 **cutblog** 52,619 followers
New York magazine's fashion blog + 405 NEW

#3 **Newsweek** 1,226,606 followers
Newsweek magazine's daily news, blogs, photo + 163 NEW
galleries, audio and vide...

#4 **THEREALSWIZZZ** 159,487 followers
THE BEST + 277 NEW

#5 **someecards** 1,607,731 followers
Welcome to the Twitter feed of somewhat acclaimed
humor site, someecards...

#6 **grubstreetny** 7,609 followers
New York magazine's food and restaurant blog + 25 NEW

#7 **RollingStone** 90,938 followers
The official Twitter of Rolling Stone magazine and + 196 NEW
RollingStone.com.

#8 EverythingNYC **EverythingNYC**
I ♥ NYC. The Greatest City in the World.
6,504 followers

Figure 12-3

6. Clicking a user in the category's list (in the eBay category, I clicked my name — MarshaCollier) will bring you to a page (**Figure 12-5**) that shows the user's one-line Twitter bio, avatar, basic information, and a list of the categories they're tagged in. If, after looking at the info, you want to follow the user, click the green *Follow this user* bar under the avatar (photo).

7. Rinse and repeat. Ooops, I mean *perform these searches*

270

over and over, and you can find lots of interesting new people to follow.

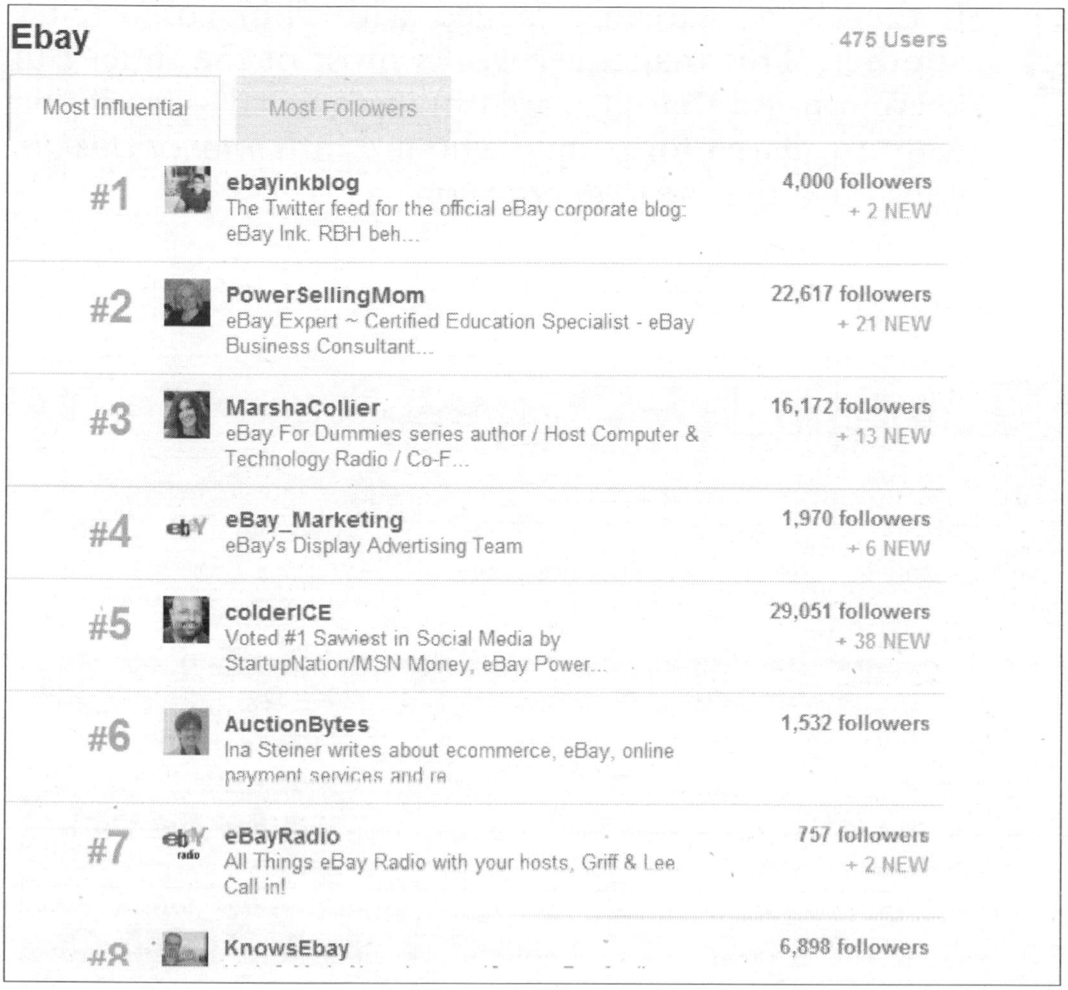

Ebay   475 Users

Most Influential   Most Followers

#1   **ebayinkblog**   4,000 followers
The Twitter feed for the official eBay corporate blog: + 2 NEW
eBay Ink. RBH beh…

#2   **PowerSellingMom**   22,617 followers
eBay Expert ~ Certified Education Specialist - eBay   + 21 NEW
Business Consultant…

#3   **MarshaCollier**   16,172 followers
eBay For Dummies series author / Host Computer &   + 13 NEW
Technology Radio / Co-F…

#4   **eBay_Marketing**   1,970 followers
eBay's Display Advertising Team   + 6 NEW

#5   **colderICE**   29,051 followers
Voted #1 Savviest in Social Media by   + 38 NEW
StartupNation/MSN Money, eBay Power…

#6   **AuctionBytes**   1,532 followers
Ina Steiner writes about ecommerce, eBay, online
payment services and re

#7   **eBayRadio**   757 followers
All Things eBay Radio with your hosts, Griff & Lee   + 2 NEW
Call in!

#8   **KnowsEbay**   6,898 followers

Figure 12-4

8. You like shortcuts? Me too. If you want to get a little daring, make a list of categories you're interested in and search directly from your browser. In the browser's address bar, type the **wefollow.com** address, followed by a forward slash (/) and then a category tag from your list. The result will look like this URL (except it'll show your category; here I wanted to find people interested in gardening):

`http://wefollow.com/twitter/gardening`

 If there's no category tagged with your subject, try another. This maneuver works most of the time. But keep in mind that tags are only one word — so if you want to search for people who are into *interior design,* you'll use the tag *interiordesign*.

Click here to follow a WeFollow user.

Figure 12-5

Add Yourself to WeFollow

1. Here's how to add yourself on WeFollow for other new users to find. Type **www.twitter.com** in your browser's address bar and press Enter. Then log in to Twitter. Open another browser tab, type **www.wefollow.com** in that tab's address bar, and press Enter.

2. At WeFollow, click the green Add Yourself to WeFollow button that appears at the top of every page.

3. Allow WeFollow to access your Twitter account by clicking the Allow button, as in **Figure 12-6**. This is safe to do; you aren't revealing your password to a new site.

4. On the next page, WeFollow asks you to input your home city and up to five different tags of subjects you're interested in.

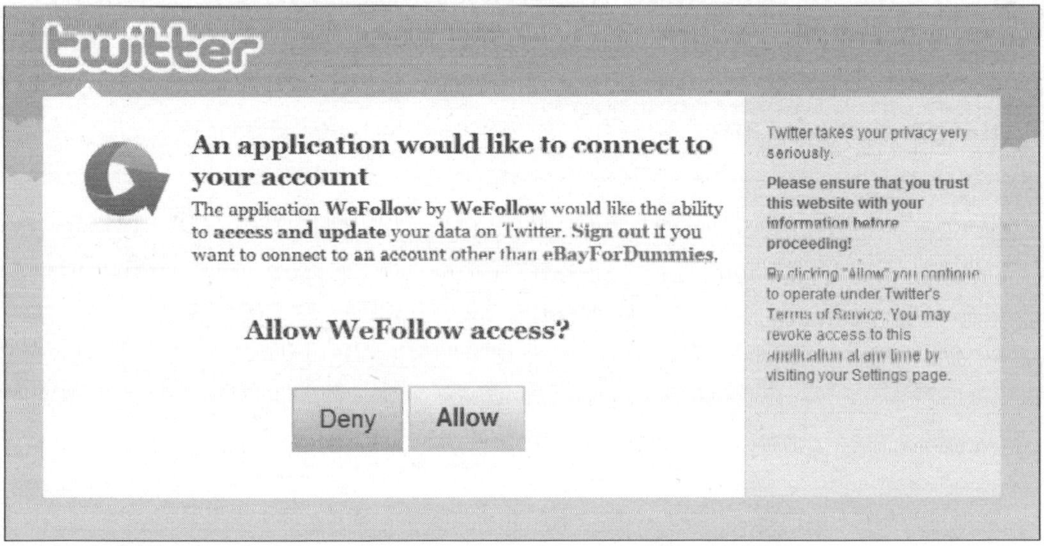

Figure 12-6

5. Click Send (when you're done) and WeFollow sends a tweet to your tweetstream, announcing to the world you are listed on WeFollow.

Find Trends with Summize

1. Summize is Twitter's own outside search capability. You can do search after search directly from your Twitter home page, but Summize does a much better job searching by keywords and trends. Type **www.summize .com** into your Web browser and press Enter; you're transported to `search.twitter.com`.

2. The resulting page is pretty blank, so I won't bore you with a screen shot. Just type a subject that intrigues you into the text box and click Search. I typed in *cookies* (as in chocolate-chip and oatmeal-raisin); I'm in the mood to see who else is baking some cookies.

3. You arrive at the search results page and see all the current tweets that have the word *cookies* in them, as in **Figure 12-7**. You can click any ID you see there to be transported to that person's Twitter page and take a look at his or her stream.

See your topic in tweets here.   Type a topic here.

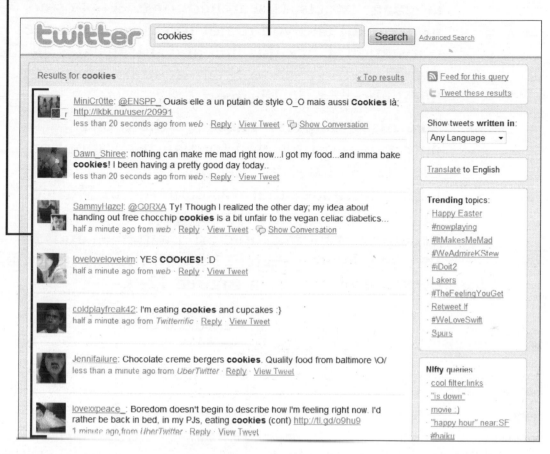

Figure 12-7

4. Then, if this new person's tweets interest you, go ahead and follow the person on Twitter (it's not just okay, it's the expected thing).

5. Notice on the right side of the page you see the following sections:

- **Show tweets written in (select language):** From the drop-down menu, you may select from a list of 19 different languages to search. The default is English, but if you'd like to meet people who tweet in French, select French.

275

- **Translate:** If you've selected to view foreign language tweets, (I searched for tweets posted in Spanish) and you're not too clear about the translation, Click this link and it translates all the tweets on the page to English. Translations are highlighted, as in **Figure 12-8**.

- **Trending Topics:** These are the topics currently most tweeted (or bandied) about on the site. As I was writing this chapter, I felt a large earthquake that was centered in Mexico, followed by nine aftershock quakes. *Earthquake* became a trending topic on Twitter — and through Twitter search, I found the tweets about *earthquakes* shown in **Figure 12-9**.

Figure 12-8

Real-time results for **earthquake**   ⊕ Save this search

erinyoungren Aaaaand an aftershock... ? #**earthquake**
less than 20 seconds ago from TweetDeck

hestaprynnmusic 6.9 **earthquake**?? Please don't tell me
Vince Vaughn is going to sing again.
less than 20 seconds ago from web

Metblogs [all city] Los Angeles Metblogs : 6.9 **Earthquake**
in Baja California http://bit.ly/dc8YNQ
less than 20 seconds ago from twitterfeed

Pinkgineer 3.6 **Earthquake** in Julian, CA
less than 20 seconds ago from Brizzly

jodenaire another **earthquake** #sheessh!
less than 20 seconds ago from web

ZAmmi More #**earthquake** damage #bajaquake
http://tweetphoto.com/17193148 (Via @elviiira)
less than 20 seconds ago from txt

ScanMyPhotos If you felt the #**Earthquake**, click on this
link and register your location for USGA tracking.
http://ow.ly/1uwK9
less than 20 seconds ago from HootSuite

naleritter Stop the world...I wanna get off. #sandiego
#**earthquake** (via @SDTechGirl)
less than 20 seconds ago from Tweetie

Figure 12-9

- **Nifty Queries:** A list of interesting queries recently performed in Twitter search. Check 'em out for a little amusement.

 Notice that when the search results page lists a tweet as an @ reply to another person, both people's avatars (pictures) appear on the left side of the tweet.

FollowFriday, FF, and Other Hashtags

1. When you've been on Twitter long enough, you'll see tweets from people with hashtags (#) preceding them. The hashtag may be followed by strange abbreviations, severalwordsthatruntogether (say what?), or single topics. Hashtags help to spread and organize information on Twitter.

 Using hashtags makes subjects easier to search for and find. Conferences, major events, and even disasters (such as #swineflu) use hashtags to put specific tweets in order and make it easier for you — and your followers — to follow.

2. Here's a list of some Twitter hashtags and what they refer to. After you look at the list, you'll get the drift. You can find more, along with their activity and the top members at What the Hashtag? (`http://wthashtag .com`) a user-editable encyclopedia for hashtags found on Twitter. After that, I give you some conventions to follow when creating your own hashtags.

- **#sxsw** — A popular conference, South By Southwest, is too long to tweet since tweets are limited to 140 characters. People at the conference include `#sxsw` in their tweets to show where they are and what they're doing there.

- **#CES** — Consumer Electronics Show. Again, too long to tweet. Let your friends know you're talking about it by using #CES

- **#musicmonday** — On Mondays, Twitter users like to tweet their favorite songs. It's like sitting around a record player (remember?) with your friends. Tweets have a link to a playable version of the song.

- **#FF or #FollowFriday** — Do you have someone you really like to follow? Someone who often puts up interesting tweets? Recommend that person to your followers by tweeting his or her ID, followed by the hashtag.

 Remember: Only do this on Fridays. Consider the people in your Twitter stream who may not approve your own private daily version of #FollowFriday.

- **#earthquake** — When someone feels the ground shake, they usually just tweet @ EARTHQUAKE because they're too freaked to say anything else. People follow up with information on damage, provide brief news reports, and append their tweets with this hashtag.

- **#tcot** — *Top Conservatives on Twitter*. This hashtag is used by a very vocal and interesting group. If you tweet something with a politically conservative slant, add this hashtag to your tweet. You're bound to get more like-minded followers.

- **#p2** — The #p2 hashtag stands for *Progressives 2.0*. Their official mission statement says "a resource for progressives using social media who prioritize diversity and empowerment, the 'progressive batchannel,' and an umbrella tag for information for progressives on Twitter."

- **#tlot** — *Top Libertarians on Twitter*. What more can I say?

- **#custserv** — A hashtag for the Customer Service chat. People participate in chats on

279

Twitter at prescribed times each week. When they take part in the chat, they follow each tweet with the `#custserv` tag.

 Rather than using search during chats, people use sites like Twubs (`http://twubs.com`), What the Hashtag? (`http://wthashtag.com`), or TweetChat (`http://tweetchat.com`) where they can see the tweets and respond to them in real time. These sites also insert the hashtag at the end of your tweets automatically. **Figure 12-10** shows the Twubs page for our #custserv chat.

3. There are many weekly chats on Twitter, and you might find one you'd like to take part in. You may use Twitter search to find a chat you might want to join. **Figure 12-11** shows a search for #petchat. Here are a few examples of chats:

Figure 12-10

- **#gardenchat** — all things gardening.

- **#dogtalk** — pictures of dogs, dog tips, and dog news.

- **#petchat** — for the rest of the animal world.

- **#blogchat** — Starting a blog? Run by blog expert @MackCollier, this chat is full of tips and ideas.

- **#journchat** — People in public relations, journalism, and related fields meet to talk.

- **#carchat** — love your car? There's a group for you too!

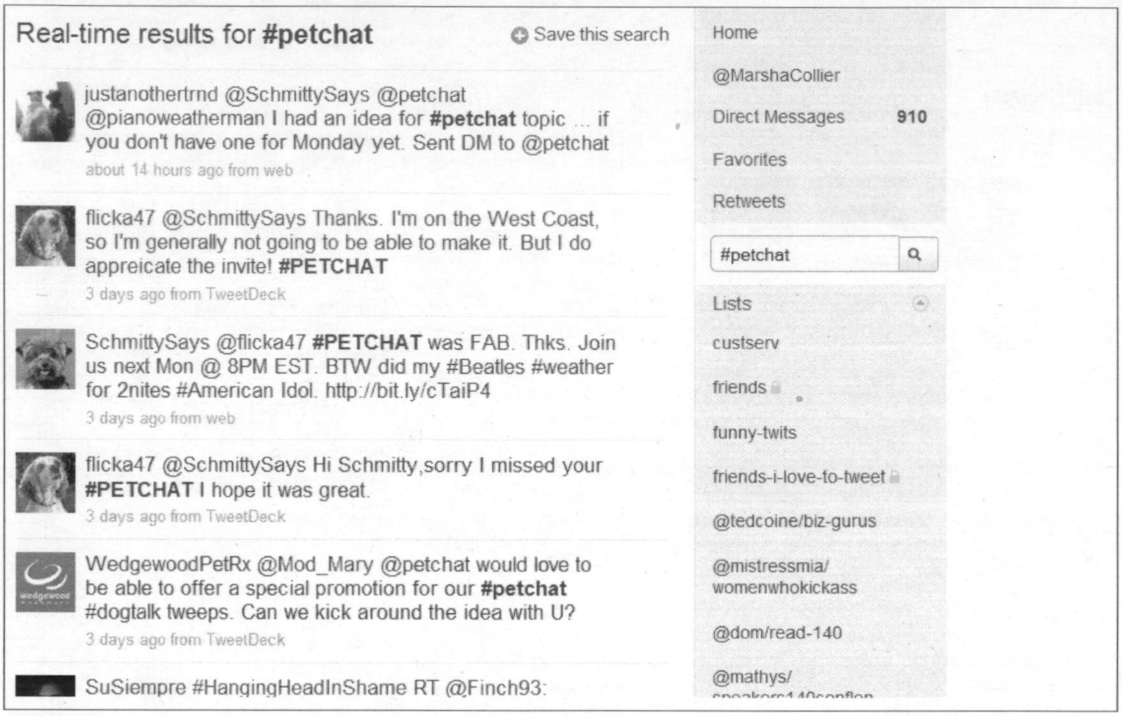

Real-time results for #petchat   ⊕ Save this search   Home   @MarshaCollier   Direct Messages   910   Favorites   Retweets

justanothertrnd @SchmittySays @petchat @pianoweatherman I had an idea for **#petchat** topic ... if you don't have one for Monday yet. Sent DM to @petchat
about 14 hours ago from web

flicka47 @SchmittySays Thanks. I'm on the West Coast, so I'm generally not going to be able to make it. But I do appreicate the invite! **#PETCHAT**
3 days ago from TweetDeck

SchmittySays @flicka47 **#PETCHAT** was FAB. Thks. Join us next Mon @ 8PM EST. BTW did my #Beatles #weather for 2nites #American Idol. http://bit.ly/cTaiP4
3 days ago from web

flicka47 @SchmittySays Hi Schmitty,sorry I missed your **#PETCHAT** I hope it was great.
3 days ago from TweetDeck

WedgewoodPetRx @Mod_Mary @petchat would love to be able to offer a special promotion for our **#petchat** #dogtalk tweeps. Can we kick around the idea with U?
3 days ago from TweetDeck

SuSiempre #HangingHeadInShame RT @Finch93:

#petchat   🔍

Lists   ▲
custserv
friends
funny-twits
friends-i-love-to-tweet
@tedcoine/biz-gurus
@mistressmia/womenwhokickass
@dom/read-140
@mathys/speakers140conflon

Figure 12-11

- **#americanidol** — Watching *American Idol* on TV by yourself? Want to make a comment and possibly get an answer? Incorporate the TV show name with a hash mark in front and look for others.

- **#sexonaplate** — Hashtag used by @ FoodPhilosophy (Jennifer Iannolo, CEO of the Culinary Media Network) when she tweets about an exotic plate of food.

282

- **#jobs** — Looking for a job? Search for tweets with this hashtag.

- **#quote** — When you post a quote as a tweet, follow it with the `#quote` hashtag for quote-lovers to find.

 Keep in mind that hashtags should be used sporadically (unless you are in the middle of a live chat). They're kind of annoying to look at, and lose meaning when used superfluously.

Connect with People

Did someone @ reply to you, and you decide you want to know more about that person? See a tweet you like? Want to know if you're following someone? Want to see who's following you? Twitter has a quick and easy tool you can use to find out more.

1. On your Twitter home page, click the link on the right side that has the @ sign followed by your Twitter ID. You'll see a list of people who have mentioned you in their tweets.

2. If you want to know more about someone (whether that person is following you, or you're doing the following, or who's following whom), put your mouse over his or her ID or avatar. An information box like the one in **Figure 12-12** appears. If you're not following the person, you see a gray Follow button; if you are following, you see a check mark and the words *You Follow*.

Find out whether you follow this user.

Figure 12-12

3. Before you follow someone you don't know, click the More link next to his or her location; the person's full Twitter information shows up in a small box (shown in **Figure 12-13**). If you like what you see, go ahead and follow.

4. If you do follow this new person — and want to know if he or she is following you — just click the little cogwheel (indicating settings). A menu like the one in **Figure**

12-14 drops down, showing the next steps to take.

If the menu says that you *can* Direct Message this person, then your answer is yes: Anyone you can send a Direct Message *is* following you.

Figure 12-13

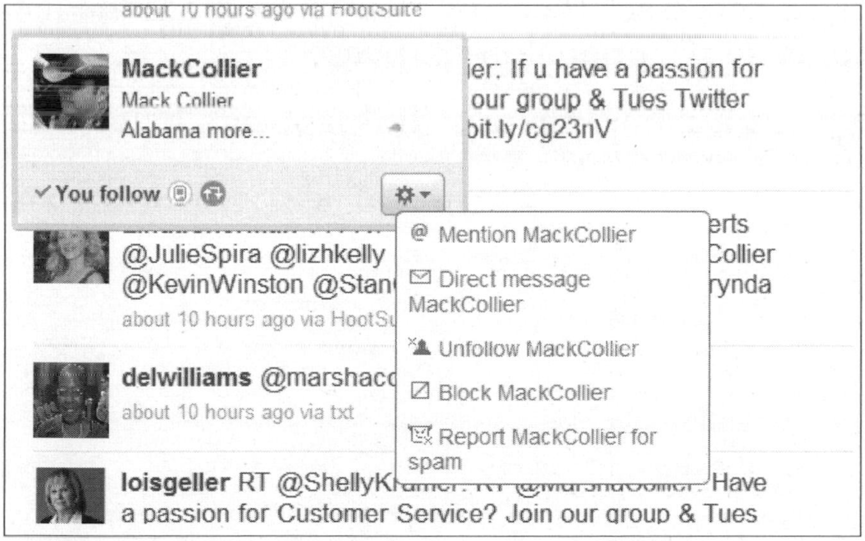

Figure 12-14

Keep Track of Hundreds, Thousands of Friends?

It's a challenge, but you'll soon be following more people than you could possibly imagine at the moment (unless you're channeling Cecil B. DeMille). The more the merrier? Sometimes. You may want to monitor a smaller group of real-life or business friends, and if you follow hundreds of people, you may never see their tweets.

1. Enter (behold!) *Twitter Lists*. You're allowed to make lists of as many people as you wish. You can choose to make them public or private. If they're private, no one can find out that they're not on the list of your personal friends (which can be tactful). Start your lists by going to your Twitter home page. Scroll down the page. Below the Search box, you'll see the Lists heading.

2. Click the New List link. A window appears, as shown in **Figure 12-15**. In the boxes provided, give your list a name and a short description. Typing a description for a private list isn't necessary (because you know what the list is about); doing so is optional in that case.

   After you type in a name, the List link appears below the Title box.

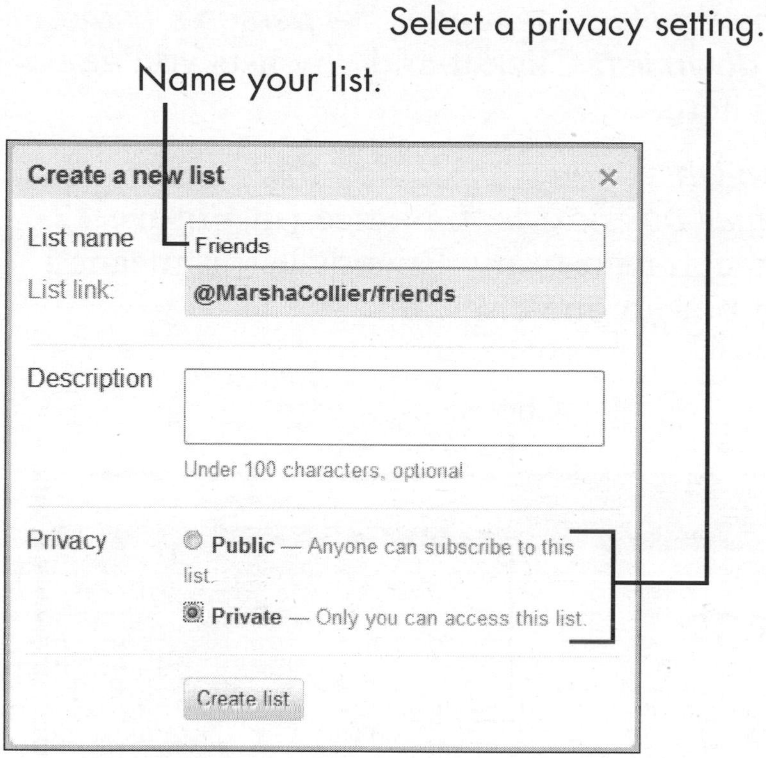

Name your list.

Select a privacy setting.

Create a new list   ×

List name   Friends

List link: @MarshaCollier/friends

Description   [   ]

                 Under 100 characters, optional

Privacy   ○ **Public** — Anyone can subscribe to this
                 list.
                 ◉ **Private** — Only you can access this list.

                 [Create list]

Figure 12-15

3. Select the Private option and only you can access the list (by clicking the link that appears under the Lists heading on the right side of your home page). If you want to share your list with others — the way I do with my Funny-twits list — click the Public option. That way other folks can follow the people on your list.

4. After you make a list, you'll want to add people to it. Here's the procedure:

   1. *You can either search for people in the Find People area (well, yeah) at the top of the page, or click a new person's ID when he or she comes up in the Twitter stream.* Clicking the ID brings you to the new person's Profile page, where you'll see a bio and other such information.

2. *At the top of the Profile page, under the person's name, is a Lists drop-down list.* Click it and any lists you've made show up here.

3. *Select the list to which you want to add this person — and click the small box next to it.* Notice (in **Figure 12-16**) a tiny lock icon next to my Friends list; it means I can see the list but no one else can.

Choose a list here.

Figure 12-16

You'll also see that you can make a new list for the person you're adding; that option is available in the drop-down menu. This is very handy if you haven't set up a list yet.

4. *After you click the box, the menu will close.* Under the newly added person's name, you'll see his or her page — which shows (only to you) that this person is on one of your lists. **Figure 12-17** shows what that looks like.

Figure 12-17

View Your Friend Lists

1. Now that you've made your sooper-secret list of those you follow, you want to be able to watch your friends' tweets, right? That's the easy part. You start on your Twitter home page, under the Lists heading, with the lists you've made. Clicking the name of a list shows you tweets from just the friends you've selected to be on the list.

2. Pretty cool, eh? But (there's always a *but*) you can't see the tweets from the other people you follow — *or* your Direct Messages *or* your @ replies! What to do? You're going to have to download some Twitter client software. But don't worry, those programs are *free* and safe to install on your computer. This software allows you to see all your Tweets, all at once.

3. There are many different programs, but two are the most popular: Seesmic and TweetDeck. They operate very

much in the same way, but you have to decide which you prefer. One may be easier to read, or you may like the way the user IDs look on the other. Here are a couple of features to note about these programs:

- Twitter client programs update tweets automatically and allow you to have separate columns for @ replies, Direct Messages (private messages), your lists, your Followers, and your searches. You're limited only by the amount of space on your desktop (and how good your eyes are). They do allow you to scroll back and forth to view all the columns.

- The software also makes a noise: a bird tweet in TweetDeck and a chime in Seesmic. You'll hear it automatically when you get an @ reply or a Direct Message. You can turn it off, of course, but that way . . . you'll never know when someone is trying to reach you.

- You can send tweets while you're using these programs, and do anything you can do on Twitter — the only difference is that you can see everything you're doing all at once. Call it a bird's-eye view.

4. **Figure 12-18** shows you Seesmic on my desktop. Notice that I have columns for my @ Replies, my @ MarshaCollier/Friends private list and my Home, which consists of everyone I follow. (You didn't really think I'd let you see my private Direct Messages, did you?)

Figure 12-18

The other client, TweetDeck (**Figure 12-19**), handles everything the same way. The major differences are that you can change the colors of the TweetDeck screen, it auto-shortens your links, allows you to post to Facebook (and other social media platforms), and has the controls and settings in the upper-right corner of the screen, versus the lower-left corner in Seesmic.

5. You can download TweetDeck at www.tweetdeck.com and Seesmic at seesmic.com. Check them both out and see what works best for you.

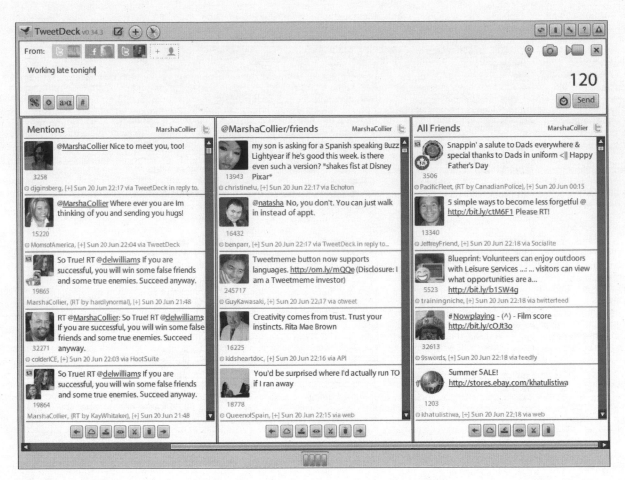

Figure 12-19

Part IV

The Rest of the Social Networking Story

The 5th Wave   By Rich Tennant

"These are the parts of our life that aren't on YouTube."

Chapter 13

Sharing (and Grabbing) Photos, Videos, and Music

One of the most fun ways to share online, in both Twitter and Facebook, is to share your favorite music and images. We've talked about sharing your own photos on Facebook, but how about treating your online friends to some of the unique items you run across elsewhere on the Web? You could share a news story, a song, or a funny video — pretty much any cool thing you find!

I've spent many evenings online with friends, pointing from a song to a video to a story. It's the 21st century version of a coffee klatch; it's also like sharing a bottle of wine with friends (only you get to drink the entire bottle if you wish).

In this chapter, I give you some advice for mannerly and efficient sharing, go over some great places to find material to share, and tell you how to easily transport the treasures you find to your Facebook or Twitter page.

Give Credit When You Share

1. I want to talk a little about the conventions — or, better yet, the etiquette — for sharing what you find online. Odds are if you hijack someone's article or photo from somewhere on the Internet, that person may never know it — but *you* will. Good manners (believe it or not) are still in fashion, but they follow new rules. Please credit any Web site and the person behind the post when you share the content. You can generally do so by including a link back to the original posting of the content, or in the case of Twitter, thank the person who originally posted it.

 I posted a video that Chris Brogan originally posted on his blog to a couple of places: my Facebook page and my own blog. Plus, I tweeted about it on Twitter. **Figure 13-1** shows how I handled giving credit on my Facebook page.

Options

Marsha Collier My favorite fan, Chris Brogan's daughter, Violette, decides to "Do it eBay" by starting out with my eBay Business All-In-One. Thank you!

Violette Reads Marsha Collier Books
www.youtube.com
For a blog post over at http://www.dadomatic.com

Yesterday at 11:07am · Comment · Like · Share · Promote

Figure 13-1

2. When you want to link to a YouTube video (see the later task "Find and Share Videos on YouTube" for more information), you can type the @ (at sign) before you type the name you want to credit. When you do that on Facebook, the names of your friends show up in a drop-down menu. **Figure 13-2** shows how that works. When you see the person's name you want to include, click it, and the full name appears in your post. Doing this also causes the post to appear on your friend's Profile page. It's what the kids call *giving a little Facebook love*.

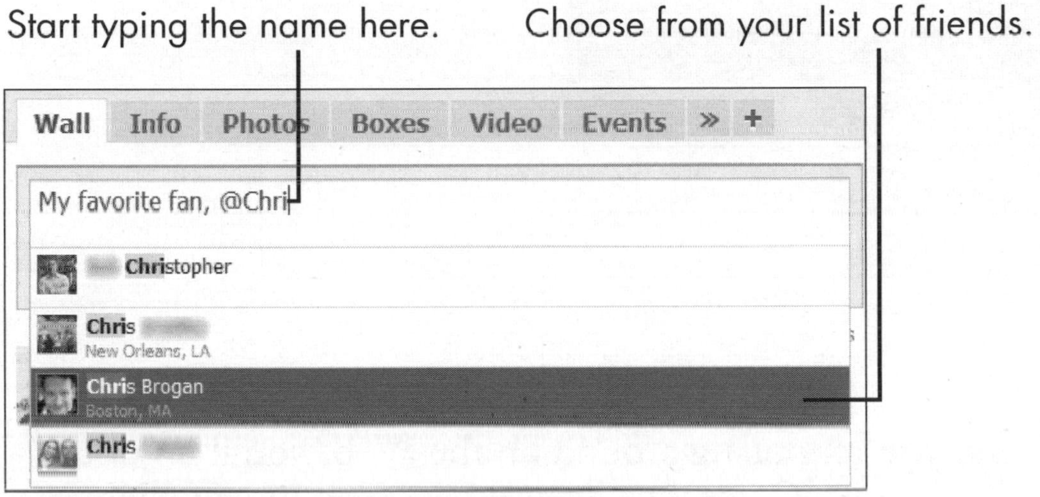

Start typing the name here.   Choose from your list of friends.

| Wall | Info | Photos | Boxes | Video | Events | » | + |

My favorite fan, @Chri

Christopher

Chris
New Orleans, LA

Chris Brogan
Boston, MA

Chris

Figure 13-2

3. Suppose you want to share a video elsewhere online, as I did a few days later when I posted Chris's video on my blog (yes, I *really* liked it). Besides mentioning the original poster by name in your blog text (see **Figure 13-3**), you can include the name in the keywords area of your blog. (Chapter 15 tells you all about blogs.) And when you do, the credit gets back to him or her through Google mentions.

Credit your source in your posts.

WEDNESDAY, MAY 12, 2010

Children Learn from Your Business Examples

I truly loved this post from Chris Brogan. He bought his 8 year old daughter a copy of my eBay Business All-In-One Desk Reference For Dummies. I'm sure she'll need a little help reading it, because the "For Dummies" title can be deceiving. I'm very proud that I've built my career writing For Dummies books. We work crazy hard to simplify the most complex of tech and business subjects. From the email I've received over the past 12 years, I know that we've changed a lot of people's lives. Good luck, Violette!

Violette Reads Marsha Collier Books

eBay Business
ALL-IN-ONE
FOR
DUMMIES

OPEN

0:00 / 0:28

Like   Be the first of your friends to like this.

Figure 13-3

4. When you're looking around on the Web, you'll no doubt see a Creative Commons license badge on independent Web sites. *Creative Commons* is a nonprofit organization that works to increase the amount of content "*in the commons* — the body of work that is available to the public for free and legal sharing, use, repurposing, and remixing." When you see a Creative Commons license icon, click it, and you'll be brought to a page where the actual license appears. This license tells you if there are any restrictions about the content that you may want to share.

Figure 13-4 shows the license that appears on my Facebook page. I really love to share, but I want to make it clear that images of mine cannot be used commercially by anyone.

298

Figure 13-4

The Creative Commons license is represented by three basic icons, and the license details are based on the order in which the icons appear. **Table 13-1** outlines a simple shortcut to the Creative Commons license rules.

Table 13-1	Creative Commons License Icons	
License Icons	*Stand For . . .*	*Which Means . . .*
	Attribution	You may distribute, remix, tweak, and build upon the work, even commercially, as long as you credit the original creation.
	Attribution — Share Alike	All of the above, with this caveat: You credit and license new creations under the identical terms.
	Attribution — No Derivatives	You may redistribute, commercial and non-commercial, as long as the work is passed along unchanged and in whole, with credit to author.
	Attribution — Non-Commercial	You may remix, tweak, and build upon the work non-commercially only.
	Attribution — Non-Commercial — Share Alike	You may remix, tweak, and build upon the work non-commercially, as long as you credit and license new creations under the identical terms. You can download and

299

		redistribute the work as is, but you can also translate, make remixes, and produce new creations based on the work.
	Attribution — Non-Commercial — No Derivatives	This license is often called the *free advertising license* because it allows download of works and sharing as long as the distributor credits and links back to the original. The work can't be changed in any way or used commercially.

 In Chapter 15, I also show you Posterous, a very simple blog format. When you have a Posterous page, it carries the credits forward automatically.

Make Your Links Short

Since we're talking Twitter here and you have only 140 characters for every tweet, using up your characters with a long Web address (and you know they can be long) is just wasteful. Even in e-mail messages and Web postings elsewhere, typing in a gigantic URL can be a real chore.

There's an app for that! Several online services will abbreviate any Web address to a nice, manageable size. You may have seen some shortened URLs when you were perusing Twitter. See any Web links that look nonsensical, with no legible words? Clicking that silly-looking link will get you where you want to go, via the magic technology of the webby-tubes.

 Two major URL shorteners — tinyurl.com and bit.ly — are in use currently. I use bit.ly because it's integrated into every Twitter application I use on my computer and mobile phone. Also, bit.ly gives you an information page where you can see how many people click your link after you publish it. (If you use Tweet-Deck for posting, it will automatically shorten your links with bit.ly.)

For example, the Web address for my radio show is

```
http://www.wsradio.com/internet-talk-radio
.cfm/shows/Computer-and-Technology-Radio
.html
```

If I use the URL-shortening application from the bit.ly Web site, it looks like this

```
http://bit.ly/3ClAu
```

If I'm Twittering about my radio show, at least the link from bit.ly gives me room to mention the guests.

1. Want to give bit.ly a try? Find a nice long URL that you'd like to shorten, type **http://bit.ly** into your Web browser, and press Enter. You'll arrive at the bit.ly site, as shown in **Figure 13-5**.

 I recommend registering with bit.ly; I promise it's safe, and the site has never sent me any spam. This way, if you want to use your shortened URL in Twitter, you'll be able to send the Tweet directly from the bit.ly page.

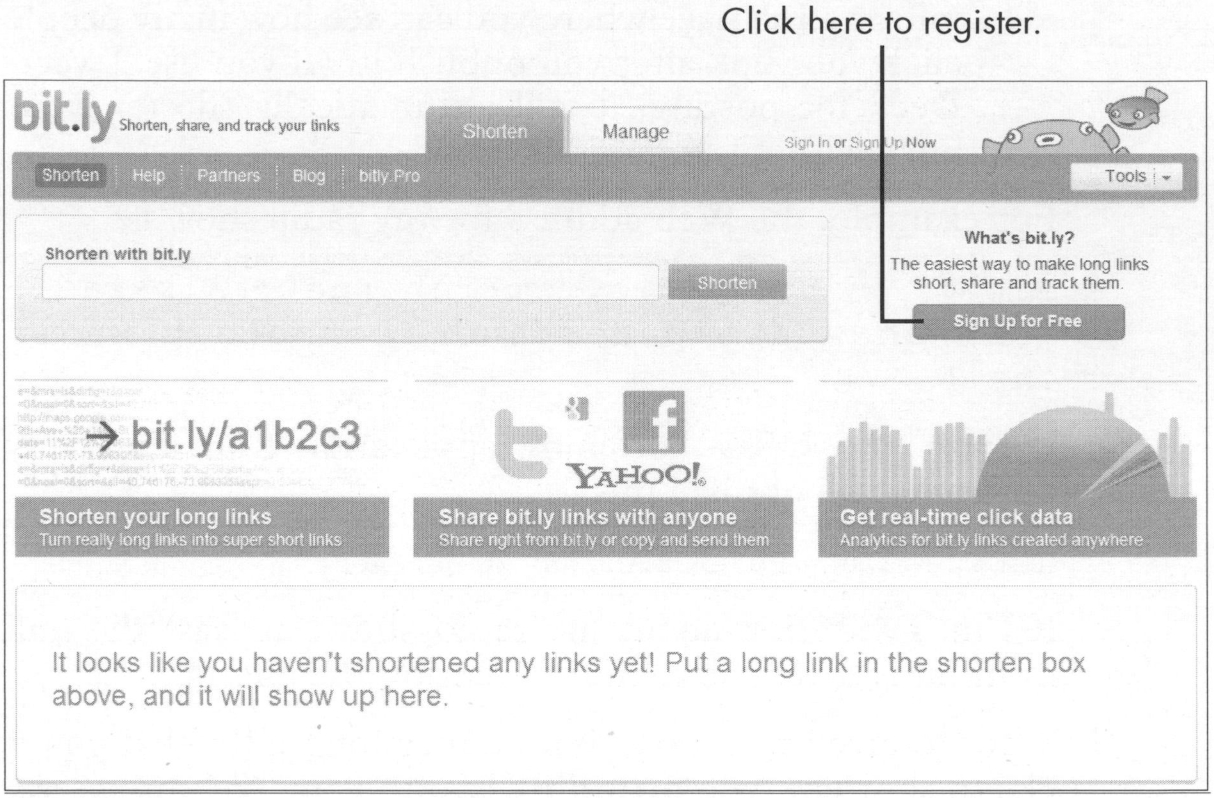

Click here to register.

Figure 13-5

2. Start the bit.ly registration process by clicking the Sign Up for Free button on the right. On the resulting page, type in a username, e-mail address, and password as prompted.

3. When you're done filling in the usual items, click Sign Up, and you're in — that's all there is to it! You're automatically transported back to the bit.ly home page, but now it will look a little different.

4. To speed up the process, if you're planning on tweeting, click the t Sign In button (the lowercase *t* stands for Twitter). This will access your Twitter account. Again, this process is safe and SOP (short for *standard operational procedure*) online.

5. Now copy the URL you want to shorten from its Web page: Click to highlight it, and then press the Ctrl and C keys together. Place your cursor in the text box that says *Shorten Your Links and Share from Here*. Paste your long URL in the box by pressing the Ctrl and V keys together.

6. Your long URL turns into a magically shortened one. If you plan to use the shortened URL in an e-mail, merely copy and paste (same procedure as above) the new URL into your e-mail message.

7. If you'd like to tweet the friendlier URL, type the rest of your tweet in the text box (as in **Figure 13-6**), along with the URL, by placing your cursor before the `http://` and typing what you'd like to say. Use bit.ly each time you come across an interesting news story, article, or video on the Web. It'll save you a lot of typing and it'll make sharing much easier.

Type your tweet before the link.

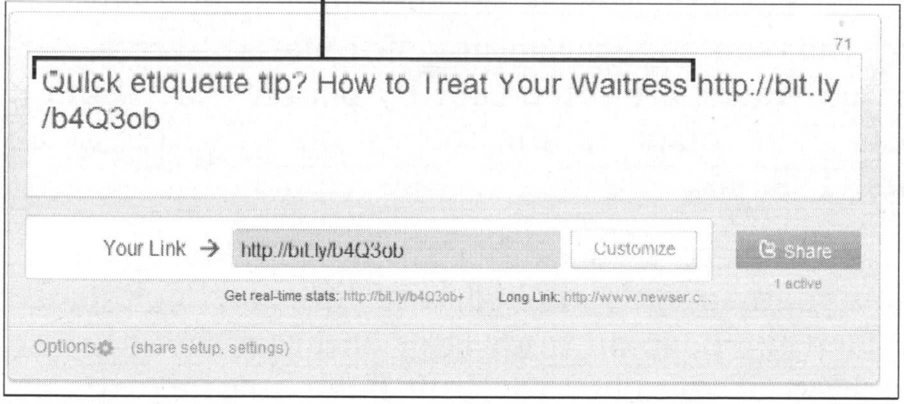

Quick etiquette tip? How to Treat Your Waitress http://bit.ly/b4Q3ob

71

Your Link → http://bit.ly/b4Q3ob   Customize   Share
1 active

Get real-time stats: http://bit.ly/b4Q3ob+   Long Link: http://www.newser.c...

Options   (share setup, settings)

Figure 13-6

A numeric countdown in the upper-left corner of the text box shows a number that decreases with each character you type. This number shows you how

303

many more characters you have left before you max out your 140-character tweet.

8. Click the Share button, and your tweet will autopost instantaneously to your Twitter-stream. **Figure 13-7** shows you the properly tweeted tweet.

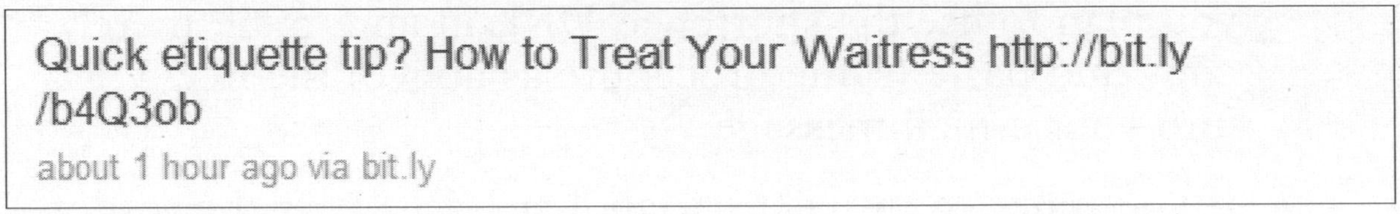

Quick etiquette tip? How to Treat Your Waitress http://bit.ly /b4Q3ob

about 1 hour ago via bit.ly

Figure 13-7

 Notice, at the bottom of the tweet I sent, where it says that the tweet was sent from bit.ly. A little-known fact is that tweets show where people are tweeting from. A tweet indicates what program the tweeter is using (either desktop applications or mobile phone), or it says *via web* when the tweet is coming directly from Twitter.com. You may see *via API* now and again, which is a sign that someone is sending automated tweets. Automated tweets are often sent by people who think it boosts their image online to be "on" Twitter at all hours. Tsk, tsk.

9. When you go back to your bit.ly page a little later, you can see how many people clicked your link to check it out. I checked the page an hour later and saw the info in **Figure 13-8**. If you click the Info Page link next to anything you've tweeted from bit.ly, you get an hour-by-hour report on the action. Kinda interesting.

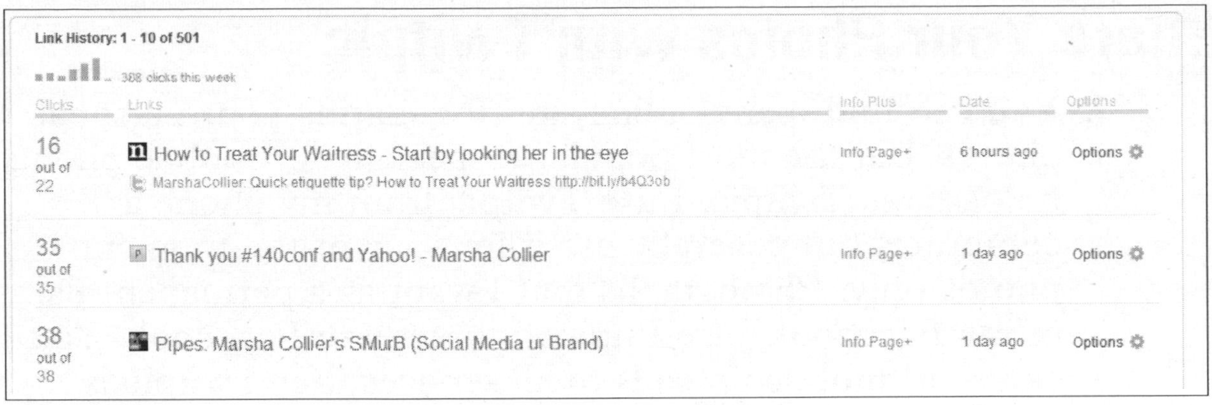

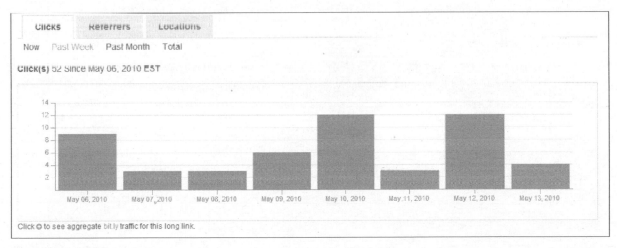

Link History: 1 - 10 of 501

▪ ▪ ▪ ▪▪▪▪▪▪. 388 clicks this week

Clicks	Links	Info Plus	Date	Options
16 out of 22	How to Treat Your Waitress - Start by looking her in the eye MarshaCollier: Quick etiquette tip? How to Treat Your Waitress http://bit.ly/b4Q3ob	Info Page+	6 hours ago	Options ⚙
35 out of 35	Thank you #140conf and Yahoo! - Marsha Collier	Info Page+	1 day ago	Options ⚙
38 out of 38	Pipes: Marsha Collier's SMurB (Social Media ur Brand)	Info Page+	1 day ago	Options ⚙

Figure 13-8

 Also, using bit.ly is a great way to shorten your own Web link in your Twitter profile. (If you don't have a blog or Web site, you can set up a free Google profile as I did at www.google.com/profiles; more on that in Chapter 15.) After you've put a bit.ly link in your profile, you can go back to bit.ly and view the statistics that show how many people visited your page. **Figure 13-9** shows my stats for a week.

Clicks Referrers Locations

Now Past Week Past Month Total

Click(s) 52 Since May 06, 2010 EST

May 06, 2010	May 07, 2010	May 08, 2010	May 09, 2010	May 10, 2010	May 11, 2010	May 12, 2010	May 13, 2010

Click ⊕ to see aggregate bit.ly traffic for this long link.

Figure 13-9

Share Your Photos with Twitpic

1. You can find many online sites for sharing your personal photos, but the most popular (especially for mobile phone uploads) is Twitpic. I use Twitpic from my phone and computer, but generally use it for spur-of-the-moment photos only. Photographs that I want as a permanent part of my Facebook page I upload directly to Facebook. You can send mobile uploads to all services, but Twitpic is handy because it's integrated into Twitter — and it gives the image a shortened URL that you can use anywhere.

 I encourage you to join Twitpic before you have a photo to post; doing so will make your first upload move quicker.

2. Joining is so easy. Type **www.twitpic.com** into your Web browser's address box, press Enter, and you see a page similar to the one shown in **Figure 13-10.**

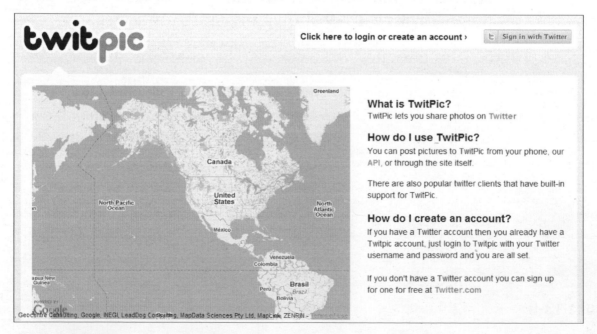

Figure 13-10

306

3. On the Twitpic home page, click the Sign in with Twitter button near the top right. Assuming you're a member of Twitter and you're not currently signed in, a screen like **Figure 13-11** appears.

4. Type your Twitter ID and password into the appropriate boxes, and click Allow. Doing so gives Twitpic permission to integrate with your Twitter account. You return to your Twitpic home page automatically, and you're ready to roll.

 You'll often be asked to sign in to a site with your Twitter account, as on the bit.ly page (see the preceding section). This safe practice uses the *OAuth protocol,* which enables users to approve that the application may act on their behalf without sharing their password. You can find more information about OAuth at `http://oauth.net`.

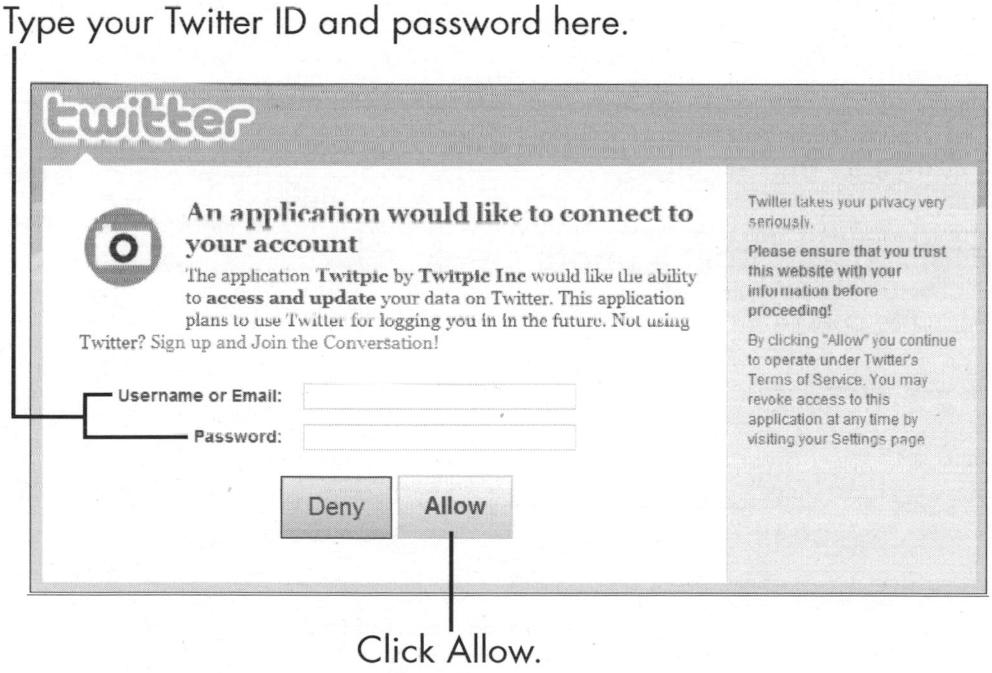

Type your Twitter ID and password here.

An application would like to connect to your account

The application **Twitpic** by **Twitpic Inc** would like the ability to **access and update** your data on Twitter. This application plans to use Twitter for logging you in in the future. Not using Twitter? Sign up and Join the Conversation!

Username or Email:

Password:

Deny   Allow

Twitter takes your privacy very seriously.

Please ensure that you trust this website with your information before proceeding!

By clicking "Allow" you continue to operate under Twitter's Terms of Service. You may revoke access to this application at any time by visiting your Settings page

Click Allow.

Figure 13-11

5. You can now send a picture in two ways:

a. *Upload from your computer.* If you're at your computer and the image you want to post is on your computer, this is the easiest way. Just click the Upload Photo link at the top left of the page. Then click the Browse button to find the image on your computer. After you select the picture you want to post online, type a message to accompany it in the Add a Message and Post It text box (what you type appears on the page with your photo). See **Figure 13-12** for an idea of what that looks like. Click the Upload button, and the photo will transport to Twitpic.

 Before you click the Upload button, decide whether you want the picture to immediately appear as a tweet with your text. If you don't — perhaps because you want to save it for a later tweet — uncheck the Post to Twitter Account check box before you click Upload.

Type your message here.

Click here to find a photo.

Upload and post a photo

Choose an image to upload

C:\Users\Marsha\Deskt Browse_
We take GIF, JPG, & PNG images

Add a message and post it

Two palm trees that have Jasmine trained to cover their trunks, a 15 year project. :)

☐ Post to Twitter account

upload

Figure 13-12

308

The picture posts with your comment and shortened link to the photo's page of your Twitter account. **Figure 13-13** shows you what it looks like. **Note:** The tweet is sent *via Twitpic.*

Two palm trees that have Jasmine trained to cover their trunks, a 15 year project. :) http://twitpic.com/1nc16u

5 minutes ago via Twitpic

Figure 13-13

    b. *E-mail the image.* If you'd like to send a picture that you've just taken directly from your mobile phone, e-mailing it to Twitpic is an efficient way to go. When you join Twitpic, you receive an exclusive e-mail address. From the Twitpic home page, click Settings to see your Twitpic e-mail address. Take a moment to input that e-mail address into your smartphone with the name Twitpic, that way it will always be at the ready.

6. You can track the images you upload by visiting your Twitpic home page. Your images appear in thumbnail form. If you want to delete one, just click the small trashcan next to the image. Click an individual thumbnail to access that photo's page. The URL of the photo page is the shortened link you can post anywhere on the Web to direct people to that image (in Figure 13-13, the URL is http://twitpic.com/1nc16u). Also, at the lower right on the photo page, you'll see a View counter that tells you how often your photo has been visited.

 When you sign in to Twitter, your computer stays signed in unless you sign out. When you first try to link another application to your Twitter account, you see a screen that asks you to allow the Web site to connect. This is a safe transaction, and the permissions will appear in your Twitter Settings: Connections area. If you want to disconnect from a service, you merely click the Revoke Access link for that service (see **Figure 13-14**).

Click here to disconnect a service.

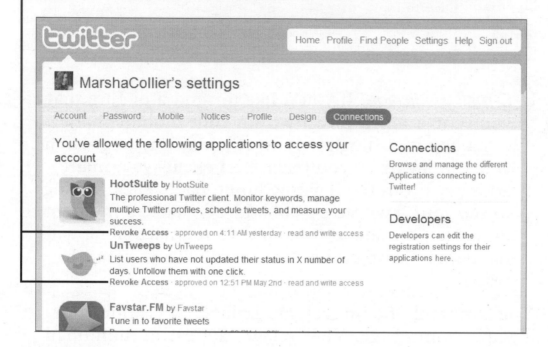

Figure 13-14

Become an Online Deejay (DJ)

1. I remember sitting around with my friends playing records, drinking wine, and having a great time. In today's so-very-busy world, we don't often have the opportunity to do that anymore. Oh yeah, there's also the fact that vinyl records have gone by the wayside, too. (Sigh.) But the Internet brings this all back to you when you visit blip.fm. Type **blip.fm** in your Web browser, and you come to the site's home page, as shown in **Figure 13-15**.

2. Joining is easy: Start by typing a DJ name in the Your DJ Name text box. You are known on the site by this name, so think twice about your selection. All your fiends will see this name when they visit the site, and it becomes the URL for your own Internet radio station. I kept it simple and used my Twitter name, MarshaCollier, so the URL for my blips is `http://blip.fm/MarshaCollier`.

Figure 13-15

3. Type your e-mail address in the Your Email Address text box and click the Sign Up button.

4. On the next page, you can connect your Twitter account by typing your Twitter username, so you can

automatically post your songs (blips). After you add your Twitter account, you see a list of people you know from Twitter.

 I recommend that you click the box that unchecks all the check marks next to the proposed DJ list names. (Can you guess that my taste in music isn't heavy metal?) You can add favorite DJs later.

5. Next, connect to Facebook by selecting Facebook from the drop-down menu. You then see a Connect with Facebook button; click it. This connection occurs through Facebook Connect, which is an authentication service for sharing content. It's very similar to OAuth (see the preceding section), and it's safe.

6. You are now set up to post *blips* (your music selections) to both your Facebook and Twitter pages. In the next section, I show you how to toggle your posting status to either service or both. The default is both.

Spin Your Songs for Online Friends

1. You may ask, "What's a blip, *really*?" A *blip* is a combination of a song and a message that accompanies it. Why not create a blip now? Go to your DJ account at blip.fm (see the preceding section to set up an account, if you haven't), type the name of a song or artist in the Search box, and click Search.

2. You see a list of songs that blip.fm matches to your search. Click the Preview link on the right to listen to a song through your computer speakers. If the matched item is a video, you will see the video in the box to the right of the search results.

3. After you find the song you want to blip, click the word

Blip (to the left of the title, as shown in **Figure 13-16**).

Click here for any song you want to blip.

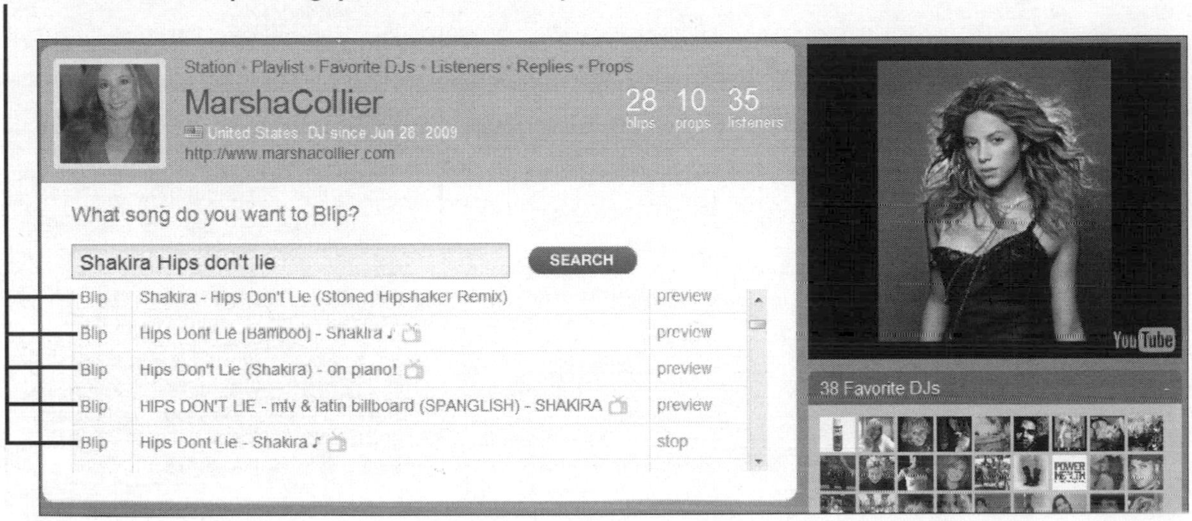

Figure 13-16

4. A form similar to the one in **Figure 13-17** opens. Type a short message that you want to appear next to the blip's link in the Add a Message text box. As you type, notice that the countdown in the upper-right lets you know how many characters you have left.

5. Click the More Options link to expose the drop-down menu. From the menu, select the registered account where you want to post the blip. If you don't want to broadcast this to your Facebook account, click the Facebook icon and it will turn gray (which indicates that it won't post to Facebook). The Twitter icon still shows in blue.

6. Submitting a blip is also referred to as *blipping,* so click the Blip button and instantly the blip posts to your Twitter account. **Figure 13-18** shows you how it will appear.

Type a message.   See how many characters you have left.

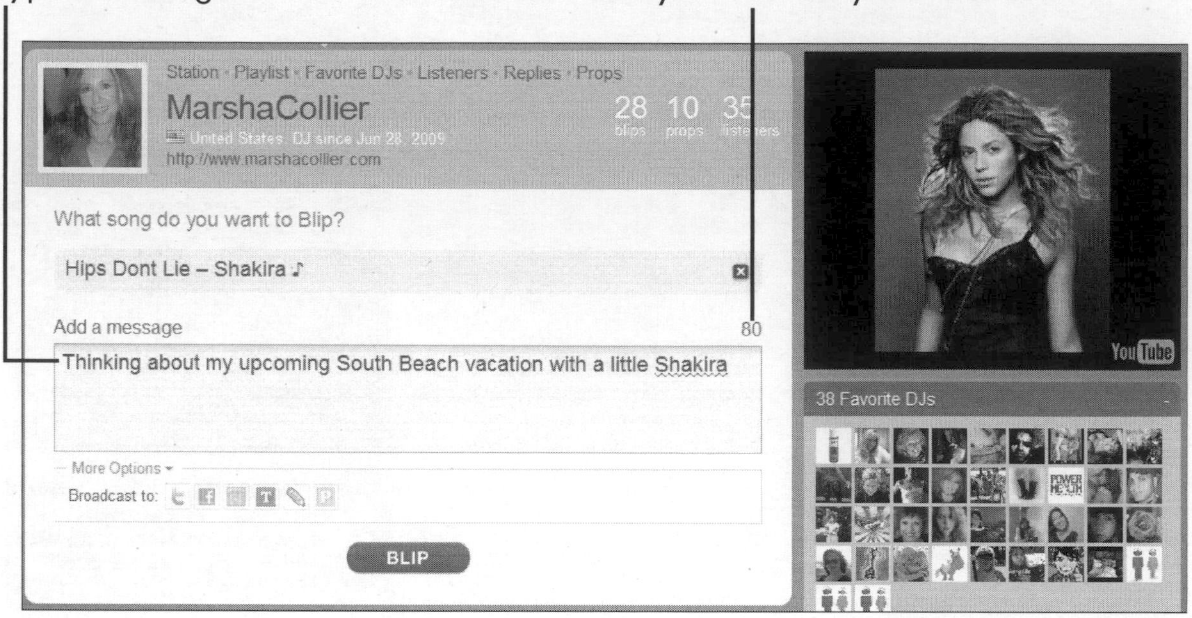

Station · Playlist · Favorite DJs · Listeners · Replies · Props

MarshaCollier   28 10 35
United States. DJ since Jun 28, 2009   blips props listeners
http://www.marshacollier.com

What song do you want to Blip?

Hips Dont Lie – Shakira ♪   ☒

Add a message   80

Thinking about my upcoming South Beach vacation with a little Shakira

— More Options ▾
Broadcast to: t f ▢ T ✎ P

BLIP

38 Favorite DJs

Figure 13-17

MarshaCollier

That's you!   ☰ Lists ▾

Thinking about my upcoming
South Beach vacation with a
little Shakira ♫ http://blip.fm
/~qalpm

less than 20 seconds ago via Blip.fm

Name Marsha Collier
Location Los Angeles
Web http://bit.ly/9h8skO
Bio eBay For Dummies
series author / Host
Computer & Technology
Radio / Co-Founder
#CustServ Chat /
Customer Service & Social
Media Influencer / Fitness
Nut

16,773 17,611 937
following followers listed

Tweets   18,100

Favorites

Figure 13-18

Find and Share Videos on YouTube

Many more hours have been burned watching videos on YouTube (www.youtube.com) than listening to songs on blip.fm. YouTube bills itself as "Broadcast Yourself" so you'd think that you might find only homemade videos. That's not the case. Big-time studios post portions of television shows and trailers from films. According to a study from Comscore, in March 2010, the total number of videos viewed was over 13 billion — and that's in *one* month! If you haven't visited the site, you should.

 As of May 12, 2010, the video that's had the all time most views — 202,638,903 — is *Bad Romance* from Lady Gaga. But, to prove that popularity doesn't belong just to the big guys, the second most popular (with over 189,049,812 views) is *Charlie Bit My Finger Again*. It's a short home movie about an infant biting his older brother's finger, as shown in **Figure 13-19**. Go figure. I guess there's a big audience for kid videos; after all, the *Little Rascals* episodes are getting harder to find these days (unless you look for a boxed set of DVDs on eBay).

Figure 13-19

1. To find a video to share, start by typing a keyword in the search box on the home page at www.youtube.com. You can search for topics, actors, singers, politicians . . . just about anything. For example, I typed *Susan Boyle* (of *Britain's Got Talent* fame) in the search box and got over 83,000 hits. And one of my favorite films is *One Six Right,* an independent film on the history of aviation. To find it, I type One Six Right into the text box and click Search. Try typing a search term for one of your favorites.

2. On the next page (the search results), you see a list of videos that match your search term. In my example, the videos have *One Six Right* in the title; I clicked the top one and came to the page shown in **Figure 13-20**.

316

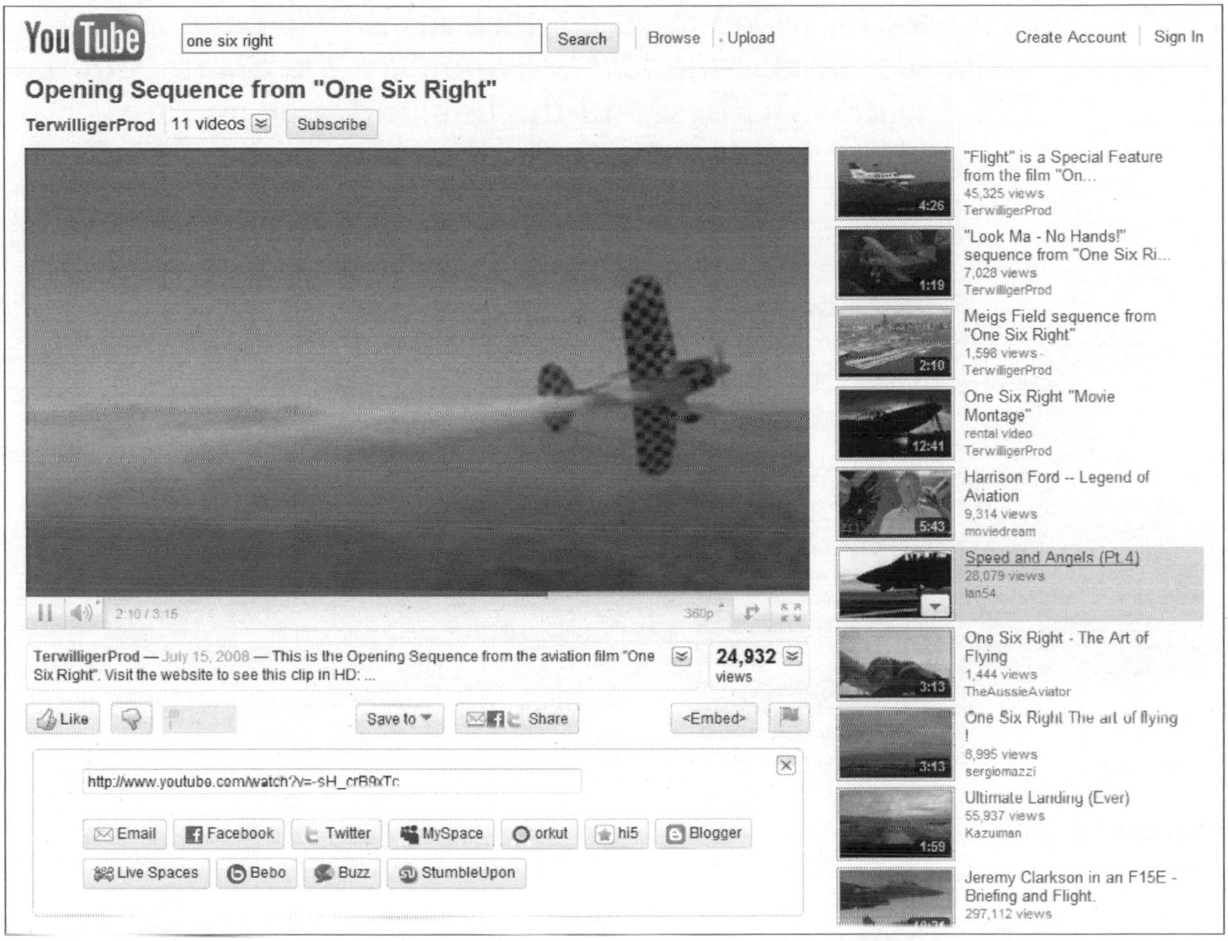

Figure 13-20

3. To share a video that you find on YouTube, click the Share button that appears below the video viewing window. (Notice that e-mail, Twitter, and Facebook icons appear on the Share button.) A box opens on-screen, showing you the URL of the video and a collection of buttons that link to various online communities — including Facebook and Twitter.

4. To share the video on Facebook, click the Facebook button; a window appears and offers you two ways to share:

a. *To post the video to your Facebook profile page, type your message in the text box and click the Share button.* The window closes, and the link and message are posted to your Facebook Profile page. **Figure 13-21** shows how it looks.

Figure 13-21

b. *If you'd prefer, you can send the video link as a message to a Facebook friend.* Click the Send As a Message Instead link at the lower-left. You then see a Facebook message window, as shown in **Figure 13-22**. Begin to type your Facebook friend's name, and a list will appear. Select your friend's name from this list, and the message is ready to send. Click Send Message to send it along to your friend's Facebook message center.

5. To share the video on Twitter, click the Twitter button and a second window opens to your Twitter home page. (If you're not signed in on Twitter, you need to do so and go back to YouTube and try again.) There will be a short message in your What's Happening text box along with a YouTube shortened URL. Edit the message (if you'd

rather say something other than *check it out*) but don't delete the link. Click Tweet. Your message appears, along with the video URL, in your Twitter stream (see **Figure 13-23**).

Type your friend's name here...and select it here.

Figure 13-22

Figure 13-23

Chapter 14

Giving or Taking an Opinion

Opinions are like bellybuttons — everybody has one. When you read reviews on the Web, realize that they can be written as honest evaluations — or they may be paid

321

promotions (remember the payola scandals?) or slam jobs by the competition and spurned ex-employees. It takes a lot of reading to narrow down the wheat from the chaff.

The power of the Internet is that it's built on the voices of millions of people. The more people post reviews and give opinions, the more the truth on any topic will surface.

Crowd-sourcing is a popular 21st century form of marketing. When a company wants to learn about the consensus on a topic or product, it sends queries on the Internet and gleans data from the responses.

You know that the "wisdom of crowds" can sometimes be the opposite of wise. Members of a crowd can be too conscious of each other's opinions — so they begin to emulate the others' comments, which brings about conformity rather than a variety of views. We see that often these days, in political arguments on both sides of an issue.

Speaking your mind on the Web is your chance to make a difference. All voices are weighted equally, and you can offer evaluations of products and services based on your experience. Plus, when you shop online, you can read the opinions of others on various sites to aide you in your personal buying decisions.

In this chapter, I show you some of the most popular sites where you can weigh in on your favorite products and businesses — and get advice when it comes to consumer purchases.

Check Out Angie's List

1. I'd like to start by mentioning an important site that I use frequently: Angie's List. *Angie's List* is a consumer review site that publishes user reviews on local service businesses and health providers. The site serves over 124 cities in the United States and provides reviews in more than 250 categories. Originally a site for local services, Angie's List has been gathering business reviews for close to 15 years and added medical industry provider reviews in 2008. Type **www.angieslist.com** in your browser's address bar and press Enter to reach the Angie's List home page, as shown in **Figure 14-1**.

2. Think about how much you might want to use a review site: You must be a paid member of Angie's List to view the member reviews. Angie's List compiles reviews for businesses and gives them grades in report card format. Just like in school, *A* is the highest grade, and *F* is the lowest. Along with the letter grades, members write descriptive reviews about their experiences with the businesses. I've been a member of Angie's List and have read reviews for several service businesses in my area.

3. You can't post anonymous reviews on Angie's List; the site expects its members to "take responsibility for their words." If someone posts a negative review about a business, Angie's List may contact the company in question to attempt to evaluate (and maybe correct) the situation that caused the bad review. At two places on the site — in its Membership Agreement and during report submission — the site states that it will share your report with the business being reviewed.

Figure 14-1

 Be advised: It's not necessarily cheap to be a member of Angie's List, and you can't find out how much it costs until you begin the sign-up process by setting up a username. I polled some people online and found that the pricing on membership subscriptions ranged from $10 to $70, and varied from city to city.

Find Anything (and Its Reviews) on Amazon

1. I must admit, I'm partial to Amazon. I've been shopping there since the site was launched in 1995. And now, Amazon is America's top online retailer. You can buy almost anything on Amazon, and almost every product has a long list of customer reviews.

 I read the reviews on Amazon even if I choose to buy an item elsewhere — although if the cost is only a few pennies different, I opt to shop at Amazon because of its incredible customer service.

2. Type **www.amazon.com** in your browser and press Enter. You arrive at the Amazon home page, as shown in **Figure 14-2**. At the top of the page is a search box where you can type in the name of any product: book, DVD, camera, cosmetic, tools, grocery items, and more. Click Go.

3. Your search presents a new page containing a list of items that match your keywords. Click the name of the item you want to read reviews about, and you arrive at the product page.

Figure 14-2

4. To get to the reviews, click the number of customer reviews just below the title at the top of the product page. **Figure 14-3** shows that you'll find 87 customer reviews for this product.

5. When you arrive at the reviews page (see **Figure 14-4**), you first see the most helpful favorable review and the most helpful critical review. Reviews are even reviewed by users of the site, so valuable reviews are often pushed to the top — and reviews without value get pushed to the bottom. Scroll down the page to see more reviews.

Click here for customer reviews.

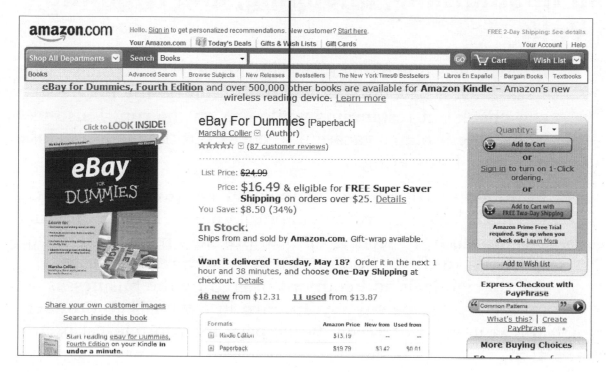

Figure 14-3

Customer Reviews
eBay For Dummies

87 Reviews	
5 star: (57)	
4 star: (15)	
3 star: (9)	
2 star: (0)	
1 star: (6)	

Average Customer Review
★★★★☆ (87 customer reviews)

Share your thoughts with other customers
[Create your own review]

Search Customer Reviews
[_____] GO
☑ Only search this product's reviews

The most helpful favorable review	**The most helpful critical review**
171 of 178 people found the following review helpful:	38 of 40 people found the following review helpful:
★★★★★ **I Was Afraid...I Was Very Afraid!....**	★★★☆☆ **Truly a beginner's book**
This review refers to "ebay For Dummies" (4th Edition) by Marsha Collier....	I've been selling on Ebay for a while and I picked up this book hoping to find some help with making my selling work better. That is really not the focus of this book so I can't fault it for not finding what I wanted. However, if you're a newbie to Ebay and want to find out what's going on without actually logging on and clicking all of the buttons, then this is a good...
I did alot of "window" shopping over at eBay, but never actually got up the nerve to bid, buy or sell over there. I felt real safe here at Amazon. I saw so many items over there that I was interested in(you name it..they got it!), but was just afraid of jumping in. Was it...	**Read the full review >**

Figure 14-4

327

Find Restaurants, Shopping, and Nightlife on Yelp

I think I was one of the first users of Yelp. I love the service — and even have its mobile application on my phone so I can check out restaurants while I'm on the run. I also use Yelp when I plan a vacation to check out the facilities close to where I'm staying.

1. Founded in 2004 by software engineers (formerly from PayPal), Yelp now receives approximately 24 million visits per month from seekers of local business reviews. You do not need to register on the site to search reviews or get the special deals and coupons offered by the businesses on the site. Type **www.yelp.com** into your Web browser, and you arrive at a Yelp home page for your closest metro area.

    In **Figure 14-5** the home page I see brings me to Los Angeles. I checked with a group of people on Twitter (crowd-sourcing) and found that *most* people got their cities pre-filled-in on the home screen. A few people in Seattle, New Jersey, and Iowa came up with San Francisco on their home page, so the little program that fills in the city is clearly not an exact science yet. If your city (or the city you wish to search in) isn't listed, just type your ZIP code (or city and state) in the box below Near. You'll be brought to the hub for that city.

2. If you want to browse businesses in the area, just click one of the links to Refine By. To refine your search further (by ratings, location, features, or prices), click the Show Filters arrow — a drop-down box with more options appears. Clicking a category (for example, *restaurants*) brings a dizzying array of results. In this case,

narrowing down the results to a type of food gives you a more manageable list.

Type a location here.

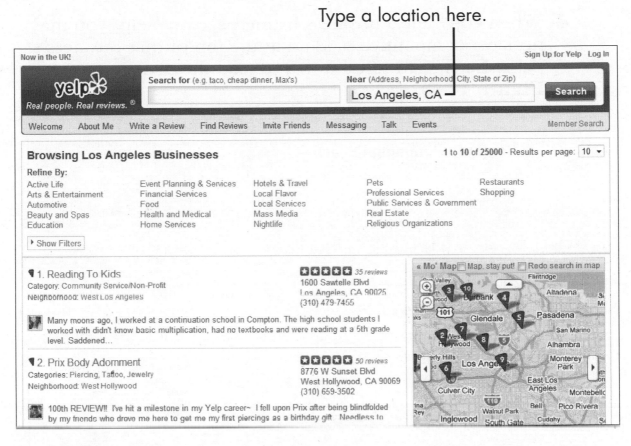

Figure 14-5

 Yelp sells advertising to local businesses, and advertisers on Yelp get preferred placement in the search results and the extra listing features. If you see top listing results that are highlighted, this means those listed businesses are paid advertisers.

3. To search directly for a type of business, type the keyword in the search box, followed by the name of the city you want to search in. For example, I typed *veterinarian Huntington Beach California* in the search box. Then I selected a listing and clicked it (because I saw a notation that this business has a Special Offer in the listing). **Figure 14-6** shows the business page and the offer.

4. When you view a business listing page on Yelp, you may notice a competitive paid ad at the top of that business's page. Be sure to scroll down to read the reviews (see **Figure 14-7**).

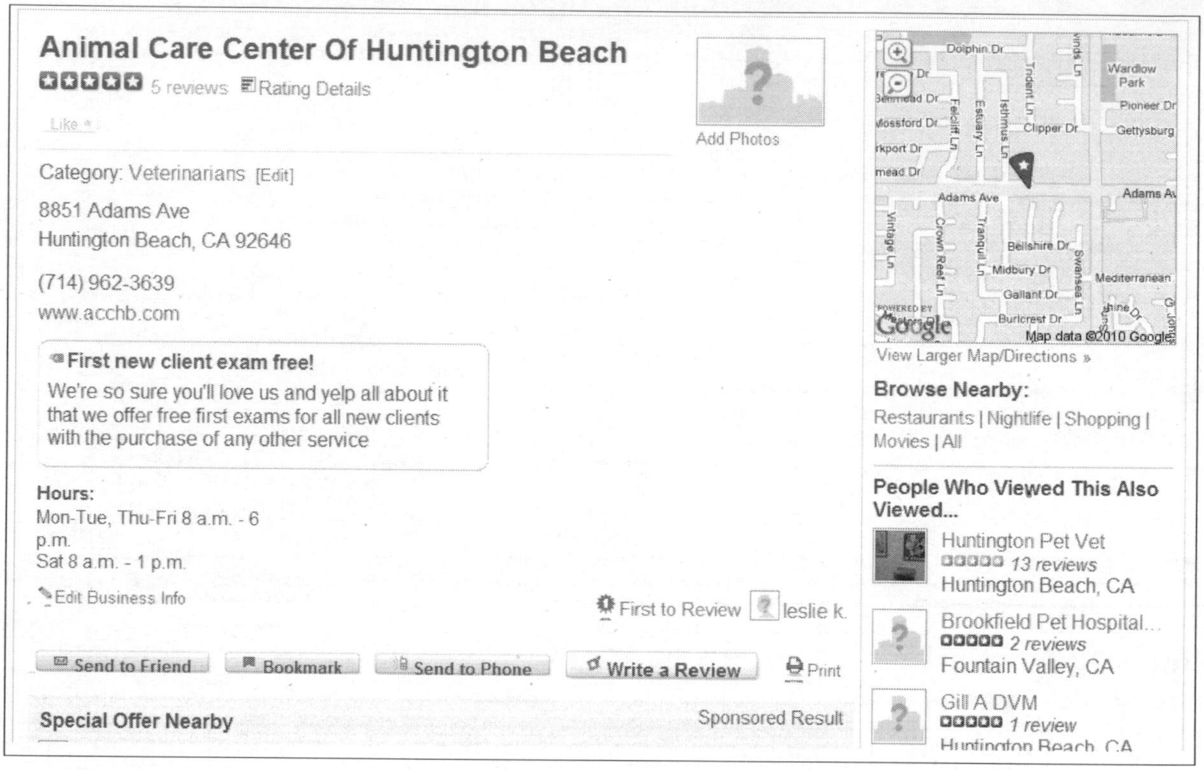

Figure 14-6

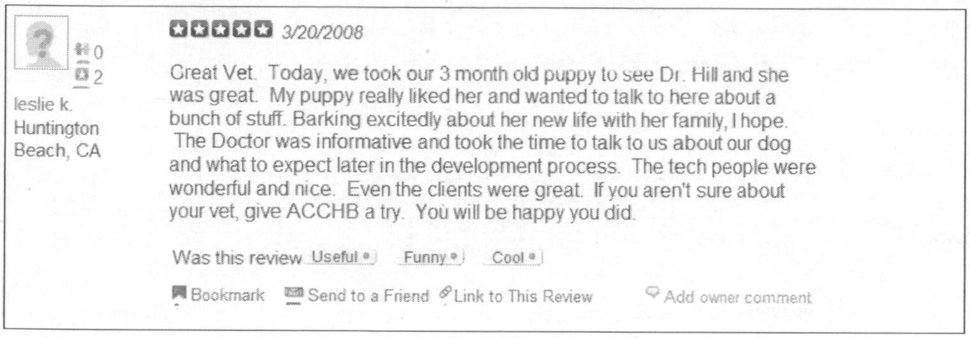

Figure 14-7

Register on Yelp to Leave Reviews

1. If you want to leave a review for a business, you must register on Yelp. On any Yelp page, click the Sign up for Yelp link. You find yourself looking at a simple registration form where you type your name, e-mail address, and ZIP code, and select a password. The form asks your gender and birth dates, but you needn't fill it in; that information is optional.

2. Next you arrive at a page where Yelp wants you to find your e-mail contacts that are on the site. You are asked to input your e-mail login and password as shown in **Figure 14-8**. Then Yelp logs in to your online contact list to see whether anyone on your list matches with current Yelp members. I'm not a fan of letting anyone know who my contacts are, even though doing so (in this case) is safe. If you squint really hard, you can see an inconspicuous Skip This Step link next to the Find Friends button. Why not click it?

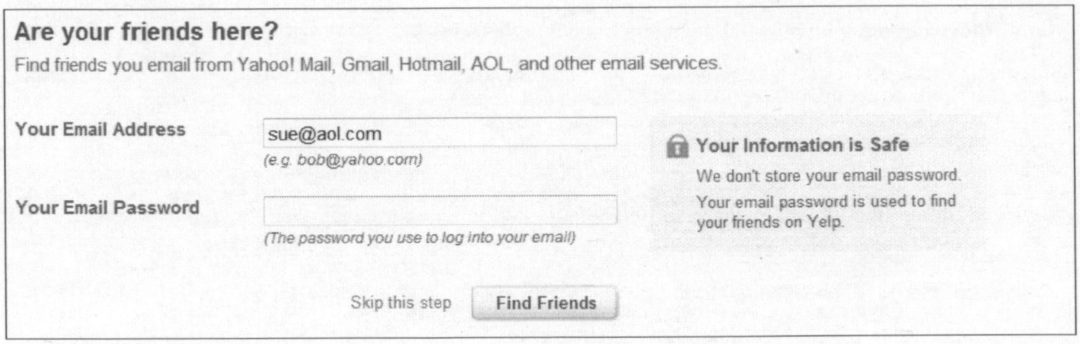

Are your friends here?

Find friends you email from Yahoo! Mail, Gmail, Hotmail, AOL, and other email services.

Your Email Address

sue@aol.com

(e.g. bob@yahoo.com)

Your Email Password

(The password you use to log into your email)

🔒 **Your Information is Safe**

We don't store your email password. Your email password is used to find your friends on Yelp.

Skip this step   **Find Friends**

Figure 14-8

3. A Welcome page greets you and offers you several options. Click Please Complete Your Yelp Registration to get to a page where you assign yourself a nickname for the site. Or you may click the Go to My Profile button where you also can fill in your nickname, as well as upload your photo and personalize your profile — as little or as much as you wish. Mine is pretty jazzy, as shown in **Figure 14-9**.

4. In the meantime, Yelp sends you an e-mail to confirm your e-mail address. It will have a link in it, when you click it; you end up back on Yelp where you confirm that your e-mail is correct.

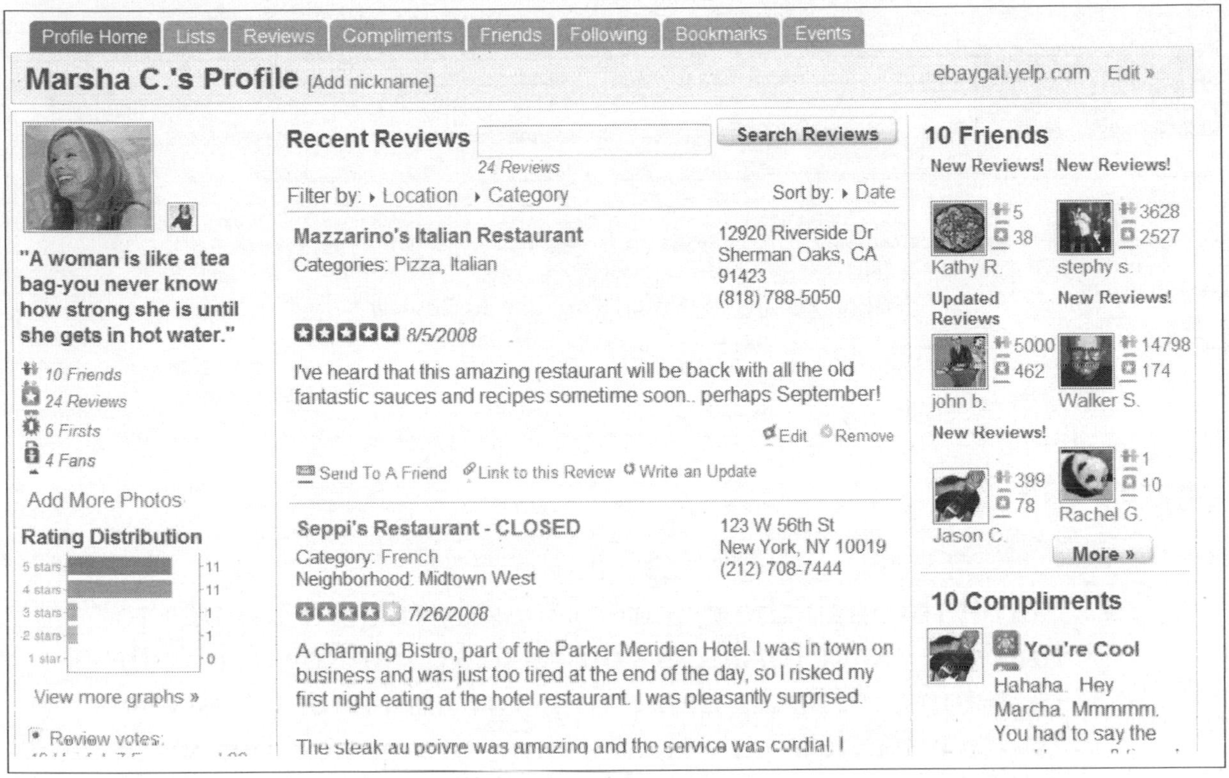

Figure 14-9

Leave a Review on Yelp

1. Every page on Yelp has a navigation bar with links to various areas on the site. Click any of those links to get to your desired area. To post a review, find the Write a Review link and click it. You land on a search page. Type the name of the business and city in the Business Name and Near text boxes, and click the Search Businesses button, as shown in **Figure 14-10**.

Figure 14-10

2. Scroll through the group of loosely related listings to find the exact business you're searching for. Click the matching business name to get to its page. Click the Write a Review link on the mini-navigation bar just below the business details (and above the reviews).

3. On the Complete Your Review page, you see the review form on the left — and other folks' reviews of the business on the right. On the review form, put your mouse pointer over the stars to select the star ranking you wish to give (one to five), and click your selection.

4. Type your review in the text box, as shown in **Figure 14-11**. Scroll down the page and optionally add an evaluation of whether you feel the photos of the business give a good representation, and click from one to four dollar signs to give others an idea of the pricing of the product or services you've received.

5. When you're done, click Post. Your review appears on Yelp for all to see — and on your About Me Profile page. From your profile, you can update a review at any time.

Complete Your Review of C the Salon - Studio City, CA
91604

Rating ⭐⭐⭐⭐⭐ *Woohoo! As good as it gets!*

Your Review

*Read our review
guidelines*

I've been getting my hair done here for five years now. If
you're looking for a colorist/stylist that truly understands
redheads, ask for Patty. She only works a few days a
week as she has a regular job styling for television. When
Patty isn't available, I've also had Claudio do my hair and
been very happy.

✔ ABC   *Auto-saved a moment ago (9:50pm).*

Figure 14-11

Read Between the Lines at Review Sites

1. Travel-booking sites such as TripAdvisor list thousands of
restaurants, hotels, and other businesses, which can make
choosing among them daunting when you're searching for
a hotel or restaurant in a particular city. You may want
to try alternative search methods to adjust the results you
get:

• Use an Internet search engine (such as Google)
to narrow down your results. You can search for
a specific city name and facility — or a desired
service — to get a smaller list of results.

• If you're looking for deals from hotels or airlines,
also visit www.bing.com/travel to widen your
choices. Bing scours many different travel sites to
get results based on price and ratings. After you
find a few possibilities this way, then go to these

sites to read the reviews.

2. While you're reading reviews, keep in mind that conditions someone else considers dreadful may not bother you at all. Here are a couple of examples:

- A friend of mine booked a trip on the east coast using Bing travel and TripAdvisor. When she and her friend arrived in a lovely hotel in Manhattan, her friend couldn't stop grousing about how small the room was. (If you've ever stayed in a New York City Hotel room, you know that almost anything over closet size is acceptable.)

- I recently booked a lovely hotel just off the Champs d'Élysées in Paris. The bulk of the reviews on TripAdvisor didn't come from happy campers. I figured at least the reviews said the room was clean and I was willing to pay the premium to stay at the location. When I arrived, I found that the small hotel was just lovely, and I was very pleased. (Of course, I knew to expect that a hotel in Paris might not have the same amenities expected from a hotel in the United States.)

3. Clearly, if you discover a hotel with a *bunch* of bad reviews, like the one shown in **Figure 14-12**, you might want to steer clear of that property.

 Keep an eye out for extra information associated with a review. I noticed that the review for the hotel in Figure 14-12 also included a photo, so I decided to click it. I saw what you can see in **Figure 14-13**. Yep, you guessed it: I'm not paying $130 a night for that. Really!

4. Individual tastes in restaurants can also vary widely. One of my favorite restaurants serves very small portions, and I love that. Others might post a review complaining that the portion size is too small. Bottom line? Use your good sense and read between the lines when you're reading any reviews.

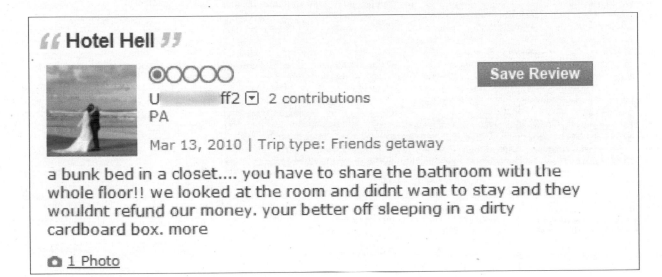

Figure 14-12

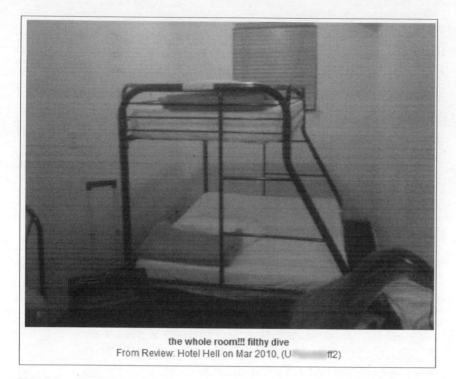

the whole room!!! filthy dive
From Review: Hotel Hell on Mar 2010, (U███████ff2)

Figure 14-13

Find Hotel Reviews on TripAdvisor

TripAdvisor is one of the most popular travel sites on the Web, netting almost 38 million visitors a month. Having so many visitors gives this site's reviews a lot more clout. If a hotel or restaurant has two reviews on one site, a visit to TripAdvisor might net 23 reviews; which would you prefer? This site currently has over 30 million independent reviews.

1. Finding hotel information in TripAdvisor is easy. Type the URL **www.tripadvisor.com** into your Web browser address box, press Enter, and you arrive at the home page shown in **Figure 14-14**. You'll see you have several options.

2. In the Plan the Perfect Trip box, you can get immediate targeted information. If you know the dates of your travel, type in the city you're visiting and the dates you plan to be there. Click the Find Hotels button and a results page shows up with full results for those dates and location.

3. Refine your search. On the top and left side of the page are options you can set to best suit your needs. You can always change these in mid-search should you not find something suitable that fits your parameters. Pare down your selections by using the qualifiers in this list:

Type where and when to find hotels.

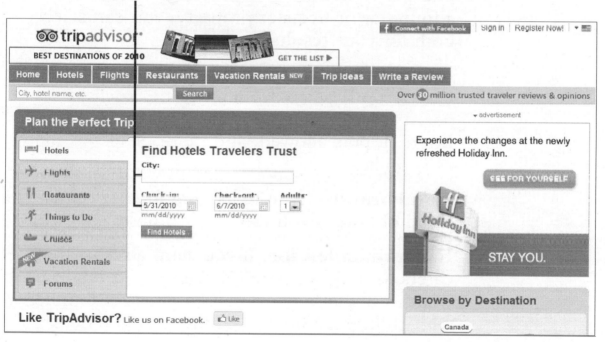

Figure 14-14

- **Price per night:** Using a sliding bar, define how much you're willing to pay and the search will be trimmed to your needs.

- **Traveler rating:** Define how highly rated a hotel you want to find. This rating is based on the independent reviews posted to the site. If a one- or two-bullet hotel (they use bullet points instead of stars) is not where you want to stay, use the slider to remove them from the results.

- **Neighborhood:** If there are nearby areas that might be acceptable, you have your choice of selecting them.

- **Hotel class:** Here's where the star ratings come in. You may select All or any combination of one star to five stars. If you only want to stay in a four-star or five-star property, you can select both for your results.

- **Amenity type:** You require a fitness center? Check it off! Select from amenities such as parking, swimming pools, room service, free Internet, pets allowed, and more. Select as many as you like.

- **Hotel brand:** If you're looking for a specific chain of hotels, you can select it here.

- **Recommended for:** If you want a resort that caters to seniors, there's a chance you might not want to stay at a place that emphasizes families with children. You can set those preferences here.

With a little tinkering and the use of your good common sense, you'll be able to find a hotel that meets your needs.

Add a Hotel Review on TripAdvisor

1. Adding a hotel review on TripAdvisor is an easy task. After you come back from your trip and have an opinion to share, here's how you can share it with the world. First you must register in order to submit your review and post it on the site. You can register before or after you write your review.

2. You have two ways to register, as shown in **Figure 14-15**.

Sign up for TripAdvisor

Sign up using your Facebook account (Recommended) - Why?

f Sign in with Facebook

The easier way to sign in to TripAdvisor

...or fill out the form below

E-mail address

Choose your password

Already a TripAdvisor member?

Sign in

Pick a screen name

Current city

☑ Keep me signed in on this computer

Sign up

Figure 14-15

a. *If you've already set up a Facebook account, you can sign in to TripAdvisor using your Facebook login details.* This method is safe — and the easiest way to join. To join via Facebook Connect (a service that allows you to keep your login info and passwords to a minimum), click the Sign In with Facebook button. If you're not already signed in to Facebook, you have to sign in at this point.

b. *If you haven't set up a Facebook account, you can create a TripAdvisor account by supplying your e-mail address and choosing a password.* Just pick a screen name and password and tell the site what city you live in. Then click Sign Up, and you're a member!

3. Find the page for the property you want to review on TripAdvisor by searching the hotel name and city. When the results appear, click the link to the hotel you wish to review, as shown in **Figure 14-16**. Then follow the rest of the steps given here as you write a review.

Figure 14-16

4. Choose one of the two places to click to enter the *Write a Review* form. Click the top navigation bar or the area to the right with the user's ratings. Clicking either one takes you to a form like the one in **Figure 14-17**.

5. The name of the property will already be on the top of the page, and the first thing to do is fill out the rating of one to five bullets in several areas. Also fill in the date of your stay, purpose of your trip, and whether you traveled alone or with someone. Now it's time to write your review.

6. Type in a title, describing the hotel in one sentence. In the Your Review text box, type your observations. Tell what you liked and what you didn't like about your stay. (Your review has to be at least 50 characters long.)

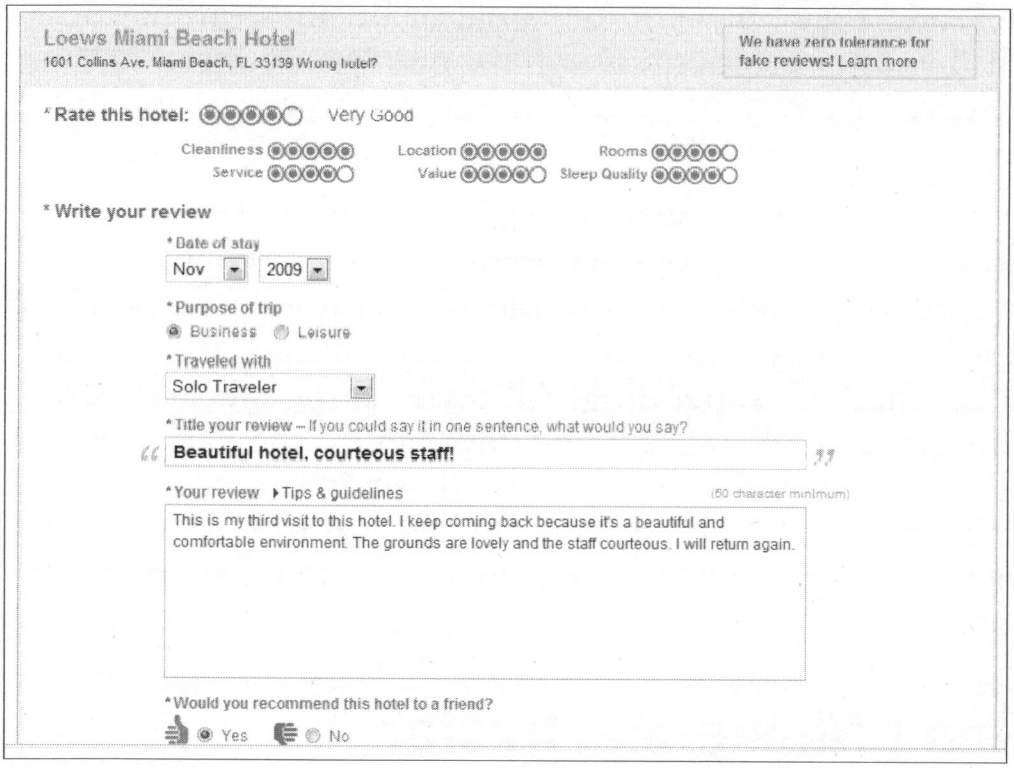

Figure 14-17

7. In the "thumbs up — thumbs down" area, click the option (Yes or No) that reflects whether you'd recommend this hotel to a friend. In the other areas, place check marks by clicking your mouse in the boxes that describe the hotel's style and amenities.

8. Optionally, upload a photo. If you've taken a photo of the hotel or its property that you'd like to share, click the *Browse* button and upload it from your computer. You also must check the box stating that the photo is yours and that you're not infringing on anyone's rights by posting it.

9. Since TripAdvisor takes the reviews very seriously, you must check the box next to the statement that assures: "I certify that this review is my genuine opinion of this hotel, and that I have no personal or business affiliation with this establishment, and have not been offered any incentive or payment originating from the establishment to write this review."

10. If you want to preview your review, click the Preview link. If you're not happy with your work, go back and make changes. When you're pleased with your work, click Submit. After you submit your review, it appears in your profile, marked as pending. All reviews are checked before posting; it usually takes a few days before they appear. When your review is posted, you'll receive an e-mail confirmation. If TripAdvisor chooses not to post your review, the site sends you an e-mail and lets you know the reason why.

Find a Good Movie on Flixster

1. Flixster is a social site where you can read movie reviews, get local movie show times, watch trailers, and post

your own comments about films. You arrive at the Flixster home page by typing **www.flixster.com** in your browser's address bar and pressing Enter. **Figure 14-18** shows you the home page where you can access a lot of information.

2. To get to the various locations on the site, use the drop-down menus from the navigation bar. Also on the navigation bar, you get a search box in the upper-right corner where you can replace the *Movies, Actors, Directors* text by typing the appropriate title or name. Then click Search.

3. Farther down the page, as **Figure 14-19** shows, is the area where you can click tabs to view the specific selections: Top Box Office hits, movies that are Opening soon, and New DVDs released. Clicking any film title takes you to the film's hub page that includes a trailer, photos from the film, the reviews from published critics, and comments left by members of the site.

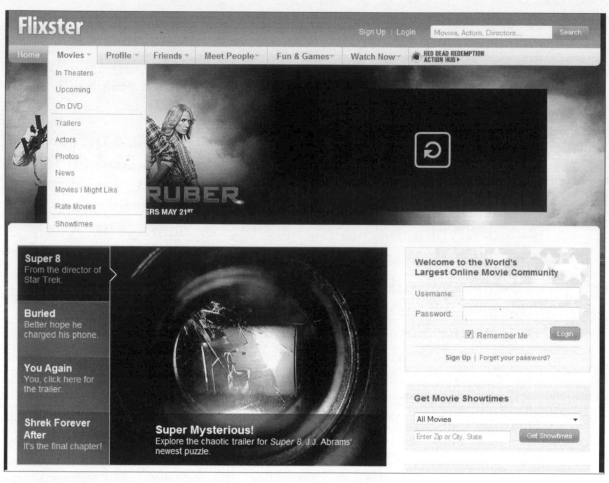

Figure 14-18

Leave a Comment on Flixster

1. To post your opinion (after you've seen the film, of course), you've got to register on the Flixster site (www .flixster.com). There's no Facebook Connect offered here, so you must create a new account. Click the Sign Up link in the upper-right corner of the page and the registration form appears (as shown in **Figure 14-20**).

2. To register, supply your name, e-mail address, gender, and birth date. You may click the check box that says

Hide my age — that way, it won't appear on your Profile page.

3. Then select a password and type the words from the Captcha code into the text box.

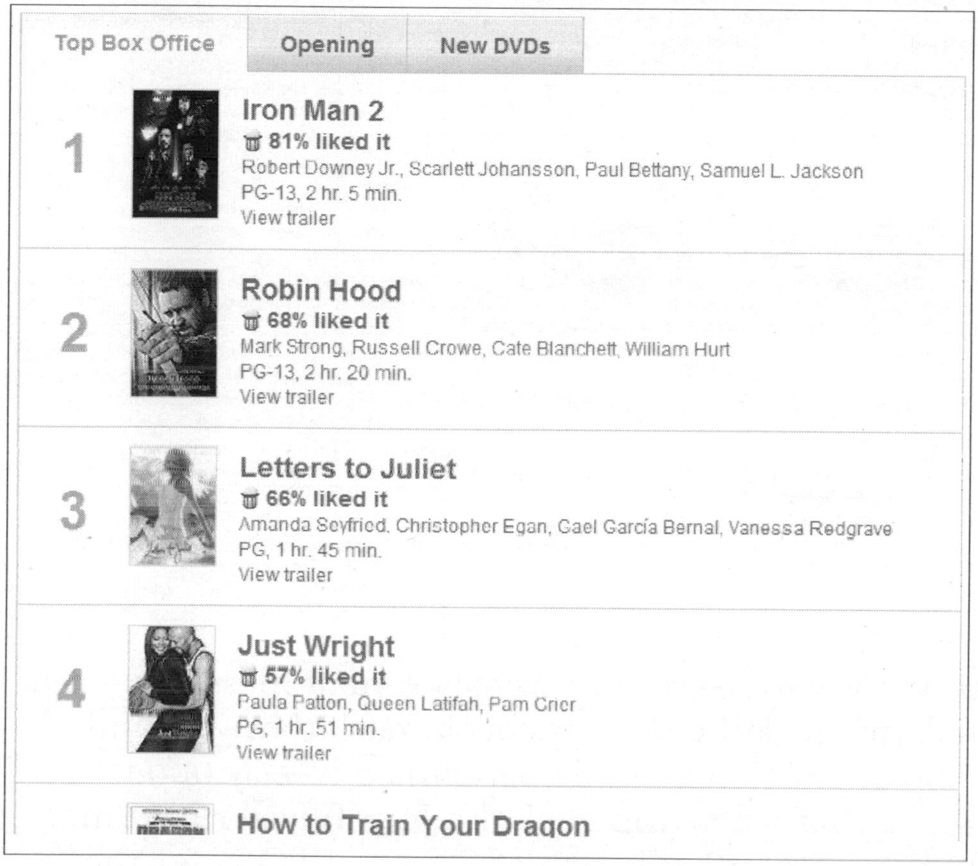

Top Box Office	Opening	New DVDs

1 Iron Man 2
81% liked it
Robert Downey Jr., Scarlett Johansson, Paul Bettany, Samuel L. Jackson
PG-13, 2 hr. 5 min.
View trailer

2 Robin Hood
68% liked it
Mark Strong, Russell Crowe, Cate Blanchett, William Hurt
PG-13, 2 hr. 20 min.
View trailer

3 Letters to Juliet
66% liked it
Amanda Seyfried, Christopher Egan, Gael García Bernal, Vanessa Redgrave
PG, 1 hr. 45 min.
View trailer

4 Just Wright
57% liked it
Paula Patton, Queen Latifah, Pam Grier
PG, 1 hr. 51 min.
View trailer

How to Train Your Dragon

Figure 14-19

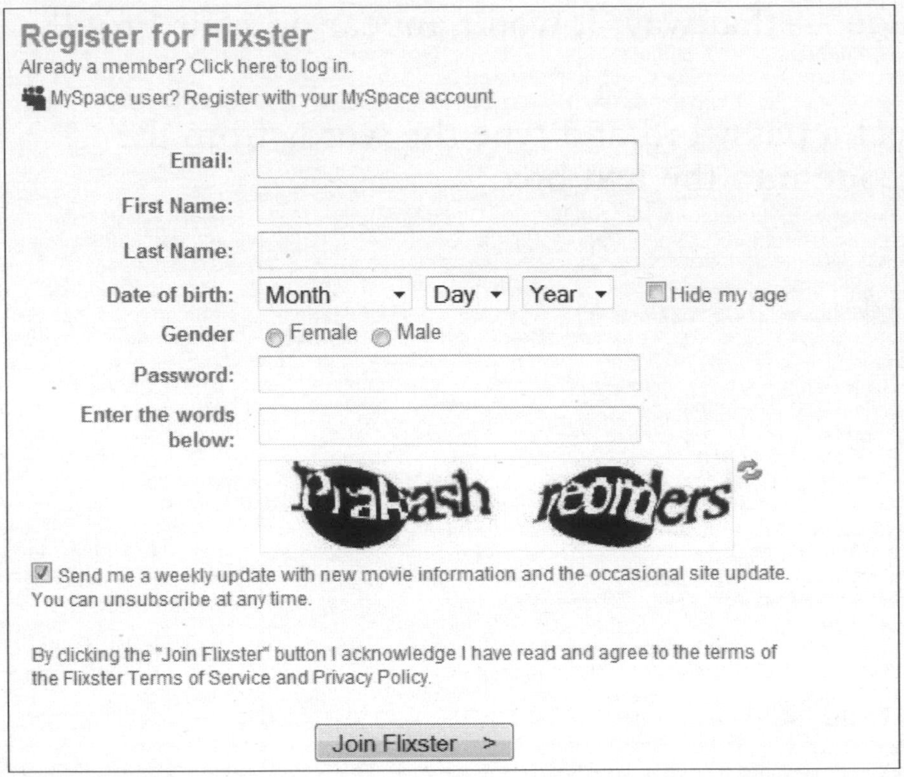

Register for Flixster

Already a member? Click here to log in.

MySpace user? Register with your MySpace account.

Email:

First Name:

Last Name:

Date of birth: Month ▼ Day ▼ Year ▼ ☐ Hide my age

Gender: ○ Female ○ Male

Password:

Enter the words below:

☑ Send me a weekly update with new movie information and the occasional site update. You can unsubscribe at any time.

By clicking the "Join Flixster" button I acknowledge I have read and agree to the terms of the Flixster Terms of Service and Privacy Policy.

Join Flixster >

Figure 14-20

4. If you don't want to receive weekly e-mail messages from Flixster, uncheck the default check mark that you find in the box next to the words *Send me a weekly update*. Recognize that when you click the Join Flixster button, you're agreeing to the Terms of Service (TOS) for the site. You can't join if you don't agree. And after you're a member, you can go to any film's hub page to leave a comment on the film.

Chapter 15

So You Want to Be a Blogger?

Get ready to...

You've heard about blogs, right? Even the learned sage Homer (Simpson) commented, "Instead of one big shot controlling all the media, now there's a thousand freaks Xeroxing their worthless opinions." Maybe not so learned, but he's more or less right — except those opinions are now online, in the millions, and are (some of them, anyway) actually worth reading. Having your own blog gives you an opportunity to write about things that interest you and add your opinions to the social buzz — and someone will probably read what you write!

Once you get involved on Twitter and Facebook, you'll see your friends linking to blog *posts* (online journal entries) and news stories. Doing a blog post is so much more personal because each one is filled with your opinions and your information.

In this chapter, I show you how to set up a blog on the Web at no cost (that means free), and give you examples of people just like you who are blogging on the Web.

Answer These Questions Before You Start

I've learned from experience that before I begin any project, I need to define some parameters that guide the project path and clarify the desired result. If you begin your blog with a plan, the blogging habit will become a pleasure rather than a chore.

1. **Who are you?** In your blog you'll have a profile. Be prepared to talk about your business background, your family, your hobbies, and even life lessons you've learned. Think about sharing pictures and videos in the future. The more information you're willing to share, the more inclined readers will be to invest time in reading your words.

2. **Why you are blogging?** If you spell out your purpose for blogging, your intentions will be clear. Are you writing for your children or grandchildren? Are you writing for your contemporaries to share thoughts? Are you writing to connect with a business community and to promote your online business (and if you're buying and selling on eBay, did you read my *eBay For Seniors For Dummies* from

Wiley)? These are all valid reasons to blog. But know that if your purpose is to promote an online business, today's successful marketing is fueled by being a real person on the Web and building a social community.

 As Mack Collier (one of the nation's premier business blog experts) says, "Consider your audience when answering this question, ask yourself, 'Why would someone come to this blog, what would they be looking for?'" (Hint: Your visitors won't be coming to your blog just so you can make a pitch to them.) Visit Mack's blog for good tips at `www.mackcollier.com`.

3. **What will you blog about?** You can blog about any subject you wish — including your family, your hobbies, your politics . . . when it comes to blogging, you're limited only by your imagination! Just let your readers know what's up so they know what to expect. In **Figure 15-1**, I show you the header of my blog. (If you'd like to check out my blog, you'll find it at `mcollier.blogspot.com`.)

MARSHA COLLIER'S MUSINGS

HI! I'M THE AUTHOR OF THE "FOR DUMMIES" SERIES OF BOOKS ABOUT EBAY AND HOST OF COMPUTER AND TECHNOLOGY RADIO. I BLOG ON EBAY, USEFUL PRODUCTS AND ANYTHING FUN. ALSO PLEASE VISIT MY EBAY BOOK WEBSITE COOL EBAY TOOLS

Figure 15-1

My blog header is purposefully innocuous because I cover so many different things. I write about my books, business, family, my garden, and my life! Stay focused and think of the header as a "mission statement" for your future blog posts.

Jessica Gottlieb, Queen of the Mommy Bloggers, has a simple statement header that appears on every page of her blog (see **Figure 15-2**). When you read it, you immediately know who she is and where she's coming from.

Jessica Gottlieb
Wife. Writer. Mother. Friend.

Figure 15-2

Visit her blog at www.jessicagottlieb.com and you may be shocked by her candid posts. She's very outspoken; named a Power Mom by Nielsen in 2008 and 2009, and averages 43,000 unique visitors each month.

4. **What will you do to get people to your blog?** Visit other people's blogs and leave comments. To find blogs from people of like mind, go to Google and search for a topic. In **Figure 15-3**, I searched for *gardening*. Then, on the left side of the page, I clicked Blogs and Past Week in the toolbar to find the most recent posts.

Choose blogs. Type a topic here.

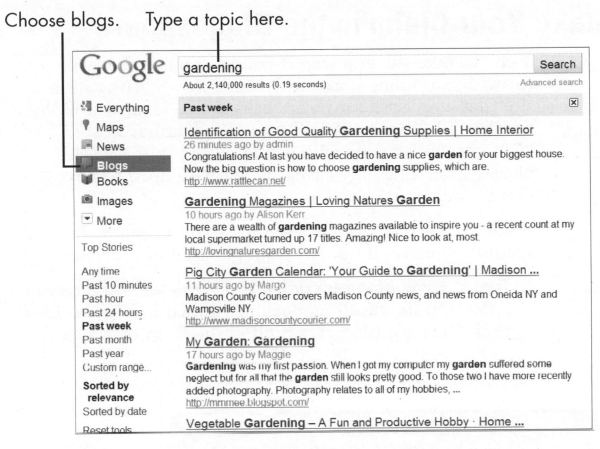

Figure 15-3

Visit, read, and comment on blogs that interest you — even ask questions to promote conversation. Other readers (as well as the blogger) may reply and click over to check out your blog. If you see a post that's on a similar topic to something you've posted on, suggest people check your blog.

5. **How do you get your audience to come back**? Expect (okay, *hope*) that people will leave comments on your posts. Be sure to comment back and visit their blogs. It's all about interacting with the blogging community. One hand washes the other. . . .

Stake Your Claim in the Blogosphere

1. Time to take the first step: Sign up at a site that will *host* (provide an online home for) your blog. Starting off at a site that won't ask for payment is a nice idea, and Google fits that bill. Since 2003, Google Blogger has hosted Web sites for anyone who wants to join in the world of blogging. The only caveat is that you need to have a Google account.

2. If you use any of Google's services, you probably have an account already. If not, you can get a Google account by

1. *Typing* **www.blogger.com** *in your browser and pressing Enter.* On the resulting page (as shown in **Figure 15-4**), click Create a Blog. Then fill in the form that appears.

Click here to create a blog.

Figure 15-4

354

2. *Establishing a Google Gmail e-mail account.* Type **www .google.com/mail** in your browser and press Enter. Look in the lower-right corner for the New to Gmail? box and click Create an Account. Fill in the short form that asks for your name, your chosen login name, your password, and a few more innocent questions (it's safe to answer 'em). When you're through, click Create my Account and bingo! You not only have a new e-mail address, but you now have access to all the Google extra-fancy services on the Web.

Google Gmail is the most popular free e-mail service on the Web; that's mainly because of large (and free!) online storage space and excellent spam filters. When you set it up, you'll be able to handle your e-mail on the gmail.com Web site, or make it so the mail gets downloaded to almost any e-mail program on your computer. (Chapter 3 offers more information about setting up and using Gmail.)

 Either way you decide to create a Google account, you get access to all of Google when you sign in to Google services and set up your blog.

Register Your Blog

1. Now it's time to jump in. Go to www.blogger.com and sign in by typing your Google username (e-mail address) and password where prompted. Then click Sign In. When you arrive at the Sign Up for Blogger form, your Gmail address is already filled in along with your name, as shown in **Figure 15-5**.

2. Fill in your Display Name. That's the name that Blogger uses automatically every time you sign your posts. Make it easy for your friends to know who you are — use your

own name. I used to go by *cre8ive* and none of my friends knew that I was commenting on their blogs!

3. Place a check mark (by clicking your mouse) in the Email Notifications and Acceptance of Terms check boxes — you want to know about new features in the application as well as the Terms of Service (TOS). To read the TOS, click the Terms of Service link, and they show up in a new tab on your browser.

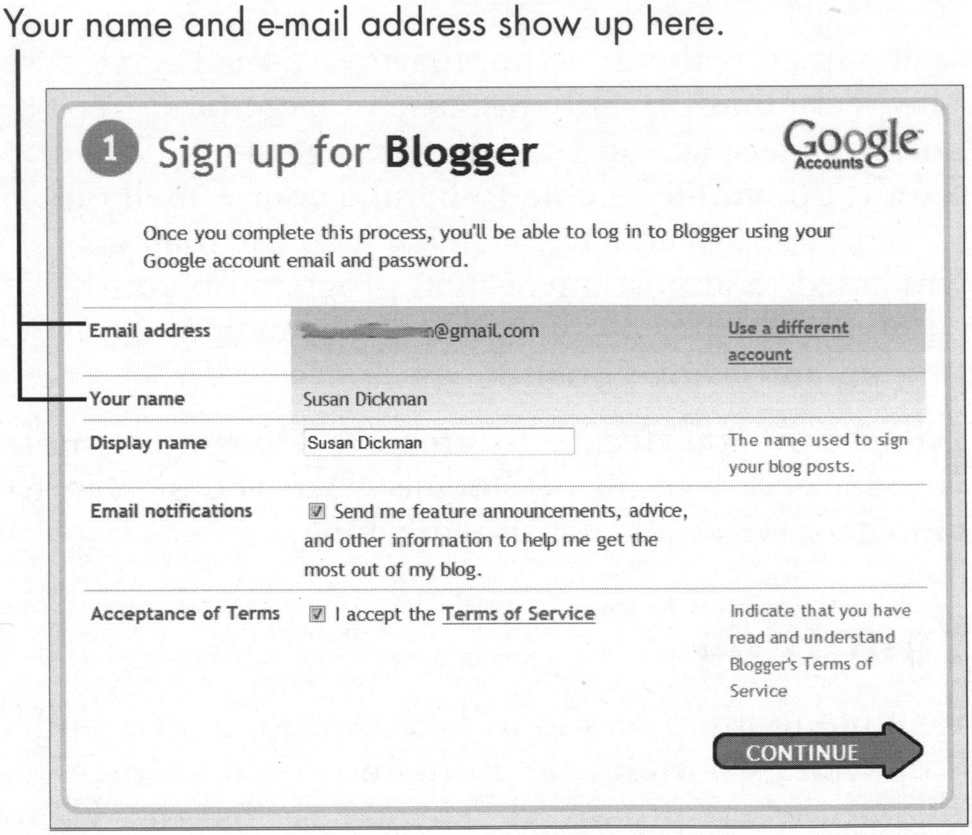

Your name and e-mail address show up here.

Figure 15-5

4. After you read the Terms of Service — and as long as you agree — go back to the Sign Up for Blogger form and click the Continue arrow. You arrive at a new page.

Give Your Blog a Name

Now that you've agreed to join the masses of people who are spilling their hearts and souls (and, in some cases, guts) on the Internet, it's time to name the baby.

1. Name your blog. This title will appear on your Dashboard and on the blog pages. Don't freak out and freeze up at this point! You can change the name of your blog at any time. So go easy on yourself.

2. Give your blog a Web address (URL). Okay, this gets a little sticky. You can change this part later, but the URL you select becomes the Web address for your blog. It's what people must type in their browsers when they want to go to your blog.

   Since there are a lot of Blogger blogs, there is a Check Availability link (see **Figure 15-6**), that you click to make sure that your URL is available.

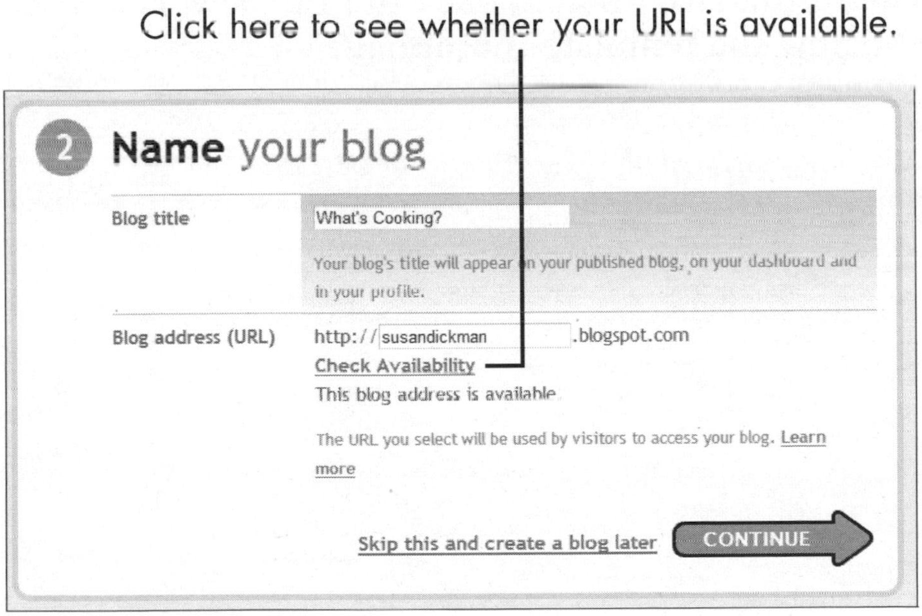

Click here to see whether your URL is available.

Figure 15-6

3. When you're all set up, click the Continue arrow.

 In the future, you can purchase a custom URL (that is, a Web address you specify) from Google and use it for your blog. It currently costs about $10 per year. Wait until your blog evolves to see whether you want to continue with it. Once you've purchased a URL, that's it — no changing your mind.

Choose a Template

1. Choosing a template is no big deal — you can always change it later. You can also make simple changes to the template — say, placement of columns and colors and such. If you're technically inclined, you can even create your own custom template after your blog is set up. But for now, you've got to pick one — so, on the page that has appeared, scroll through the available templates (as in **Figure 15-7**).

 To see a full-size version, click the Preview Template link below the template thumbnail.

Click here for a full-size preview.

Figure 15-7

2. When you've settled on one, click the option button next to the template name and click the Continue arrow. Congratulations! **Figure 15-8** shows the Your Blog Has Been Created page. Now it's time to click the Start Blogging arrow.

✓ **Your blog has been created!**

We've just created a blog for you. You can now add your posts to it, create your personal profile, or customize how your blog looks.

START BLOGGING

▶ Advanced Setup Options

Figure 15-8

Post Your Story with Photos

Posting to you blog is as easy as using a word processor. The New Post page (**Figure 15-9**) has everything you need.

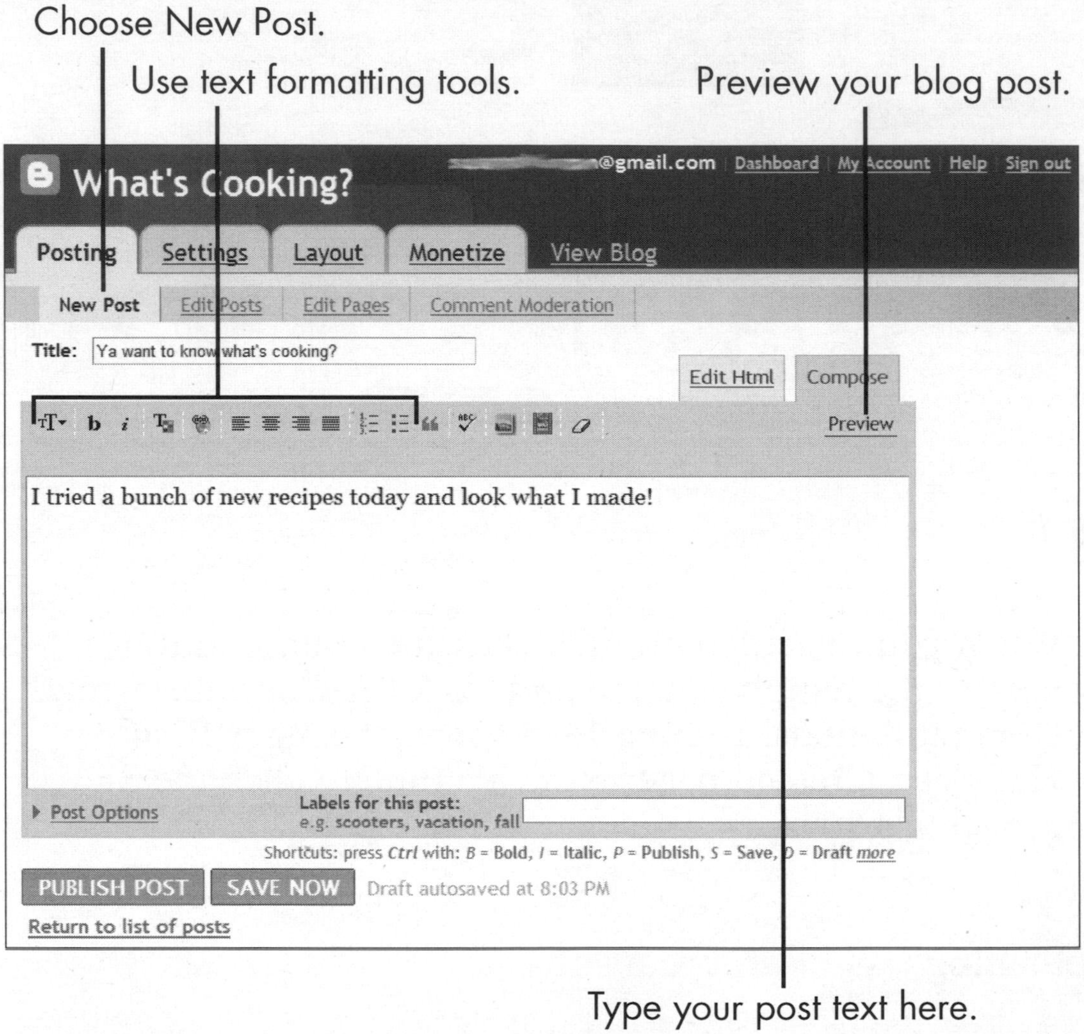

Choose New Post.

Use text formatting tools.

Preview your blog post.

Type your post text here.

Figure 15-9

1. Give your post a title: Make your title catchy, with keywords that reflect the topic.

2. Write your post: Compose your blog post in the text area. Use the toolbar to change the formatting of your text if you wish. Use bold, italic, colors, or numbering — just as in a word processing program.

 Don't use a word-processing program if you pre-write your post. I know spell checking is handy, but when it comes time to copy and paste what you've written, some of the characters won't transfer properly. If you want to pre-write, use a plain "text editor" program like Notepad.

If you're writing your post in Blogger, don't worry about having to hurry. Take your time. Blogger autosaves your work every few minutes.

3. Add a picture. People love pictures! Click the icon of the photo in the toolbar (**Figure 15-10**). You're brought to another page (**Figure 15-11**) where you can click Browse to look for a photo to upload from your computer. You may upload an image file of almost any format — JPG, GIF, BMP, and PNG. Just make sure the file is no bigger than 8 MB.

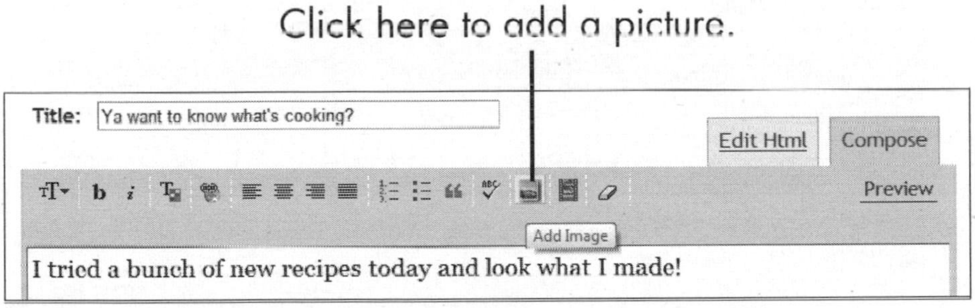

Click here to add a picture.

Title: Ya want to know what's cooking?

Edit Html | Compose

Preview

Add Image

I tried a bunch of new recipes today and look what I made!

Figure 15-10

 When inserting a photo, you can also type in the Web address (URL) for an image elsewhere on the Web.

Before you "liberate" a photo from another Web site, be sure it's not a copyrighted image: Check Chapter 13, where I talk about Creative Commons and copyright issues.

Decide what size you'd like the image to have when it appears on the page and click the corresponding option button (Small, Medium, Large). Not to worry — you can preview your past choice and change it at any point (even after you publish it).

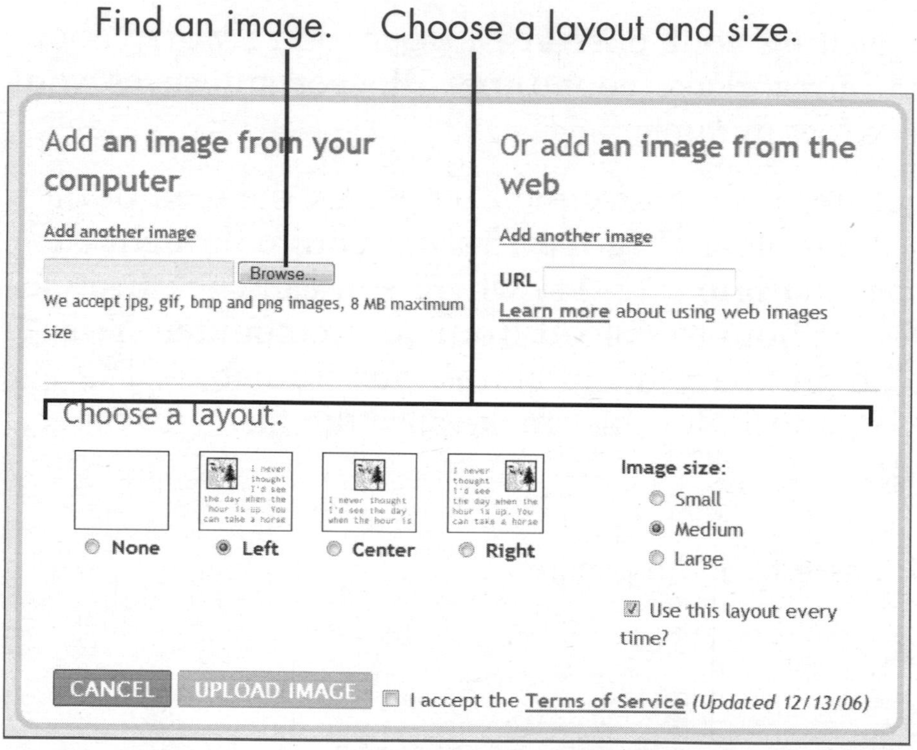

Find an image.   Choose a layout and size.

Add **an image from your computer**

Add another image

[   ] Browse...

We accept jpg, gif, bmp and png images, 8 MB maximum size

Or add **an image from the web**

Add another image

URL [   ]

Learn more about using web images

Choose a layout.

None   Left   Center   Right

Image size:
○ Small
● Medium
○ Large

☑ Use this layout every time?

CANCEL   UPLOAD IMAGE   ☐ I accept the Terms of Service (Updated 12/13/06)

Figure 15-11

Since I'm setting this blog up for a friend, I want to use one of her photos from Facebook. To do that using my Firefox browser, I go to the photo's page on the Web. Right-click the photo and select Copy Image

Location from the resulting menu. Go back to the Blogger page and paste the URL into the URL box, by pressing the Ctrl and V keys at the same time. In Internet Explorer, you'll find the photo's URL by right clicking and then by clicking Properties.

4. Put a check mark in the box saying you agree to the Terms of Service and click Upload Image. This uploads your image and takes you back to the Post page. After a little chugging, your browser (**Figure 15-12**) will let you know your image has been added. Click Done and that window will close and you'll be back on the posting page.

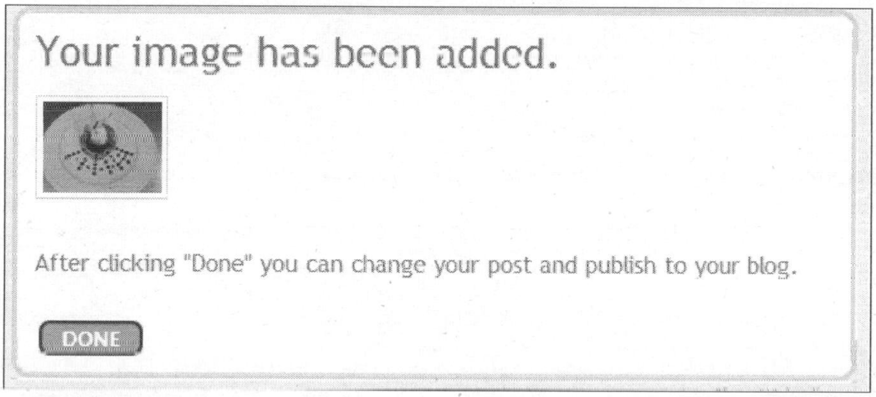

Your image has been added.

After clicking "Done" you can change your post and publish to your blog.

DONE

Figure 15-12

If you get back to the composition page and the photo looks too big, you can grab one of the corner handles of the image and make it smaller. When you resize the photo using the corner handles, go to the lower-right corner one. It's easier to maintain the perspective from that control point.

5. Select keywords: In the Labels for This Post text box, type in the keywords that best describe your post. These words will be picked up by search engines when they index the Web to help people find your post.

6. Check out your work: If you want to see how your blog post looks when it's posted, click Preview (refer to Figure 15-9). The page will change and you'll see the post as it will appear on your blog page. To return to editing, click *Hide Preview* at the top of the page (as shown in **Figure 15-13**).

7. If your post is ready and you want to put it live on the Web, click Publish Post. If you'd rather give it extra thought, just click Save Now and it goes into your posting area. You can then find the post in your Dashboard (see **Figure 15-14**) on the Edit Posts tab, and it will be marked as *Draft*. You can add to or edit the post at any time.

Publish your post.

Or save it for later.

Figure 15-13

8. Notice some other options and handy items on the Edit Posts tab. You can schedule a post to appear on the Web at a prescribed time. And on the left side of your list of posts, check out the Labels (keywords) that you used in your posts.

Perhaps you publish a post to your blog and notice a misspelled word. Don't worry: You can go back to the Edit Posts tab and make changes easily, so don't worry about anything you do!

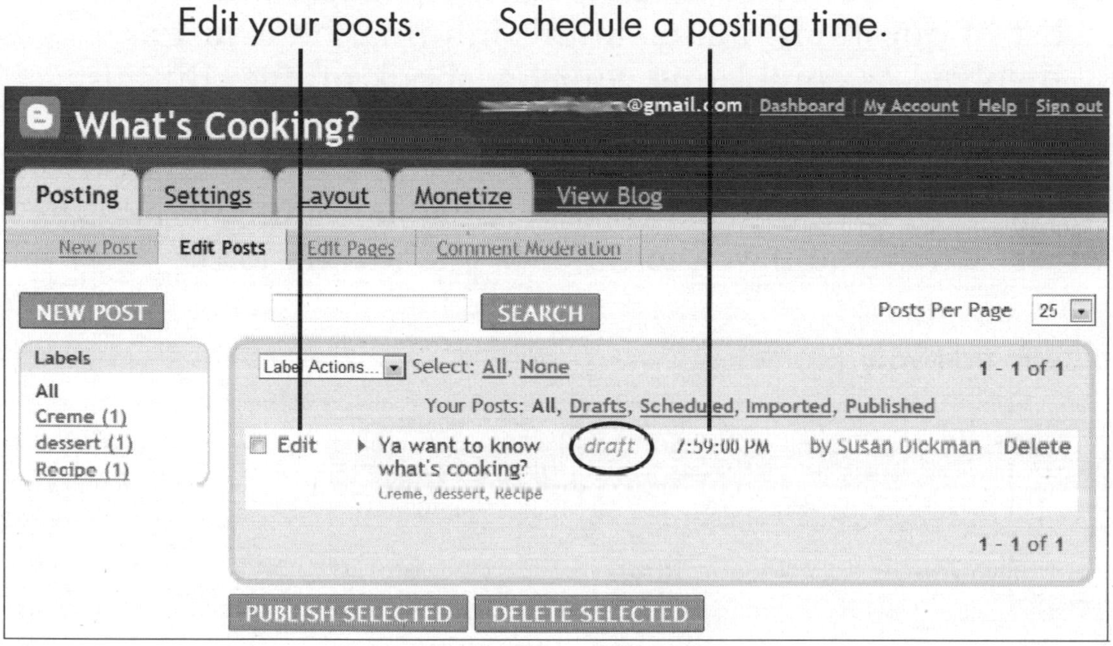
Edit your posts.
Schedule a posting time.
What's Cooking?
Dashboard
My Account
Help
Sign out
Posting
Settings
Layout
Monetize
View Blog
New Post
Edit Posts
Edit Pages
Comment Moderation
NEW POST
SEARCH
Posts Per Page
25
Labels
All
Creme (1)
dessert (1)
Recipe (1)
Label Actions...
Select: All, None
1 - 1 of 1
Your Posts: All, Drafts, Scheduled, Imported, Published
Edit
Ya want to know what's cooking?
draft
7:59:00 PM
by Susan Dickman
Delete
Creme, dessert, Recipe
1 - 1 of 1
PUBLISH SELECTED
DELETE SELECTED

Figure 15-14

Set Up Your Profile

You can't have a blog without a profile. You lose a lot of credibility when people can't put at a face to the blog. Some people don't use their own photos and, instead, use avatars to remain anonymous. Perhaps they don't like the photos they have of themselves, and an avatar is fine to use. But you do need to offer a little background about yourself. After all, your readers can't always relate to you without some idea of who you are.

1. To set up your profile on your blog, click the Dashboard link on the navigation bar at the top of the page. You arrive at your blog's control panel, as shown in **Figure 15-15**. Find the Edit Profile link (under the missing picture of you), and click it.

2. You arrive at the Edit User Profile page and face a long list of questions. Filling in this information is just as involved as completing your Facebook profile. But just like on Facebook, you can fill in as much or as little information as you wish. You can add a lot of data, so you might want to start with a small amount and add the rest when you have the time (or the inclination).

Click here to edit your profile.

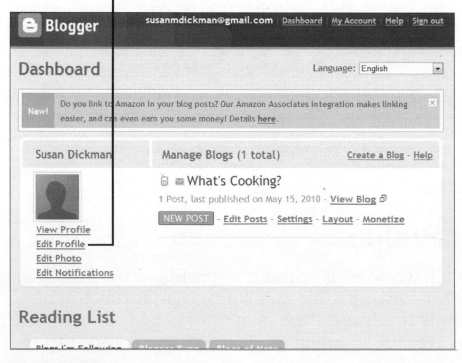

Figure 15-15

3. Most of the questions are self-explanatory, and pretty benign. A few are important to fill out on your first pass — especially these:

- **Share my profile:** Clicking the box here makes your profile page appear as a link from your blog; it puts a face on the words in the blog.

- **Show my real name:** If checked, your first and last name will appear on your profile; if not checked, just your first name will appear.

- **Show my e-mail address:** I recommend declining to check this box. People can comment on your blog and Blogger will send the comments in the form of e-mails to your Gmail account. Showing your e-mail address only invites spam.

- **Profile photo:** There's an option to either upload a picture from your computer or to use a photo that's already on the Web. If you want to put in a photo from the Web, just type in the URL of the photo in the text box (as in **Figure 15-16**) and the second you finish typing it in, it will magically appear on the page.

  If you want to upload an image from your computer, click the Browse button to open a window to your hard drive, navigate to the folder where you store the very best photos of yourself, and Double-click the photo. In a moment, it appears on the profile page.

- **Birthday:** It's not such a terrible thing to let people know when your birthday is, especially because Blogger lets you leave off your birth year.

Click here to pick up an online photo.

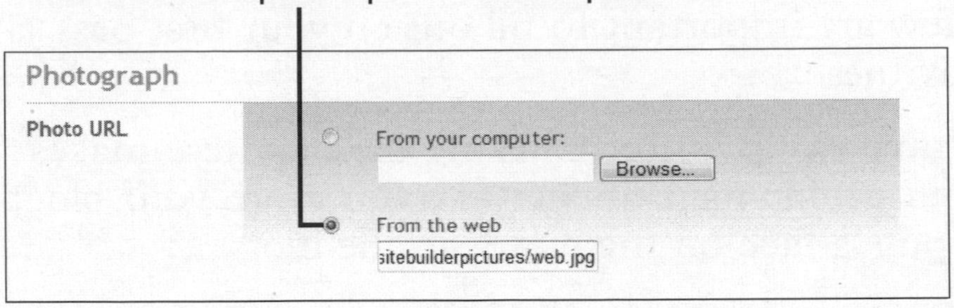

Photograph

Photo URL

○ From your computer:

[   ] [Browse...]

⦿ From the web

[sitebuilderpictures/web.jpg]

Figure 15-16

4. Fill in whatever else suits your fancy and, when you're done, click the Save Profile button at the bottom of the page. Your Edit User Profile page reappears, bearing the reassurance that *Your settings have been saved*. To view your profile, click the View Updated Profile link and you see the fruits of your labor, as shown in **Figure 15-17**.

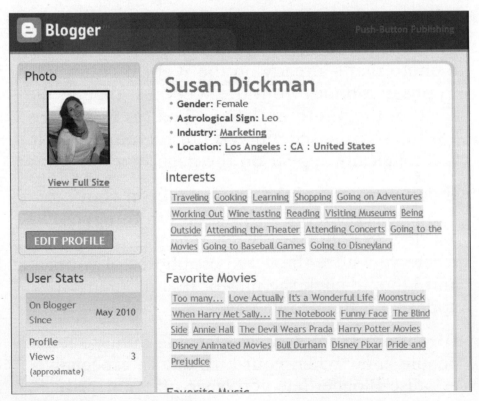

Figure 15-17

Index

369

music Monday, 278
mutual friend, 164–65
MySpace, 101–2

N

O

Notes

Notes